Welcome to
INDIA

Sumeet,
Best regards,
Victoria

44/100

Welcome to INDIA

A Westerner's Spiritual Journey

Victoria Kjos

VICTORIA KJOS

TATE PUBLISHING
AND ENTERPRISES, LLC

Published by Tate Publishing & Enterprises, LLC
127 E. Trade Center Terrace | Mustang, Oklahoma 73064 USA
1.888.361.9473 | www.tatepublishing.com

Tate Publishing is committed to excellence in the publishing industry. The company reflects the philosophy established by the founders, based on Psalm 68:11,
"The Lord gave the word and great was the company of those who published it."

Book design copyright © 2014 by Tate Publishing, LLC. All rights reserved.
Cover design by Jan Sunday Quilaquil
Interior design by Jimmy Sevilleno

Published in the United States of America

ISBN: 978-1-63185-400-2
1. Body, Mind & Spirit / Healing / Prayer & Spiritual
2. Travel / Asia / India & South Asia
14.05.12

To all of my spiritual teachers and guides,
and especially to Mom and Dad,
my first and most important teachers,
whose continuing guidance is ever-present.

Acknowledgments

I AM DEEPLY GRATEFUL to the many long-term special relationships with dear friends, students, former colleagues, and family members, who have been supportive of me throughout the twists and turns on life's journey leading me to this place. Especially to siblings Sherryle, Sandy, and Nick and to nephews and nieces, I appreciate their love and support. For the privacy of friends mentioned, they have been given pseudonyms.

I am especially appreciative of all who read my journal meanderings and encouraged me to proceed with this book—Doriane, Camy, Maryanna, Kim, Ocotilla, Joan, Jim and Judy, Bob and Barbara, Paulina, Carol, Sherry, Betty, Chuck, Bill, Ron, Norbert, Josh, Liz, Mary, Terri and Jack, Nancy, Catherine, Nick, Nathan, Jenifer, Bonnie, Barbara, Caralee, Linda, Elaine, Jerry, Rick, Larry, Brooke, Emily, David, Ted, and Nils and Carolyn.

Special thanks are given to those who provided the foundation for this quest: my yoga, qigong, and meditation teachers, Master Hong Liu, Sandra Summerfield Kozak, Judith Lasater, Ian Rawlinson, Gary Kraftsow, Mary Beth Markus, Radha,

Elise Miller, Jordan Kirk, Rama Vernon, Erich Schiffman, David Holloway, Phyllis Pilgrim, and Leslie Kaminoff.

I am profoundly thankful to the people of India who touched my soul and allowed me to share in their fascinating culture and spiritual traditions. Aside from individuals affiliated with spiritual communities, names of others have been changed to permit anonymity.

To my editors and terrific team at Tate Publishing, Trinity, Stacy, Josh, Germaine, Maria Jeanette, Jan, Jimmy, Cheryl, Roxanne, and Amanda, I offer deep thanks for their assistance, direction, and kindness in bringing this to fruition.

Contents

Wisdom from the Sages

"When you are inspired by some great purpose, some extraordinary project, all of your thoughts break their bonds: Your mind transcends limitations, your consciousness expands in every direction, and you find yourself in a new, great and wonderful world. Dormant forces, faculties and talents become alive, and you discover yourself to be a greater person than you ever dreamed yourself to be."

—*The Yoga Sutras of Patanjali*

"When we find our core certainty within, then we no longer look for certainty outside. The unfathomable nature of the ever-changing world ceases to be a source of anxiety and instead is a source of joy and adventure."

—Deepak Chopra

"Look within. There is no difference between yourself, Self and Guru. You are always free. There is no teacher, there is no student, there is not teaching. Going within means just listening to your own Guru. And this Guru is your own Self. The real Guru will introduce you to the Guru within and ask 'you' to keep quiet. This is your own grace. It comes from within you. No one else can give you this grace."

—Sri H.W.L. Poonja

"Guru is God embodied in human form to Liberate souls from ignorance. Guru is the divine doctor, who cures us by giving us knowledge of Self."

—Swami Papa Ramdas

Prologue

MOTHER INDIA HAD been gently beckoning for several years. As a yogini and yoga teacher for more than twenty years, traveling to the sacred birthplace of yoga was a longstanding dream. Circumstances seemed to be directing me, and the timing felt propitious. The little adage kept spinning about: "If not now, when?"

Examining my life, I had been unhappy and bored for some time. Generally upbeat, however, my nature is not to mope around or complain much. Nevertheless, something was missing that I wanted to remedy. Suspecting many people feel similarly disillusioned, dissatisfied, or discontented, most of us just continue on the same treadmill, taking us nowhere new. Others have affairs or marry younger women. Some drink too much or use other substances to dull reality. Many find escape through shopping, decorating, remodeling, or gambling. I kept changing jobs.

On probably my tenth career, with many more jobs, I was then working as a realtor. But my storied employment history involved work as a lawyer, deputy treasurer of a state, bank vice president, insurance agent, sales representative, consultant, government department head, political campaign manager, bank teller, and yoga, meditation, and qigong teacher. Although loving most of those positions, I continued searching, needing new challenges.

Academically inclined, I was a perpetual student, evidenced by an accumulation over the years of multiple advanced degrees, teaching certificates, and professional licenses. In recent years, my study had gravitated to Eastern philosophies and spiritual traditions. Yoga and meditation, along with other experiences, perpetuated me further down that path.

As my personal quest deepened, more questions arose. Why did the Taoists, Buddhists, and Hindus I met always seem so happy and serene? Why were they more content than Christians and Jews? And without exception, everyone I knew who had traveled to Asia talked about how happy the people were there, despite having few possessions or monetary wealth. Comparatively, Americans flush with material goods never seem to be satisfied.

My mantra, received decades ago from a Chopra-trained instructor, had been the basis of my meditation practice. Stacks of Wayne Dyer's tapes were my daily traveling companion in my car for years. A plethora of other spiritual guides and writings provided study materials. I read the India section of Elizabeth Gilbert's *Eat, Pray, Love* a dozen times. All helped me arrive at the simple conclusion that there *really* had to be more to life than replaying the same old tapes, listening to repeated complaints, and going through mindless motions.

So despite my own study and practices, although perhaps a trite refrain, I longed for greater meaning in my life. Notwithstanding a commitment to dwell in a deeper spiritual place, my emotions varied. But the prevailing ones were not the uplifting, enlightening ones I craved. Instead, I often felt: Weary. Bored. Lethargic. Unenthusiastic. Absolutely believing that it is my personal responsibility, and within my control, to change my feelings… and ultimately, to be happy, I spent a few years studying, thinking, and preparing for what might next unfold.

In my fifty-some years of living in the United States, I did know—at least in my soul—with absolute certainty a few things. That the accumulation of money meant little to me. That I no longer wanted to associate with people who obsessively focused on money. That to find my personal spiritual compass, I needed to leave our money-centric, materialistic environment. That America's obsession with wealth bored me.

The other certainty was that my focus had to be on the spiritual, believing that is where the only true answers, and happiness, lie. A core spirituality is what sustains true humanity and is all that matters at the close of each day, at the end of one's life. I wanted a transformation. Or simply…to find God. People have sought answers for centuries in India, most recently in the past seventy years or so, but for thousands of years, seekers have journeyed to the cradle of sanctity, the holiest of holy places.

Once the intellectual and emotional decisions were made, the rest were merely details. Selling my house and car and disposing of the vast majority of my belongings. Winding down my real estate practice and ensuring clients received a good referral. Unsure if I would return or not, I allowed myself a safety net, keeping the basics in a storage unit to set up a small apartment. For me, the basics consisted of books, art, clothes, some linens, and a few kitchen and household items.

Some called me brave to set out all alone on this spiritual quest to India. Never having considered myself particularly courageous, I admit to being not in the least afraid and of being inquisitive, enthusiastic, and thriving on change and diversity. Several friends verbalized that they thought I was crazy. Others may have felt similarly, but remained silent. A few thought it sounded adventurous and were encouraging.

Making reservations on Air India from Phoenix via Chicago, then Chicago to Delhi, and on to Chennai, my spiritual quest commenced on April 25, 2012. I was very excited!

The Journey Begins:
Major Jet Lag and Initial
Impressions of Mother India

WEDNESDAY, APRIL 25, 2012

TOWARD THE END of my flight from Chicago to Delhi, for some inexplicable reason I felt compelled to start writing. Pulling out my laptop, I am amazed to have not seen anyone using a computer as I meandered through the cabin in more than twenty hours' flying. My writing experience, however, is brief because soon, our Delhi landing announcement is made.

Never planning to journal since all similar efforts over the years have always been in vain, the longest I ever managed previously, despite many attempts, to faithfully write was for a few weeks. That I am keeping this journal is testament to one of the many gifts India has bestowed upon me. But I have continued for the next couple of days to write. Always loving writing, and perhaps because it was the most vigorous activity I could manage in my jet-lagged fog, I typed away.

The Air India flight from Chicago to Delhi on Air India is absolutely phenomenal! Frequent travelers always tout the laurels of international carriers over American ones, and indeed, I understand why. Entering the plane, a beautifully sari-garbed attendant asks, "21 Delta?" Yep, that's me, Seat 21D. Finding my seat in the large carrier with multiple cabin sections, I notice immediately a welcome entirely empty row of three seats. Imagining the intense joy of having more room, I ask Lovely Flight Attendant if the flight is full to which she responds, "No, you possibly may have the whole row."

Nearly delirious at such a prospect, I had only gotten about two hours' sleep the night before. My intentions were to be asleep by 10:00 p.m. to arise before the crack of dawn for my 4:00 a.m. cab for the 6:00 a.m. flight. Nephew Zach, who earlier had been at my apartment, was right. Explaining my plan to get six hours' sleep, as he looked around at the remaining sorting and packing, his reply was, "No way!"

Soon, Lovely Flight Attendant returns to inform me that, indeed, there will be no other passengers seated in my row. Thanking her profusely, I cheer silently and thank my angels, God, the universe. Next, I notice wooden foot massagers at every seat. I am in heaven. Then I see three, yes, three pillows and three blankets, a little net holder with a bottle of water, and individual television screens at every seat, of course, featuring a multitude of movies, radio, and music.

In flight, it is delightful to listen to Indian music and watch my first Bollywood movie, recommended to me by my attentive Exquisite Steward Vivek. When inquiring if a particular movie is good, he replies with complete seriousness, "No, none of them are any good, but you have to watch one." I laugh. At least, it lulls me to sleep.

My fantasy of an entire flight spent sound asleep, however, doesn't materialize; nevertheless, I manage a few mini-naps. Taking several little walks around the cabin, I do yoga stretches frequently in alcoves. Immediately upon take off, a hot meal is served. Preparing for Hindu India, I choose vegetarian (lamb and chicken are also available), and the food is delicious. During the flight, two more meals are served as well as having access to an open kitchen, with unlimited beverages, cookies, and sandwiches available throughout. I am amazed.

About my personal flight attendant, not too far into the flight, an Exquisite Steward Vivek "adopts" me. At my age, I sincerely doubt his interest is anything other than being attentive and kind. Perhaps he thinks I look in need of a friend. Or is it because I am one of a handful of Westerners on the flight? Whatever the reason, he is endearingly sweet, asking me if I need this or that, bringing me bottles of water, and offering assistance if I come to Mumbai. Comparing this level of service to that of a typical American carrier, it is truly like comparing apples to oranges.

It is nine hours into the flight before I notice a gaggle of amazingly gorgeous male stewards. Where have they come from? Have they been stowed in a closet somewhere and just released? Or on these long flights, does the staff work in shifts and have they been in the back sleeping? Central Casting handsome, with impeccable manners and a proper, reserved kindness, they serve tea and coffee with white gloves. I don't think they are an apparition, but as mysteriously as they appear mid-flight, when we land, they are nowhere to be seen. As we exit the plane, only beautiful, sari-clad women bid us a pleasant farewell.

During the flight, another very nice Indian chap, across the aisle in his own three-row grouping of seats, starts a conversation with me. Kindly, he offers me his contact information when I am in Delhi along with his friend's name, who works in an Agra hotel. Then when wandering into the kitchen, I comment on the beautiful attire of a lady there with me.

Another Delhi resident, who owns a boutique there, she says to call her when I get to Delhi, gives me her mobile (pronounced "moe-bile" by Indians) number, and says that she will help me however she can or send her driver for me. Oh, yes, just as in America...sending our drivers. Not in my world. Again, the most remarkable kindness from a woman with whom I speak for perhaps five minutes.

One always hears about the generosity, kindness, and inherent need to be of service of the Indian people. Longing for these experiences, already all around me, it is abundant from the flight staff and these total strangers offering assistance. How excited I am for what lies ahead.

The Delhi airport is mesmerizing. Later, I learn that it is relatively new, having been built within the past couple of years. Greeting passengers in the lobby is a magnificent, mammoth brass statue of Surya, the sun god. Positioned above the ticket counters are sculptures of humongous hands, each posed in a different mudra. I am entranced.

In addition to its beauty, however, what I am most struck by is the silence. There is no noise. How can the airport in India's second largest city in a country of 1.25 billion people be this quiet? Airports are always noisy and chaotic with bustling crowds, loud announcements, crying children, and people shouting on cell phones. It is as if a meditative calm permeates the entire place. Already, I love India!

The Delhi-Chennai leg is a more typical flight – a hot, crowded, small plane. My luggage has arrived by the time I clear customs, which surprisingly doesn't take long. Conveniently, there are luggage carts—free of charge—available at baggage carousels in all Indian airports.

I am now in Mother India. Prepared for cacophony and madness, it is far less intense than anticipated, perhaps because this is Chennai, not the larger Mumbai, Delhi, or Kolkata. Or possibly because from hearing and reading so many over-the-top tales about India, one expects to be dazed or blown away. For example, I expect gut-wrenching stenches, crowds of people smothering me, unbearable humidity and temperatures, and assaults by beggars and thieves. None of those yet feel overwhelming.

Chennai, though, is hot and humid or "close" as my mother would describe it. However, a desert rat who has survived Phoenix's 100- to 123-degree summer temperatures for decades, India certainly is not nearly as oppressive, at least not yet. The only wee glitch is that the prearranged car from my hotel has not arrived. The wait is probably forty-five minutes or so, but having thought a lot about this journey and the importance of acceptance, patience, flexibility, and simply "being," as well as what India is supposed to teach me, I relax. I locate a water stand and stock up with a couple of bottles of *cold* water. When the car arrives, it is modern and, happily, has frigid air conditioning.

My driver chats nonstop, warning me about the touts and cheats who will offer to take me to shops earning their commission for merchants' overpriced goods. Then without missing a beat, he offers to be my guide for two days hence–*and for a very good price*–if I need one. My first sales pitch. Welcome to India!

On the trip to the hotel, I am utterly intrigued by women attired in gorgeous, bright-colored saris sitting sidesaddle on motor bikes behind the drivers, zooming along with long scarves flapping wildly behind them. There is an added seat on motorcycles to accommodate that mode of transportation for ladies.

The hotel welcoming staff is fabulous, engendering more high praise for the Indian service model. Most likely, they are well-accustomed to foreign bleary-eyed, disoriented guests arriving at night. By now, I am nearly catatonic and have limited memory whatsoever of check-in, shower, and subsequent collapse.

One of the reasons I allow myself this luxury of such an expensive hotel is the desire, after more than twenty-four hours in transit and little slumber in two days, to sleep in a wonderful bed with magnificent linens. What is it about linens in first-rate hotels? I realize that they are high-thread count and good quality, but there is something else special about them. Is it because they have been laundered so frequently that they are inexplicably soft? And they have been ironed. Whatever the magic of hotel sheets and poufy comforters, I sleep like the dead for eleven hours.

The hotel is a gorgeous, colonial-style that appears to be quite old, but I learn that it was built only eleven years ago. With the charm of the Hotel Bretagne in Athens or The Fairmont in San Francisco, a massive Hollywood movie set–looking marble and wrought-iron staircase leads upstairs to my room. Featuring lush tropical grounds, the view from my window is of massive palm trees and a water fountain.

Upon awakening from my corpse-like collapse, I start to recall the sensation of jet lag, mostly because I am experiencing it big-time. Having not traveled internationally in some time and with myriad things to address before leaving Arizona, the concept of jet lag never crossed the synapses of my brain. In my hotel room, I spin around in circles like a whirling dervish, trying to focus. It is weird, as if I unintentionally ingested a hallucinogen.

Hungry and awakening too late for room service breakfast, I hobble down to the twenty-four-hour restaurant. Clueless what food is best to minimize the effects of jet lag–protein, carbs, or sugar, I decide to order what sounds appealing: fish and chips. Chennai is on the Bay of Bengal, and as a lover of fish, it seems a good choice. And indeed, it is; the meal is delicious, possibly some of the best fish and chips I have ever eaten anywhere.

At lunch, reading the newspaper, which is delivered in a darling little cloth bag hung on my hotel room door, I stumble across a brief article with photographs of ASU students in Tempe, Arizona, stripped down to their skivvies for some end-of-year ritual for charity. Unbelievable; what is the likelihood that I would read this story in India? Having both lived in Arizona for thirty years *and* attended ASU, never before have I heard of this event. It feels as though I am in some bizarre cartoon.

Remembering two aspects of dealing with jet lag, they include resetting one's watch to local time and immediately starting to function on the time zone where one has landed. If it is night, go to bed, and if day time, stay awake. Attempting diligently to follow these two credos, I manage not to nap, spending the majority of the day horizontal on my bed with the television tuned to any non-sports programming and writing in my journal.

Deciding a massage might be nice, happily, no appointment is needed, and a female therapist is available (one is cautioned not to use male therapists in India) at the hotel "spa," a term I use guardedly. The massage room temperature is about 90 degrees F, and the table is circa 1950, very hard with one-inch thick padding and no face cradle. There is no ambience whatsoever, no soft music, no frills, fluffy bathrobes or thick white towels, or yummy spa products.

Technically, the therapist is adequate, and she is very strong. Claiming to have been doing massage for fifteen years, the extent of our communication is her telling me, "You have cracked feet. You need a pedicure." Although the massage room is hot, the steam room is not. This feels more like a Russian spa of a bygone era, definitely providing only the basics. And she uses about two quarts of olive oil on me, yep, olive oil. I cannot wait to shower it off. In my jet-lagged state, however, I am happy for any reprieve, and crawl back to my bed at its conclusion.

Now on my second day here, I remain very woozy; it is a punch-drunk feeling. Although the hotel has a gorgeous pool, my body lacks the energy to limp out there. Lying in the sun seems too daunting, as does trying to swim.

Navigating a most complicated remote light system in my room, however, still remains an impossible task. To activate electricity, the key card is inserted into an electronic gizmo at the door when entering the room. It's a good idea to conserve power, with the only negative being that without air conditioning when out of the room, it becomes a tad toasty. Activation of a dozen lights throughout both the room and bath is controlled from a panel beside the bed, and it remains a hit-and-miss system as I experiment with which button switches on what light.

Not having even left the property yesterday, I force myself to do something today. I first attempt to hire a personal guide to visit various temples and centers, but Travel Desk Chap and I never manage to get on the same page. My brain is firing on even fewer than its normal cylinders, and there are definitely "communication" challenges with the English I speak and that spoken here.

An American, Roger, who lives here and is a friend of a lawyer working for my friend George in a Florida law firm, kindly e-mailed me before my arrival. My only local contact, he mentions Pondy Bazaar as something to experience. A street bazaar seems the perfect mindless outing and introduction to India.

Having not fared too well with Travel Desk Chap, I approach the only Female Desk Clerk at front reception. Indeed, we sisters communicate much better. Responding to my question, she thinks I seem confident enough to leave the hotel property to hire my own cab and head to the bazaar on my own; however, she cautions, "It's all junk jewelry and other things. You probably won't want to buy anything." Adding that a couple of hours' time will be sufficient, she is right on both counts.

Off for my first outing in India, it lasts for all of about *five* whole whopping minutes! The heat is oppressive, my brain feels dead, and the prospect of getting myself to Pondy Bazaar seems overwhelmingly challenging. Doing an immediate about-face, I return to the travel desk and hire the hotel car for four hours. Driver, although pleasant enough, speaks so little English that I quickly give up trying to chat with him.

My first venture in South India is interesting and reminds me of parts of Mexico and undoubtedly, many other developing nations where I have not been. The pollution, which I have been warned is hideous, doesn't seem so bad. The traffic is insane, but actually it might be rather fun driving here. It is one giant free-for-all, vehicles driving wildly anywhere with no designated lanes, cutting in wherever a spot opens with incessant horn-honking.

Everyone blasts his (I have seen no women drivers) horn of cars, taxis, auto rickshaws (also called tuk-tuks), scooters, motor-cycles, trucks, and buses. The non-stop horn blaring is bizarre, and I am told that the purpose is to alert other drivers of one's presence. Really? That sounds preposterous. If *everyone* honks his horn, would it not make more sense simply to look around for oncoming vehicles? And they do have rear-view mirrors. It seems to me a testosterone-driven reason to be noisy and aggressive. But what do I know? I do not live here and have been in India for a whopping two days. My yoga teacher Erica, who was here a couple of years ago, advised me to bring earplugs. I now under-stand why.

Originally, I think, although due to communication limita-tions I am not entirely certain, that Driver plans to await my return in the car at a designated spot. But for some inexplicable reason, he changes his mind. Perhaps he thinks I am too hap-less to negotiate the place alone or considers this foreign lady his charge to safely deliver back to his employer. Whatever the reason, he decides to follow along behind me. In my fatigued state, I conclude it is fine to have a male wearing a hotel uniform to help me navigate.

I experience my first Indian beggar, a woman with a badly deformed nose asking for money. Apparently, often the beggars have gross physical deformities, and I have heard stories about children being intentionally maimed to present more sympathet-ically for their destined lives as beggars. Locals counsel not to give money because many are professional beggars with pimps or handlers to whom they give much of the day's take. She well may be one of those because her sari looks pretty new and clean. At least, she doesn't exhibit the destitute condition of the homeless living on Phoenix streets.

Driver shoos her away. Later, as we are about to leave, when Driver goes for the car, she finds me and plants herself in front of me with hand extended. Deciding to make my response kindness, a smile, and negative head shake, she is not discouraged in the least and remains standing directly in front of me. If that is her occupation, I guess she has nothing better to do. It is, however, rather unnerving, so after a few minutes, I move a few stalls away. She follows and repeats the same thing. Actually, it is a pretty effective ploy because had there been any small rupee coins in my bag, I would have given them to her simply out of discomfort.

Female Desk Clerk was correct; there is little of interest to buy. A gigantic flea market, reminding me of Mexico on steroids, the Pondy Bazaar is comprised of multiple streets lined with thousands of stores and vendors selling all manner of merchandise. Of the two items I contemplate, Driver says, "No, no, take you to better place." Looking at cotton handkerchiefs, after some negotiation with the seller, Driver does not like the price and refuses to let me purchase them.

So what, they are only handkerchiefs? And as for the silk scarf I consider, he indeed takes me to a lovely silk shop on the way back to the hotel. A very old, established company with silks from the region of Kanchipuram, an area in south India, a photograph of Queen Elizabeth touring their silk factory graces the wall. So perhaps I can claim to have shopped at the same silk shop as the Queen of England.

Undoubtedly, Driver gets his commission (thank you, American visitor) because upon our arrival, immediately scarves are presented without my requesting them. Obviously, Driver calls ahead when retrieving the car. Refusing to negotiate prices, "One price only," the sales clerk tells me. A novice in the Indian marketplace, I wonder how the process would have transpired had I replied, "Oh, that's too much," and began to walk out.

But I don't do that; I am already in love with the silk. These scarves can be worn with daily clothes, dress-up, or casual.

Having no idea what the price should be, the quoted price seems very reasonable. Although I buy a few, our stay is brief because even shopping is too taxing in my altered brain functioning state. A woman knows she is in trouble when too disoriented to shop. Mark *this* day on the calendar.

About saris, I find myself mesmerized by them. Not only are they beautiful, but women wearing them look flawlessly put together. How does one wear six meters, a bit more than six yards, of silk or a blended fabric in this weather and not melt?

I am told that women do not really wear them much any longer, but that certainly is not the case in Chennai. One person says that women wear saris to dress up or for special occasions; however, most of the women on the streets are in saris. They do not look terribly comfortable to me. Perhaps it is a generational thing, worn by older women but not as much by the younger ones.

A few hours out of the hotel is all my fatigued body can manage. The usual collection of well-uniformed hotel staff greets me upon my return, asking how my shopping was, if I want something, have I had lunch, do I need this or that. There are always at least three or four young chaps around, and affirmative action apparently allows one token woman; she works in the pastry concession area.

Their behavior ranges from extremely solicitous to pretty inappropriate, at least by American hotelier standards, exemplified by Karan asking me if I would bring him to America and help him get a job and the bar supervisor inquiring about the cost of my necklace and if I bought it myself or if someone gave it to me. Having read about the Indian penchant for questioning and general inquisitiveness, I still am unprepared for this overt level of grilling and prying.

Tonight, Roger joins me at the hotel for dinner. An American who has lived in Chicago, Miami, and Los Angeles, surely a thirty-five-year-old has more interesting things to amuse himself on a

Friday night than dining with a woman whom he has never met and is old enough to be his mother. Asking him, he replies, "You need to understand that I haven't talked with another Westerner here for more than a year!" Tomorrow he and an Indian friend, who has a car, will serve as tour guides for the day.

A Tour of Chennai

THE NEXT DAY in mid-afternoon, Roger, Anish, who works with Roger, and Anish's darling girlfriend, Sharma, pick me up. Having prepared a list of places, but realizing that visiting all in one afternoon is not possible, I suggest they decide the itinerary. Hideous traffic times and a late start somewhat dictate our choices as the temples are already closed. Both Anish and Sharma, in their twenties, are lovely kids and great resources.

Shopping at a different silk shop, Sharma negotiates prices at one-third of what I paid at yesterday's store. I guess I overpaid. She tells me later that they have to offer her better prices because she is a local. A very established shop, she has gone there since a child with her parents and grandparents. I buy more scarves as gifts.

After shopping, Roger suggests eating so we head to a restaurant they all like that specializes in biryani. Arriving at an off-hour between lunch and dinner, our choices are limited to chicken or goat. With no vegetarian option, I order chicken and try to eat around the meat. Tasty, this is my first attempt eating Indian style, *sans* utensils using only one's right hand. I rather like it; it's like playing with your food, a return to childhood. After eating, everyone goes to an open washroom at the side of the dining room to soap and wash our hands.

Later, we head to the best beach in Chennai, Marina Beach, which apparently is the second longest beach in the world. We all guess which is the longest. Sharma, on her phone, Googles it, finding much to our surprise that it is Chicago. Even Roger, a Chicagoan by birth, does not guess that. Later when researching further, however, the longest is actually in Rio de Janeiro. Both the beach and the Bay of Bengal are gorgeous.

We are off to the San Thome Cathedral, a huge, beautiful Roman Catholic church where mass is being conducted in the Tamil language. Beneath the chapel grounds is the tomb of St. Thomas the Apostle. Unknown to me is that Thomas went to India and died here; legend has it that he was killed.

After a long and hot day, everyone is tired. The Indian couple offers to come again early tomorrow and go to temples. Declining, I thank them saying they have already been too kind and need to have their day of rest, the typical Indian work week being Monday through Saturday.

I can always return and visit important sites, including the home of Vivekenanda (the famous scholar and patriot, who introduced the United States to yoga at the World religious conference in Chicago conference in 1893), the Theosophical Society, the brand-new Krishna temple, the Krishnamurti Center, and other temples. Desikachar, the famous yogi and son of the renowned teacher Krishnamacharya, is also here, but according to my guidebook, one cannot just drop in to study with him. Having studied yoga with some of his protégés and liking his viniyoga style, I would love to study with him.

Also, interestingly, by Indian standards, I am from Norway. Never mind that I have never lived there, nor even been there for that matter; it's the home of my ancestors. When asking someone if he or she is from Chennai, the answer may be in the affirmative, but more likely will be, "No, I am from Kerala." Yesterday, Sharma tells me that, and in asking when she moved to Chennai, I learn that she has *never* lived in Kerala. Born and raised in Chennai, her grandfather moved here long before her birth. But she is still from Kerala.

On my fourth full day in India, after a good night's sleep, I leave this glorious luxury hotel and head for more modest digs. Referred to as "serviced apartments," a concept with which I am unfamiliar, my next place seems comparable to a mid-range hotel or inn in the United States. With room service available from local restaurants, regular housekeeping, laundry service, free in-room Wi-Fi , and breakfast buffet are included in the rate.

After checking in and getting the lay of the land, I venture out for food and to the Pondy Bazaar again. The front desk refers me to a great veg (the abbreviated term here for vegetarian) restaurant, one with locations throughout the world, including New York and California. Although not entirely sure what I eat, it is delicious. Again, the staff is phenomenal. I have no idea if it is standard protocol or because I am Western, but at least three or four persons hover about to serve me.

Eating my second meal quasi-fingers only, although given a spoon here, after finishing, I go to the rest room to wash my hands. The floor appears to be flooded, but then I remember the Indian custom of using a water hose to clean oneself. Hoisting up my pants, I walk in, opting to use the toilet paper tucked in my bag. I also have brought some soap sheets in a small plastic container, recommended by world-traveling former clients, but alas, those are in my hotel room. My introduction to the proverbially wet bathroom floors of India.

Upon arriving at the bazaar, I note the strong, distinctive odor of ganja. Although having no particular shopping list, I purchase a Casio black watch for about $3 (150 rupees), cotton t-shirts for approximately $2 each, and two cotton skirts for about $5 each. I am happy with my purchases and negotiations. Some of the sellers are persistent and aggressive, but most are not.

On my way back to my hotel, I stop at a wee temple. Small neighborhood temples abound everywhere. With beautiful, bright-colored statuary atop or surrounding them, inside is the altar with various idols. A kindly chap wearing a crisp white lungi, which is a longer white sarong-type garment, greets and blesses me, placing colored ashes on my third eye. I leave a few rupees as an offering.

Returning to my hotel, I have a few more uniquely Indian experiences. First, I am nearly hit head-on by a speeding scooter. That is my fault for having walked around a parked vehicle directly into oncoming traffic. And I walk past a male urinating on the side of the street. Gratefully, his back is toward me. Walking past a larger temple with long lines of people waiting to enter, outside, there are many beggars. None are aggressive; all just sit with their hands extended. One assumes donations are more generous outside temples.

A temple that I pass en route to Pondy Bazaar is open on my return. Having seen multitudes of women along the street stringing flowers, I wondered who buys them and why. When arriving at the temple, there is a flower-selling lady out front. Obviously, temple offerings are one use for those multitudes of flowers. I buy some. Shoes are left at the bottom of a rather tall stairway and my shopping bags at the rear temple door.

Although a few stools are available for the infirm and elderly, everyone sits on the floor. The priest in charge is preparing a fire, and soon, bells ring; he walks down into the temple proper, and we move toward him and receive flowers. The beauty and peacefulness are moving even though I don't understand what the ritual means. At that instant, it becomes abundantly clear to me that it matters not how one worships, to what deity one prays, or where blessings are received, we are all one. Catholic mass one day, two Hindu temples the next. How special this trip already is. I am floating as I walk back to my hotel.

Concluding last night that these additional two nights in Chennai are enough, I feel ready to head to sacred Tiruvannamalai, populated by saints, rishis, and yogis alive and not. It is best known for its sacred Mount Arunachala and the ashram of another famous realized saint, Ramana Maharshi, who has devotees across the globe.

Until today, I have communicated only by e-mail with a German fellow about staying at a guest house maintained by their small ashram, which is essentially their home. How I discovered this place was again synchronistic. In preparation of my trip, I commenced reading *From Here to Nirvana*, a guidebook for spiritual spots, ashrams, and holy places in India, cowritten by a former *Yoga Journal* editor and another frequent seeker in India. Somewhat dated, having been published in the late 1990s, it was the only book of its ilk that I found.

In reading the book, Yogi Ramsuratkumar sounds authentic and interesting. Something about him resonates with me, perhaps his humility. When the book was written, he was still alive, but he has since passed, or in yoga-speak, "left his body" in 2001.

Known as the Godchild of Tiruvannamalai, he referred to himself as a beggar, despite having been extremely well-educated, fluent in several languages including English, and a teacher before leaving the profession on his own spiritual quest in his late twenties. His claimed teachers were other famous yogis and saints, Swami Papa Ramdas, Sri Aurobindo, and Ramana Maharshi.

In the guidebook, when available, contact numbers for United States organizations are provided. Interestingly, the one for Yogi Ramsuratkumar is in Prescott, Arizona. That devotee also has since died, but someone at the Arizona location returns my call, refers me to the Tiruv fellow, and the rest as they say, is history. In preparation, I began reading an extremely well-written and researched book by another devotee and former Catholic nun, *Only God: A Biography of Yogi Ramsuratkumar*. Arriving only a few days before my departure, I brought it along and am still reading it.

Off to Sacred Tiruvannamalai and My First Indian Ashram

TODAY, THE REAL spiritual piece of this journey begins.

It is a holiday in India, May Day or Labor Day, and the day I arrive in the sacred city of Tiruvannamalai. I am determined to soon learn how to pronounce it. Despite a dozen people in Chennai correcting my mispronunciation, I cannot seem to master it. It is embarrassing.

The ordered taxi arrives fifty minutes early. My driver Rajesh is a nice guy who speaks limited English, so there is little chatting en route. About two hours before leaving Chennai, my bladder starts exhibiting the telltale symptoms of a urinary tract infection. Oh no, why today? I have felt fine until the one day I have to sit four hours in a cab. So I begin my familiar regimen – lots of water, cipro, more vitamin C, and cranberry tablets, hoping for the best. There is really nothing much else to do except say a small prayer.

Already needing a pit stop before we even get out of Chennai proper, I inform my driver and he says, "Yes, in thirty kilometers." I say, with an urgency that he seems to understand, "No, now!" Absolutely willing to stop on any pathway off the highway, as any woman who has ever been in such a predicament well understands, he finds a petro station, asks if they have bathrooms, and points the way. It is reassuring to know that gas station rest rooms exist in India as well.

Badly in need of immediate voiding, I rush to the toilets; the signs are in what I assume to be Tamil. I think, *Well, maybe they're unisex* (later, when thinking about that possibility, I realize that in conservative India, unisex bathrooms are rather unlikely), and because I am nearing the point of pain, asking someone for directions to the ladies' stall never crosses my mind.

This is my first "hole in the ground" Indian squat toilet, but it is not nearly as bad as I am prepared for. Essentially, it is a porcelain toilet seat surrounded by a cement slab. And as a yogini, squatting is a piece of cake for me. That is one position that I can maintain for a very long time.

Oh my heavens, I feel so much better; however, as I exit the bathroom, there is a young guy waiting to get in. Taking one look at me and at the wad of toilet paper sitting in the toilet, he is at best incredulous, more likely disgusted. Although possibly having committed the worst of sins, I care very little at this stage. So I just chalk it up to one of those "early in India mistakes" that I shall not make again, knowing to look for signs indicating gender at the next bathroom stop, which thankfully is not far away because I need to use it again. This time, there are signs in both English and Tamil. I try to decipher the difference in the men's and women's in Tamil, but cannot discern any.

When stopping by Roger's office yesterday to deliver a small thank you gift to the Indian couple, I notice a small altar in his office with fresh flowers. They begin each day with a puja, which is worship or prayer, and buy fresh flowers daily. And when one buys a new car or opens a new business, there is a special puja for that event.

Today, the cab driver has two small statues of deities on his dashboard, one of Ganesha and another I don't recognize, along with a small string of jasmine flowers, which provide a wonderful aroma. Now I understand who buys all of the flowers I see at stands everywhere—everyone for every imaginable purpose. No wonder everyone becomes quickly mesmerized by the magic of this country.

On today's drive, I think frequently of Sister Sandy and Nephew Zach, but for different reasons. The driving here is utterly amazing, nearly defying description. Sandy would need to be drugged and passed out, and Zach would love driving. Having some memory as teenagers playing "chicken" with other kids on the road—cars driving directly at each other until one swerved, that is the *normal* driving mode here. It appears certain that yours and the fast vehicle approaching head-on will crash, but at the very last moment, the appropriate car, truck, bus, motorcycle, or scooter turns, weaves, or moves ever so slightly. Just enough to avert collision.

It is absolutely fascinating, like a dance of crazed road warriors or daredevil race car drivers. Not frightened by it, I have always believed that when my number is up, it's up. And driving fast is not necessarily an unknown activity to me, evidenced by a fair number of speeding tickets accumulated over the years. So dying in an India car crash would be fine with me.

At one point today, two vehicles are zooming straight toward each other with motor scooters or motorcycles speeding simultaneously on both sides of them as well. But with the requisite loud horn honking and swerving, all is well. I guess if raised here, the locals know no other approach to driving. But for Westerners, a love of carnival-style bumper car rides or secret desire to be an Indy race car driver might be good traits.

Passing through rural villages, there are multitudes of shacks, hovels, and shanties of every imagination and configuration, tin-roofed, grass huts, and other very modest housing. Eons of wee businesses and stands line the roads; roadside vendors sell fruits, vegetables, and juices. Lots of men sit about talking and drinking chai or coffee. Occasionally, I see a spanking new, bright blue, modern tractor amidst other ramshackle vehicles and implements, wondering if it is driven by a particularly prosperous farmer, or perhaps a cooperative buys one together.

Rajesh clearly has made this journey many times. The drill is that there are two designated stops en route, in addition to my earlier required bathroom stops. At one stop, toilets have English signs. I buy ice cream bars at the first stop; they are tasty, just like American ones. Even though not much of an ice cream eater, I take note because if in the future, I am craving chocolate, they will suffice. Thus far, the two times I have purchased chocolate here, I have been pretty underwhelmed by the flavor.

On a subject about which I am intimately familiar—and dearly love—chocolate, India may not be the best place for finding it. Cadbury is a major brand, but I have yet to sample it. Hopefully, it will taste like ours at home, however, I have not seen my favorite, caramel. Gratefully, the couple of times I have tasted what are referred to as "sweets," the Indian desserts, I do not care for them. It is pretty much like mainlining pure sugar.

Approximately four hours later, we arrive in Tiruvannamalai. On our way into town, Rajesh points out the most famous ashram of the beloved Ramana Maharshi, known as Ramanashram. Ramana and his ashram is what gave this town its initial spark; he is widely renowned and revered.

Ramana too was the real thing. His benevolent, loving eyes, like those of Paramahansa Yogananda, have always captivated me. He spent about twenty years or so living in the caves on the mountain. When I later ask whether there remain hidden saints on the mountain as I have read about, a local says that there are, but that they wish to remain in hiding. Hence, finding them is not so easy. Understandably, western guru seekers would flock to them if people knew who or where they were.

Sri Ramana Maharshi and Yogi Ramsuratkumar are the major players here. Their photographs even grace real estate sales bill-boards. One wonders how these holy men would feel about that blatant advertising. Given their enlightened states, they probably would care not one whit. Ramana, as everyone calls him, is by far the major draw as he is much better known throughout the world, and especially in the West.

Arriving at the guest house where I shall stay, a lovely woman, Leela, shows me to my room, one of several sleeping rooms in an upstairs apartment-like space. Very basic but spotlessly clean, it features marble tile floors, beautiful wooden doors with gorgeous brass locks, and relatively comfortable beds. It reminds me of the monastery where Olivia and I stayed in Santa Barbara several years ago, but with a bit more ambience and comfort.

Normally, this entire suite can sleep up to seven people in a large open dormitory-style room, my room with two single beds, and another bedroom with a double bed. Mostly, I am thrilled to have an attached bathroom with a western toilet, shower, and sink. A sign indicates toilet paper cannot be flushed down the toilet and is to be deposited in a little covered plastic bucket. I experienced this custom many years ago in Greece, where even the best hotel in town, the Hotel Bretange, due to the age of its plumbing, could not accommodate toilet paper.

Amenities are sparse but adequate; there is a fitted sheet on the bed and one pillow in a pillowcase. My travel silk sheet set is much too hot to use the first night. And there are no tow-els, details about which I forgot to inquire. Improvising, I use a pair of baggy linen shorts for a towel until tomorrow, when I shall borrow or buy one. There also is no hot water, but frankly, it doesn't matter much as the cool shower is incredibly refreshing.

When Leela shows me to my room, she turns the ceiling fan on at maximum speed, so although the room is hot, it is bearable. It would be pretty miserable without it, perhaps not tolerable at all. Apparently, the temperatures are below normal for this time of year; I am not sure but think they are in 80s with, of course, higher humidity. Taking the same approach that I have adopted after decades of living in Phoenix, I prefer not to know how hot it is, ignorance being blissful.

My room is up two short flights of stairs on the second floor of the building. The windows have screens so they can be left open, however, there is not much breeze circulating because there are multistoried buildings constructed very close on both sides. I am struck by the massive, beautiful doors, colorfully painted gates, and impressive brass locks throughout the property.

Deciding to find the Yogi Ramsuratkumar Ashram, at the end of my street is a house with a sign that says, "SheRaSur" or something like that with many sadhus sitting and lying about. Later, I learn that they do not actually reside there, but the owner allows them to hang out and have access to water. There are always a few sadhus sleeping on the street as I pass. Some ask for money; others smile; most ignore you.

In India, there are the true sadhus and others who have simply taken up the life of wandering. Some have serious training with their own gurus; others do not. The locals tell me that one learns to discern the "real" from the "pretenders." I suspect that the younger chap with blue jean shorts under his orange sarong may fall into the latter group.

The ashram is just down the street, only about 100 meters away. En route, I pass the Yogi Ramsuratkumar primary school, where the children recite aloud after their teacher says something to them. Days later when I pass, the teachers are sitting on the step so I stop to chat with them, and they tell me there are no written lessons, only spoken. They are teaching in Sanskit, the ancient Indian language of yoga.

Tall signs and a massive Yogi Ramsuratkumar photograph grace the ashram's entrance. Shoes are left at the front gate of the ashram grounds, and everyone wanders around barefoot. That is a little rough for me; although not a terribly long distance, it is farther than I am accustomed to walking *sans* shoes on blisteringly hot sand, dirt, sidewalks, and cobblestone. My feet will have to toughen up, and so much for following my chiropractor's advice to wear supportive shoes.

Footwear is left outside everywhere, when entering shops, homes, government offices, and other establishments. The reason quickly becomes obvious. Nearly all of the roads are dirt and mud so tracking that into homes, temples, and shops would be a nightmare. All of the shopkeepers are meticulous, frequently outside hosing off steps or sweeping with straw whisk-like, hand brooms.

I feel like a drenched rat after being outdoors a few hours in this weather. Nevertheless, I constantly see men with perfectly pressed shirts and trousers and women who look immaculate in their gorgeous saris.

The ashram is pretty overwhelming on my first visit. Having no idea what or where anything is, I just wander around. The grounds are fairly large, although not the multitude of acres apparently some ashrams have, with various buildings scattered about. Uncertain of what occurs or where, there is a daily schedule posted in front of the main temple/auditorium, in both English and Tamil. Unfortunately, it provides me little assistance because I am clueless as to any of the specific events and ceremonies listed.

First, I go to the Hall of the Mahatmas, a very large circular room with black marble floors attached to the main temple hall. Upon entering, it feels cooler, making it seem like a sanctuary. But what mesmerizes me is the extraordinary collection of oversized paintings and photographs of great well-known yogis and saints hung along all of the walls.

Some are mentioned in the biography of Yogi Ramsuratkumar, *Only God*, a book I would heartily recommend to anyone interested in the history of Indian saints and sages. Although a biography of Ramsuratkumar, so well-written and researched, it provides a great introduction to, and explanation of, many greats from Krishnamurti to Sri Aurobindo and Mother to Ramana to Papa Ramdas and a plethora of others. For example, I learn from the book that there are five high priests or spiritual leaders in the Hindu tradition, known as Shankaracharyas, whose status is comparable to that of the Catholic pope.

Many of those represented that I recognize include Vivekananda, Gandhi, Ramana Maharshi, Ramsuratkumar of course, Paramahansa Yogananda, Ramakrishna, Swami Papa Ramdas, Sivananda, Satchidinanda, Mother and Sri Aurobindo, Guru Nana, Muhammed (no image), Buddha, Jesus Christ, and both of the Sai Babas (the original one, whom many believe is the only authentic one, always sits with one leg crossed over his knee and wears a white turban. The Afro-haired one, who died only about a year ago, is toward the end of the wall as I exit).

There must be fifty or more photographs. In addition to providing a lovely introduction to the ashram, the room has a powerful, yet calming, energy. Already, I know that I shall visit this hall often. In both this hall and everywhere, there are signs posted: "Please switch off your cell phones." Hallelujah!

Next entering a giant auditorium-like hall, it is the main ashram space and temple. Originally, I think it is the Meditation Hall, but later learn that is located next door up a couple of long flights of stairs. A glassed-in room overlooking this huge auditorium, it would be a magnificent place to meditate, if not for the stifling heat. Many people are milling about outside, and I feel conspicuous in my dress and sweater. Nearly all of the women are clad in saris. I shall have to buy at least the pants and long top outfit; the sari looks too unwieldly to tackle.

From the large board with posted activities, I learn that activities begin at 5:30 a.m. and continue until about 8:00 p.m. Serving meals is a tradition at ashrams. Most only allow those people staying at the ashram to partake; however, meals at the Ramsuratkumar Ashram are open to anyone and are free. That apparently was Yogi Ramsuratkumar's wish, and Ma loves to feed people. Breakfast is served from 8:30 to 9:30, and the two lunch sittings are at 12:15 and 1:30 p.m.

The next day, I return to the ashram earlier in the morning where a small group of women are seated chanting inside the main hall. Surrounding the entire space close to the ceiling, two or three stories above, are various six- to eight-foot photographs of Yogi Ramsuratkumar, massive "om" figures, and the mantra that is chanted all day long from the time the ashram opens until close. It is "Yogi Ramsuratkumar, Yogi Ramsuratkumar, Yogi Ramsuratkumar, Jaya Guru Raya." In a biography about him, someone asked why chant his name, to which he replied that if his name is chanted, "This beggar would always be with the person chanting it."

WEDNESDAY, MAY 2, 2012

Amazingly, I awaken only a couple of times during the night, having slept in my skivvies on top of my sheet. It is hot enough so no other bedding is necessary. And by morning, I actually have pulled my multipurpose sarong/ashram shawl/bedcover over me. About 6:30, I arise, take another cool shower, dress, and head to the ashram for early morning chanting.

Upon entering the ashram, Ma Devaki, the resident manager and Ramsuratkumar's long-time devotee, warmly greets me and asks where I am from. Although I immediately recognize her from photographs in the book, I have been told she is the one *always* wearing a white sari and large, heavy shawl...regardless of how hot it is. She is incredibly lovely and warm, telling me about the depth of spirituality from all the saints, both deceased and alive, whose energy populates the surroundings and the mountain. She says that if I do just a few tapas, the result will be very powerful. I feel welcome and so happy to be here.

Asking a couple of questions to get the lay of the land, Ma explains the chanting and tells me to participate or not, meditate wherever I want, and points to the upper level for meditation as well. She tells me when breakfast and lunch are served. Later when seeing her, she inquires to ensure I ate breakfast and reiterates the lunch times. Breakfast, however, is so substantial that I cannot possibly eat lunch as well.

Joining the chanting is lovely; there are only a few people here. I try diligently to chant it properly. Throughout this main ashram hall are various statues of Ramsuratkumar, a poured cast of his feet, and a beautiful inner sanctum that extends up to the multistory-high ceiling where his body is buried sitting up, the standard practice for sadhus, saints, and other godly figures.

After chanting until 8:40, I decide to find where breakfast is served. Asking another smiling young woman who has been leading the chanting and is now outside on the grounds, she escorts me to the dining hall and becomes one of the breakfast servers. The room is empty, so I protest, saying, "Oh, no, I don't want to be the first. I'll wait." Urging me to sit, she manages to explain that others have already eaten. Soon, more folks arrive; men sit at one table facing the women across from them. No one speaks after entering the room.

The food is very good—rice with some sauce or gravy, but the quantity is too great. Having previously been told this as well, a sign at the dining hall entrance explains that food is Prasad (sacred), that many people go without food, and that it is considered adharma to waste food. Hence, one is to eat whatever one takes. I gesture with hand signals to the servers to stop filling my plate or to indicate serving a smaller portion.

Food is served on stainless steel plates, which are like small rimmed platters. Cups, in which water and milk are served, are also stainless steel. Although my bladder issue seems resolved, taking no chances, I continue to drink lots of water. Noting at breakfast that Indians never let the cups touch their lips. Instead, they very adeptly tilt back their heads, pouring water into their mouths without spilling a drop. I try it, and water runs down my face.

The International Shipping
and Parcel Department

IT IS DIFFICULT to remember what day it is.

Sitting and chanting for too many hours, the first day takes its toll on my back. I vow to practice yoga daily. After all I am in India, the birthplace of yoga, so I should have a faithful, consistent asana practice here. And I decide not to stay for such extended periods of chanting. Doing the Bikram hot yoga series, with my own additions, feels normal in this sweat box, that's for sure. The marble floor in my room is great for yoga.

After asana and meditation, I go to the ashram. There is a beautiful ceremony at the temple, which apparently is performed at any temple where a saint or yogi is buried, i.e., his samadhi site. The lingam of Yogi Ramsuratkumar is positioned above his body, and an extensive ritual occurs of washing it, clothing it, and then burning something. Only the priests performing the ceremony are allowed inside the inner sanctum. Upon completion, very loud, shrill bells and drums are played by an automatic machine, and the flame is brought out. People touch the fire and then themselves as a blessing. Vibhuti, the sacred ashes from the fire, is passed out, and we apply it to our foreheads; then coconut water from the washing is distributed. It is a beautiful ritual.

There is always Prasad that has first been offered to the gods and then given to attendees at the door. Today's is a tasty sweet concoction of honey and something else, which is placed in one's right hand. In India, the right hand is used for eating, the left for other duties, such as wiping one's butt, putting on shoes, and other less sanitary functions. In past visits, the Prasad has been rice, nuts, garbanzo beans, and coconut.

There are regular devotees whom I see daily, including an elderly gentleman who comes assisted in a cart driven to the door. He chants loudly and heart-renderingly the entire time, usually for a couple of hours in the mornings. Today, he leads the chanting.

Even though not a devotee of Ramsuratkumar, and I think having known or seen any of these saints in person would make it easier to be a devotee, I certainly feel enveloped in warmth at the ashram. Ma Devaki, who radiates love, is so magnanimous to everyone. The other ashram regulars, women both young and old who are there each and every day, all day long, also are extremely nice. Usually, I offer the Namaste greeting, or they do and I respond.

The few that have spoken to me always ask where I am from. One older incredibly kind lady, Vijayalakshi, was another of Yogi Ramsuratkumar's major devotees, along with Ma. She and Ma were two of four women who served as his devoted servants and were referred to as the Sudama Sisters.

Ma Devaki has an interesting background. Born into a Brahmin (the highest Hindu caste) family, she was well-educated with either a master's or PhD and teaching university physics, but she had been searching for years for a guru. When she met Ramsuratkumar in 1986, she became immediately lost in bliss, quit teaching in 1993, and remained with him until his samadhi in 2001.

Intriguing to me is the concurrent activity buzzing all day long in the ashram main hall. Not only is the main chant continuous, but in the afternoon, other chants are also offered, and in a twice-daily temple ceremony, yet different chanting occurs. Some may be reading or writing, while chanting simultaneously. Today, a woman pushes a floor cleaning machine. Women cut flowers and place them in designated locations. Others copy the main chant in little books or address envelopes. One day, I assist stuffing envelopes with a brochure about an upcoming event.

Various people come and go throughout the day; some confer with Ma. Often, there are families or mothers with children who may sit quietly or race around the hall. Ma may be chanting, opening mail, paying homage to Yogi Ramsuratkumar at his statues, greeting visitors, or talking with staff. It seems to be a well-oiled, busy operation.

Initially, rather taken aback by people talking, comparing my own experiences in church services, I now understand that this is more of a gathering place, and although sacred, an ashram is different from a church. One major activity is the serving of meals. A big production, many people serve, prepare, clean, and coordinate them. Ashrams also engage in a variety of community services, including feeding regular folks and sadhus, providing medical care to sadhus and the community, and educating children. They are a vital aspect of social services provided in Indian society.

Yesterday, I had my first real "yes, this is India experience!" When telling a Westerner at dinner that evening, he surprisingly replies, "Really, you've been here this long, and you're just having your first?" Having purchased my scarves in Chennai as gifts and deciding to send them back to the United States now, I inquire about posting items and am told to go to the post office, where there is both a packaging area and mailing counter.

Arriving at the counter, I am amazed to find no line and no wait. A post office with no lines, and in India, no less with a population of more than a billion people; how can this be? In Phoenix, there is always a wait at the post office. Showing Pleasant Postal Girl the items to comprise four small parcels and asking if she can package them, she tells me yes and then says, "Follow me." We exit the post office and walk to a tiny building a few doors away, on which a posted sign reads: "International Packaging and Shipping Availble (sic) 24 hours."

Upon entering the wee stucco hut, the stench is so overpowering that I can barely breathe. Having both heard from travelers and read in guidebooks about the intense and memorable smells of India, I have not noticed anything terribly offensive, until now. The stink is mind-numbingly overwhelming, a combination of humid heat and smell of cows and other livestock from behind the house.

Pleasant Postal Girl introduces me to a lady Seamstress. The "24-Hour International Packaging and Shipping Department" is her shanty. It has concrete floors, corrugated tin roof, bed, chair (where I am directed to sit), treadle sewing machine, table stacked high with various items, and color television. Around the corner, I see another room.

The Indian pace of life is very slow, as it should be I suppose, given the heat here, but it is also part of the culture. Seamstress is in the midst of watching her soap opera, and my arrival is clearly not propitious timing for she remains far much more interested in her program than my business. I discover that the plan is for her to sew tiny bags out of cloth that reminds me of the cream-colored muslin flour bags of my childhood.

The interminable process begins.

First, Seamstress rummages around to find this and that odd-sized plastic bag for each of the four parcels, places the items inside each, and securely tapes the bags. This takes fifteen to twenty minutes. Having walked the distance from my room, and although it isn't far, it is noonish, the day is hot, and her room is excruciatingly stifling. Everyone has been commenting today about how hot it is.

Next, she digs around to find cloth, lays each parcel on it, and cuts the cloth. Another fifty or more minutes pass. Beginning to feel very uncomfortable, not only from the stifling heat and odors of cow manure, but also because I realize that I am about to send delicate silk to America in cloth bags.

Knowing how the US Postal Service handles parcels, I have visions of shards of silk arriving in muslin rags. Although this is seeming an imprudent plan, I feel rather stuck. Having not inquired as to the cost, I finally ask her. She tells me fifty rupees. Total or each? Each. Okay, $1 per bag. Fine, whatever; it seems a little pricey given the Indian marketplace, but at this juncture, I care not. I want only to get out of this room...preferably alive and without suffering heat stroke.

Finally, the bags are cut. Clearly a real seamstress, she has a pair of those gargantuan, spiffy scissors, the kind I have never owned, but that are used in fabric stores. Next, she goes to her vintage 1930s sewing machine, flips an electricity switch on the wall, and stands, using the treadle to sew up the bags.

To expedite things, I begin turning the bags as she completes them. She protests, but worrying that I well may perish in this place, I say, "Oh, I can sew, my mother taught me at a young age," and begin to package the items. One bag is too small. Terrific, more time to sew another. She is still sewing the remaining two. When she finishes, I show her the bag that is too small. Not believing me, she tries mightily to cram in the items, but finally concedes that they don't fit. So there is more rummaging for fabric, cutting, sewing, and turning the bag again.

I am beginning to feel faint. At least an hour has passed since we began this process. Watching her and contemplating the situation, I conclude that sending silk to the United States in cloth bags, albeit wrapped in plastic, is just a bad idea. *Finally*, three sides of all bags are sewn, and the scarves are stuffed in the bags with not 1/8 inch to spare on any side.

Seamstress then comes to the bed, which serves also as her work table, with thread and a gigantic needle about three or four inches long. Realizing that the plan is now to hand-sew the remaining open side of each bag, I envision another hour's time in this smelly sweat box and know I cannot survive it!

Nearly delirious from heat exhaustion and the reek, I decide to abort the exercise then and there and find a box or sturdier packaging. Telling Seamstress, "This is not going to work," I hand her 200 rupees, thank her, and dash out the door.

Back at the post office, I try explaining to Pleasant Postal Girl my concern about silk getting damaged during shipment. She is probably offended, and although trying very hard to be respectful of this culture at all times, my physical discomfort has simply overcome me. Now, I feel stupid for getting this far into the process. My first major lesson of India: *ask enough questions!*

Amazingly, when I ask Pleasant Postal Girl if they have any small boxes, she says, "Oh yes, we have boxes," and produces the perfect small size. Asking if they have four, Pleasant Postal Girl replies, " "Oh yes, they are sixty rupees." I say, "Fine, this cloth simply isn't going to work." She looks puzzled, but is very compliant.

Asking for scissors to open the plastic bags and unpackage some of the items to transfer, I label the boxes. Then I complete *four* individual customs forms, one for each box. Writing "Kjos, India" as my return address, it isn't sufficient; she needs a real address. I don't know it. Using the name of the ashram is good enough, and another lady behind the desk, perhaps the Postmistress, knows how to spell the name of the ashram.

Now, Pleasant Postal Girl can meticulously and *very, very* slowly, tape, weigh, recalculate, and reweigh. This whole procedure takes at least another forty-five minutes. But at least I am

happy that my scarves are properly packaged and most appreciative of her help. Actually, I am surprised that including the cost
of the boxes, each parcel probably cost approximately $10 to ship.
It costs me that much to ship a small parcel from Arizona to
the Midwest.

By the time I leave the post office, I am thoroughly spent and
stagger back to my room to collapse. Later in the afternoon, fear-
ing I may have experienced a bit of heat stroke, I am unable to
cool off despite numerous showers and cold compresses on my
forehead. Eventually, I take a nap and feel recovered.

And as for Indian time calculations, I learn quickly having
been told my numerous people, "Oh, that's five or ten minutes
away." Either I am a very slow walker, cannot tell time, or it is
like being in Russia. There, everything was "tomorrow." Having
been told that day after day, we finally grasped that back then
in Russia, "tomorrow" meant "never." Here where everything is
either five or ten minutes, using thirty instead, at a minimum,
is wiser.

SATURDAY, MAY 5, 2012

Feeling guilty about being unkind to Seamstress yesterday and
deciding to make amends, I take to her today a pair of linen
shorts with a ripped seam for repair, tip her, and am kind. She
quotes me twenty rupees; I give her thirty. She is very happy and
gives me a Namaste thanks of bringing one's hands into a prayer
position. I feel better. Kindness is the most important of human
virtues, and I do not like myself when I act otherwise.

Yesterday, having what I referred to as my first real India
experience, today I encounter the flip side of that—and another
real India experience. Walking back from Shanti Café the same
way I walked earlier, after exchanging dollars for rupees, I man-

age to step in the middle of deep muddy sludge from yesterday's monsoon.

Sinking in muck, my shoes and socks are totally covered in mud up to my ankles. Looking down, my only thought is where I can possibly wash them off, and I say aloud, "Welcome to India!" It is to become my mantra for these uniquely Indian moments.

Continuing down the road, I hear a woman calling, but have no idea what she is saying. Shortly, I meet a Second Lady who motions me. The woman behind has been trying to get my attention to direct me to a water faucet located back at the area where I stepped in the mud. Second Lady ushers me to the location, where I wash off my shoes. I thank them both profusely and am terribly moved by their kindness. One really does find God in myriad ways and places.

The ashram lunch drill is different from breakfast, where one drops in during the one-hour serving period. There are two lunch sittings. Arriving too late for the first one, I go to chant. At 1:30, we are allowed entry to the dining hall. Ma greets everyone and directs them to sit, the majority on the floor. Likely thinking this Western woman is not yet floor-ready, kindly, she sends me to a table with another lady. It appears that first the floor is filled, then the overflow along with others such as me and the elderly are assigned to tables.

Ma makes some greeting in Tamil. We chant as plates are filled with a very tasty round fritter, a deep-fried sweet concoction, some carrot mixture, rice, and a gravy/sauce with veggies that is called sambar. Everything is yummy. For the first time, I get a reasonable-sized portion, always passing on the milk.

The serving is well-orchestrated, taking only a few minutes to fill everyone's plates, whereupon Ma says something else—perhaps meaning something like, "Okay, you can eat now," and we commence. Servers come by frequently to refill water glasses and offer additional helpings of rice and gravy, served from large silver buckets. No one speaks while eating.

Upon completing meals, the stainless steel water cup is deposited in a large plastic container in the dining room. Then we exit outdoors to a long metal trough to wash our stainless steel plates under one of several water spigots and place them in another big tub. Wondering if this is the only washing the plates receive before being reused again, I prefer not to know.

Having now been in this spiritual hotbed of India for a full three days, I contemplate how I have been affected thus far. How do I feel? What do I want to do? The conclusion I reach is to continue trying to be present, grateful, and loving. It will take time to unwind, decompress, and start to shed Western attitudes, expectations, and biases.

Having tried to focus over the past few years on "being" versus "doing," "having," "accumulating," and "wanting," with varying degrees of success, I may be a few steps down the road toward my own awakening. For now, it feels fine to live in a non–air-conditioned place, learning how to cope with being very hot and occasionally even uncomfortable. It is important to find reserve within myself rather than things always being easy. I know instinctively that I am ready for whatever God has in store for me on this journey.

Getting Thrown Out of the Ashram Dining Room

I THINK IT WAS yesterday—the days start running together—when at breakfast I am seated one seat away from a beautiful young woman, Jerri. Obviously Western, so I, always the friendly one, inquire about her origins. From Toronto, Canada, she has been in Tiruv for two and a half months. She is delightful, and we chat away eating our breakfast. Soon, one of the servers yells loudly at us and motions for us to leave. We had finished eating, but they inhale their food here, and upon finishing, you apparently are immediately supposed to leave the table. There is no dillydallying. Perhaps we also were not supposed to talk. So we sheepishly slink out, and I take her to the main ashram hall.

This is a particularly interesting experience for only a day or so ago, I had a conversation with another foreigner who pointed out that Indians, unlike as is our custom, do not use meals as a socializing time. They eat, but there is no chitchat.

One thing I learn from Jerri is that she rents an apartment *with air conditioning* for only 250 rupees a day, approximately $5. I begin salivating. Rental rates are lower now after the high season is over. The recommended donation suggested where I currently am staying is much higher and would normally include all meals. Since I am not getting those, I may scout around to find a better rate for a place with air conditioning. To date, that has really been my only challenge. My room is very hot, despite the fan running twenty-four hours daily.

Reminding myself that it is all right to be uncomfortable and that it is part of the process, I try not to focus on it too much. And only a couple of nights have been rough, one being last night. Despite drawing from tricks learned in Phoenix when air conditioning goes out during the hottest summer temperatures—cold towels, water sprinkled on sheets, cold showers, and cooling ties around my neck, it is a night of many wake-ups. Happy to have packed three of them, I keep two in a bucket of cold water, and if really hot, simply keep alternating them.

The closest shop I frequent is a tiny nearby spot with a quirky owner. Upon asking what to call him, the locals say to call him "Sir," which is fine since he always greets me as "Madam." Here you address people depending upon their jobs and/or their ages. For example, "Watchman" is the name to call the building security guard. I stop at Sir's market daily for snacks, mango and cranberry juice, nuts, soda, and cold water, which is a real treat.

And in the United States, I cannot recall the last time I drank a Coca Cola (diet Coke, unfortunately, yes), but out of boredom, I drink one here for a change of pace. Without my beloved Celestial Seasonings herbal iced tea, it is my little guilty pleasure. I am surprised by how many people drink coffee here also rather assuming that everyone would drink tea.

Finally, a Cooling Rain

NOT LONG BEFORE leaving the United States, there was an interesting piece on *60 Minutes* about how Indians love their gold. Girls' families begin buying them gold when they are very young and keep buying it through their lives. Essentially, when women marry, they then have a stash of gold. Not really like a traditional dowry in that apparently, it is not given to the groom's parents, but rather it provides security for the woman. One wonders if women really keep it or if their husbands do receive it.

The gold is very bright and shiny, not the 14-karat that we typically wear. It is probably is 22-karat. Brother Nick brought me an 18-karat gold puzzle ring from Saudi Arabia, and this gold looks brighter and shinier than that. The women wear gold necklaces, small gold pierced earrings (sometimes with other gemstones), and gold bracelets. No doubt there is status affiliated with how much gold one wears. I also am beginning to notice with respect to saris those trimmed in gold versus the plain cotton ones, again no doubt indicating the status or social position of the wearer.

Having just read in a copy of the *Nirvana* guidebook, recently secured from the library, having lost mine somewhere in Chennai, when the Ramana ashram chanting schedule is, I shall return for a formal chanting session. Perhaps too, if I read some of his works, his energy will come through for me. Ramana, a realized great saint, spent many years of his life in silence. Revered far and wide, nearly everyone I have met and spoken with here is a Ramana devotee.

Pondicherry is supposedly lovely, and everyone recommends going there. Interestingly, Pondicherry too has a new name like the other major Indian cities, which names were adopted a decade or so ago replacing the British designated ones. It is Puducherry, which I discover from my *Lonely Planet* guidebook. No one refers to it as anything other than Pondicherry or Pondi. I still prefer the old names myself—Bombay, Madras, Calcutta, Delhi. No one uses the "New" with Delhi either.

Sri Aurobindo's ashram is in Pondicherry. Educated in England, he returned to India and was one of the great scholars of his time, as well as a leader of the Indian independence movement along with Vivekenanda, Gandhi, and others. Mother Mirra (referred to as "Mother"), a French woman and mystic, was his full-time partner and major disciple. Interestingly, many of the great realized saints of India had primary female disciples, including Ramakrishna, Vivekenanda, Papa Ramdas, Yogi Ramsuratkumar, and others. Ramana's mother was his disciple, coming to Tiruv to take care of and live with him later in her life.

While at Pondicherry, Aurobindo spent most of his time in seclusion, rarely giving audiences; Mother was the day-to-day person in charge. He died in 1950 the same year as Ramana. I only know of his work, but have never read any of it. Yogi

Ramsuratkumar credits Aurobindo and Ramana as his first two teachers and Swami Papa Ramdas as his last and most important.

Pondicherry was a French colony so it has tasty, more diverse food, charming architecture, and is on the sea. Not far from here, the journey is about three and a half hours by bus or car. Auroville too is appealing. Located just outside Pondicherry, the universal city was conceived by Mother and is apparently comprised of multiple communities, but it is hard to get a good flavor of it from my guidebook.

One of the little endearing customs I keep forgetting to write about is that men and boys walk down the street holding hands. Or they may stand together and hold hands or sit with their arms wrapped around each other. It has nothing to do with their sexual preference, but rather a sign of friendship. The first time I noticed this was at the Le Meridien Hotel in Chennai where the waiter introduced me to his supervisor in the lobby outside the bar, took his hand, and the two continued to stand holding hands. Later, when we were out in Chennai, Anish kept teasing Roger about how he didn't like being touched by men, which would be a typical reaction from a straight American guy.

Oh, and how could I have not yet written about the indigenous head bobbing? Having been told about it by other travelers and the fact that one cannot assume that the bob or side-to-side wobble indicates either assent or dissent, today when asking Sir a question, his reply was a head bob. Asking, "Yes?" he replies, "No." The women do it also, but it seems more prevalent among men, or at least I notice it more with them.

Another interesting, uniquely Indian experience is walking about town and coming upon two gents ironing away at a street corner. I have no idea what their power source is, but clearly, that is their business. And another day, lost on my way back from the restaurant Dreaming Tree, in the middle of nowhere on a little road is a lady with her sewing machine inside a very small hovel. Battery-operated perhaps?

When Brother Nick lived abroad those many years, including in Pakistan, Thailand, Mongolia, Yemen, and several other Middle Eastern countries, he frequently commented that we Americans have no idea how the majority of the rest of the world lives and how spoiled we are. One does appreciate the little things we take for granted—like big fluffy towels, air conditioning, *ice, ice, ice*, Celestial Seasonings Red Zinger tea, *ice*, and air conditioning. Actually, that's really not much of a list so far though. Mostly, I remain grateful both to be here and for my many yoga teachers over the years, who began illuminating this path.

Some friends have sent e-mails with various questions. One is whether the food and drink are safe? Yes and no. Food at ashrams is fine because they have water filters and apparently take special caution to ensure food is safe. There are certain restaurants where one can eat safely—essentially better restaurants or those catering to foreign travelers. One is counseled *not* to eat street food sold by the vendors because the cooking oil might be rancid or utensils unsanitary and the like. The usual plethora of flies swarming on street food makes it rather unappetizing anyhow.

The basic advice for eating in India is to eat only cooked food, boiled water (unless bottled), and fruits that can be peeled, such as apples, oranges, mangoes, pineapples, melons, and bananas. Except for the oranges, which are pretty tasty, the fruit eaten thus far, even at the hotels in Chennai, has been pretty marginal. I have not yet had mangoes or pineapples.

Interestingly, however, while still reading newspapers (which I no longer do) in Chennai, an article about the city water there said that it is so horribly contaminated, it is recommended that *no one* drink it, not even the locals. Various prior India travelers offered me advice, in addition to information I read, which included recommendations to bring lots of vitamins and any possible medication one might need. I brought a sizeable array of both and take a plethora of vitamins as well as probiotic supplements.

On a related subject, one of the most difficult things for me is to throw trash on the ground, which is the custom. I still really do not unless absolutely necessary. The amount of trash littering the streets and ditches is staggering; it reminds me of Mexico. One wonders if that issue will ever be seriously addressed or if there are far more pressing concerns for the country. Occasionally in a back alley in Chennai, I saw large metal garbage bins, but that is exceedingly rare. Sir, who is meticulous about keeping his floors and property clean, however, has a plastic receptacle for garbage. And Roger told me that plastic water bottles are collected and recycled in Chennai.

Whenever not at my computer, observations, thoughts, and ideas that I have forgotten to write about pop into my mind. One is that Pattabi Jois, the famous elderly Ashtanga yoga teacher from Mysore, died, which I learned from reading the April *Vanity Fair* issue on the plane. Having been outside the mainstream yoga world for a while, I had not heard of his passing.

To my knowledge, the venerable B.K.S. Iyengar in Pune, father of hatha yoga, is still alive. The *Vanity Fair* article indicated that one of Jois's exceedingly wealthy East Coast students is setting up Jois Centers (or some similar name) throughout the country, supposedly at his bequest. This is causing much controversy in the Ashtanga community because apparently some of his long-time early teachers, such as Tim Miller and others, have been treated badly. How sad.

The transport of yoga to America, indeed, is now big business. And of course, capitalists must increase capital and profit. Hopefully, the real transmission of its import and soul will not be completely subsumed as the physical aspect continues to be the primary focus in this country. I keep thinking that perhaps as we boomers and others age, we may better appreciate yoga for its myriad benefits, not merely the physical. Inevitable though I suppose when anything develops such popularity in the United States, mass marketing and packaging result. Bikram, certainly the forerunner of yoga as a for-profit big business, figured that out decades ago.

Before departing, I read several books about the sadhus, India's holy men who are renunciates and maintain various spiritual practices and austerities, renouncing all worldly possessions and interests. The bona fide ones begin their lives anew after initiation by their gurus when they receive sacred mantras and new names.

Not only was I unaware that there are many different sects, formal initiations, and hierarchies within these branches, it amazed me to learn that still many millions of sadhus wander throughout India, their lives solely devoted to worshipping the Divine and surviving from alms. In reading a biography about Sivananda, the great saint and swami of Rishikesh, I learned that many sadhus also simply choose to live the mendicant lifestyle without any formal tutelage from a guru.

Most sadhus continuously travel about, often on pilgrimage from holy site to holy site; others stay put in various cities or dharamsalas. This is a tradition and culture totally incomprehensible to ours in the West, and as far as I know, unique to India. Yogi Ramsuratkumar fervently believed that sadhus were a critical part of India's culture—past, present, and future—requiring protection. He maintained that the sadhus were what gave India her soul.

Having read that many Indians consider sadhus as merely a lazy, chillum-smoking lot unwilling to support themselves like normal folks, I think Hindus with a strong spiritual background believe that they are holy men, treating them with great reverence. Many sadhus, especially the followers of Shiva in the north smoke chillums (tobacco and hashish or marijuana) regularly as part of their practice and lifestyle. And according to my guidebook, there have been since time memorial, wanted criminals who don the robes to avoid the law as well.

Many sadhus frequent this neighborhood. All wear orange garb of some form, which is usually a dhoti or lungi. Not particularly moved or enamored by those I see routinely, I have nick-names for the regulars: Sincere Sadhu, who makes several rounds through the ashram daily, prostrates, gets blessings, and appears to be very devout; Green Shirt Sadhu, who is at the ashram every morning; Swimmer Sadhu, whose sunglasses look like swimming goggles; Boy Blue Sadhu, a young guy who wears blue jean shorts under his orange dhoti; Screaming Sadhu, who always yells as I pass; Sweet Sadhu, who only smiles and offers Namaste' greet-ings; and a new fellow who appeared within the last couple of days, Bicycle Sadhu, who has a bicycle and more belongings, including a radio. The true hard-cores carry one shoulder bag with all of their earthly possessions.

Swamis also wear orange, which is considered a holy color. As I understand the difference, swamis, although also having taken vows as holy men, do not live on the streets as renunciates. They may have an organization, an ashram, or a group supporting them, or perhaps not. Obviously, the local Internet Café Swami runs a business, is married, and has children. When out of curios-ity, I ask him today how long he has been wearing the robes, he says three years.

One fascinating book is *Autobiography of a Sadhu* by Rampuri (originally printed under the title *Autobiography of a Blue-Eyed Sadhu*), who came to India at a young age of seventeen or thereabouts from California searching for more meaning to life. His father was a Beverly Hills surgeon. Ultimately, he was initiated into the Naga Babas (an order of warrior ascetics who are naked and often castrated), the first Westerner ever to be so permitted. That was a very "big deal"—a white sadhu, and he was not readily accepted by the sadhu community.

Until I read his book, I was unaware of the various groups and lineages. An amazing peek into that culture, Rampuri describes the Naga Babas as the "Hell's Angels of the Babas." Someone in Phoenix sponsored him a few years ago, and my yoga teacher friend Bonnie met him and says that he is the real deal. He now has an ashram in Haridwar in northern India.

Another incredibly well-written, fascinating book, which I have only begun, by a French author, Patrick Levy, who actually lived the life of a sadhu for a time, is *Sadhus: Going Beyond the Dreadlock*. Although compelling on so many levels, one thing that I am struck by is that a sadhu has a life of ultimate, complete freedom. Owning nothing except what fits in his bag, which might include a food bowl, a blanket, some sacred writings, and the like, a sadhu arises before dawn to see the sun rise (an important ritual), and then spends his days as they unfold—no commitments, no requirements, no needs, no stress, no deadlines, no plans. There is something intriguing about such a lifestyle that seems magical to me.

FRIDAY, MAY 11, 2012

My ambivalence is notable. Two days ago, my plan was to purchase another fan to provide more comfort in my room, and yesterday, it definitely seemed time to leave Tiruv. Today, I feel that I should stay a while longer. Ambivalence means that it is not yet decision-making time.

When I left for India, my plan was simply to follow my heart and my intuition. Ergo, I have no preplanned itinerary. My only real plans were to consult the nadi scroll readers, go to ashrams, and see the Taj Mahal for, of course, it would be heresy to come to India and skip her most famous landmark.

My Angel Card Reader told me that the reason I am drawn to India is because I lived here in prior lives. I think that is accurate because my reaction to India has not been what many others report, feeling neither dismayed nor overwhelmed by much. Intrigued and fascinated certainly, but generally, I feel pretty comfortable with the conditions of India. So is it because I have spent past lives here?

Who knew that I would write so much here either? My long love of writing has just taken hold. My friend Suzanne, who has been here many times, told me that creativity comes easily in India. That certainly has proven true for me.

For forty rupees, or roughly eighty cents, I lunch at a little café in a nearby ashram with an exceedingly long name. My plate is a massive banana leaf (how very charming), and my female server actually hands me a spoon just as I am about to dive in with my fingers. Some folks really get into the playing with food routine, engaging in quite a ritual of stirring, molding food with sauces, rearranging, scooping, and organizing. A kid's eating paradise this place. Not a restaurant in the typical sense, there is no menu; I eat what is available that day.

Today's repast tastes pretty similar to that of the Yogi Ramsuratkumar ashram—as if the same cook may have prepared it. Essentially, it is the same food; in addition to rice, of course, beets are served, cut into the tiniest of pieces with a delicious seasoning. Given five or six little cups of various sauces, two of which appear to be milk or yogurt that I do not eat, some are pure liquid with seasonings that are beginning to taste familiar. Others have some veggies in them. Later, I learn that this is a classic Indian "thali" meal.

Another unique aspect of Indian restaurant protocol is that anyone may join you at your table if there is no room elsewhere. No one speaks to each other, however. As a single woman in a conservative country, I make a point not to chat with any man who sits at my table for fear of seeming too friendly or available. Today, a man sits at my table. Earlier this week, at Abriani Restaurant, it was a large family, several of whom sat on the table bench across from me while the rest stood waiting until I finished, and then took my side of the bench. It is rather unnerving to have a group of people hovering over you while eating. One certainly does not linger completing the meal.

Having my second Indian massage from a fellow recommended by two Western women, the masseur is originally from Kerala. Telling me the ten-syllable name of the town he is from, I inquire if it is the locale of the famous nadi scroll readers. He says, "Yes," but then quickly adds, "But don't waste your time with that stuff, it's nonsense, magic." *Really?* I think amusingly to myself, but say nothing. In a country where your major religion has 330 *million* different forms of gods that represent its Supreme Being, some folks might think that's a bit out there too! It is interesting how we all see reality through the prism of our own upbringing, experiences, and understandings.

As I age and study more cultures, religions, and belief systems, I decide that I believe in everything. Why not? There are so many judgments and musts and do's and don'ts in many organized religions. Sins and sinners. Who is to say that one belief system is better or right? Each person trained or brainwashed in one belief system, whether Christian, Jewish, Hindu, Buddhist, Jain, Sikh, or Muslim, can find a plethora of materials, teachers, sacred books, and studies to support that religious tradition.

It has always seemed preposterous to me to believe that simply because I was raised Christian—solely a function of the location of my birth and parents—why my belief system should trump another or be considered more correct than that of someone raised in the Middle East, India or Africa. Even more limiting, in Christian traditions, Protestants often believe that their beliefs are the "right" ones, superior to those of Catholics. No doubt there are Catholics with the same biases about the Protestant faith.

If one believes in a Supreme Being, it shouldn't matter what path one follows. These narrow attitudes are why so many people find "religion" in a more traditional sense unappealing, preferring a spiritual approach instead. Certainly, believing in everything resonates more with me. Or as a friend said about religions many years ago, "They are all the same."

Melissa's Fan, a Godsend, and Serving Sadhus

MOTHER'S DAY. THINKING about my own mother, she was a truly amazing woman. How blessed I feel to have been raised by her. The epitome of motherhood, she always put her family first. She was the first "saint" I knew; although growing up, of course, I certainly didn't appreciate that until Sherryle first referred to her as that, and I realized she was so right. Gratefully, as I matured, I came to understand and value what a wonderful human being she was. Everyone loved Annie, a kind, gentle, and thoughtful woman.

I honor you today, Mom. I love you and think of you often. I know that your spirit continues to guide me. The greatest compliment anyone could ever give me would be to say that I adopted any of your traits of selfless love, compassion, and generosity.

Melissa has invited me to her house for a visit. Using the auto rickshaw driver, Majinder, who gives her reasonable prices all year long (not surprisingly, they take advantage of the seasonal visitors and raise fares substantially), she sends him to pick me up. My afternoon out in the country with her is delightful. Although only a ten-minute rickshaw ride away, it is pretty rough terrain so I am grateful to have emptied my bladder before departing. Delightedly, there is a palpable temperature difference between town and out there, and she serves iced tea (what a major treat) and biscuits.

Built for her by a local Indian friend, Melissa's home is lovely. A two-story, concrete structure on a fair-sized lot entirely surrounded by a high wrought-iron fence and large gate, the house is simple but pleasant with a living room/kitchen, bedroom, and bathroom, certainly sufficient space for one person to live comfortably. With windows on all sides, the ventilation is much better than where I stay, and it is actually comfortable in her home.

Melissa gives me a battery-operated fan to use that someone left it at her house and she doesn't use. What an appreciated gift! It will be an absolute blessing during power outages.

When we discuss my interest in going to Pondicherry and Auroville, Melissa asks if I want company. I am thrilled. She has lived here off and on since 2000, so it will be nice to have someone who knows the ropes.

Spiritually, I am experiencing many positive things, not necessarily as I might have anticipated, but rewarding nevertheless. If nothing else, perhaps the heat will burn out my ego. My friend Betsy from New York City e-mails that it sounds like an eternal summer here. It's a perfect description. Not unlike the blistering hot Phoenix summers in that if outdoors, one feels a stifling, silent kind of energy. I move slowly as does everyone. The dogs are asleep in whatever shaded spot they find. Sadhus recline under trees. It reminds me of that Tennessee Williams play where everyone is withering in the southern heat.

MONDAY, MAY 14, 2012

Going to the ashram later for the morning puja, I eat lunch there, but it is too hot to stay and chant in the main hall. As has become my habit, I wander through the Hall of Mahatmas on my way out of the ashram grounds. The same fellow is always asleep against the wall inside the grand black marble room, where it is cooler. Sleeping amidst all those saints must generate good energy. The Mahatmas Hall is my favorite place on the property—peaceful, humbling, and meditative.

By the time I arrive back at my room, only about 100 meters away, my clothes are drenched in perspiration. Ripping them off, I jump under a tepid shower for a cool-down, turn on my wonderful new fan, say *major thanks* to Melissa (my own little angel), and lie on a towel on my bed. Just breathing and chanting the Ram chant: "Om Sri Ram, Jai Ram, Jai Jai Ram."

My pants at Seamstress' are to be finished today. Her door is closed when I arrive; tomorrow I shall try earlier in the day. Other pants purchased from the little Kashmiri guy, Omar, have a small hole in them, which I didn't notice at the time. Popping in to return them, he prepares me a tasty saffron tea, which has saffron, sugar, cardamom, and another spice.

Omar shows me "some very special shawls that he does not show just everyone." It is quite the spiel. If to be believed, the wool is derived from the scruff of some special rare bird and comes in only three colors: taupe, brown, and black. Incredibly soft, and indeed beautiful, they do not wrinkle, which he demonstrates by rolling one into a wee ball and stuffing in his pants pocket. Explaining that it is much, much better than pashmina (wool from the scruff of the pashmina goat), it is "only $250 American, special price for me, charge more in season, I would look so smashing at a party."

Tales abound about scams of shopkeepers. Later, I learn from another Kashmiri shopkeeper, who becomes a friend, that the rare bird with special fur from its neck is nonexistent. No such creature, no such wool. Gotta love India!

In my discussion with Omar, who is Muslim, he says that naturally he eats no pork, considering it so unclean that if he is walking on a street and a pig approaches, he will move to the other side of the road. Regarding Hindus not eating meat, it is unclear to me how strenuously this custom is followed. One regularly sees restaurant signs that read "veg" or, my personal favorite, "high class veg" (whatever that means). Food served in ashrams is always vegetarian, but milk products are used. The concept of "vegan" is not one recognized here; everyone seems to drink and eat dairy products: curd, yogurt, milk.

When with Roger's two Hindu friends in Chennai, they both eat beef and love it; their parents do not. Most likely how rigorously various dietary proscriptions are followed depends upon how devout one is and perhaps, of which generation. Apparently, one fast food chain here, one of the pizza chains I believe, serves beef. In Chennai, there were advertisements for both Domino's and Pizza Hut. McDonald's does not serve beef, and I was told that because of its size and reputation, it wanted no hassles in this primarily Hindu country. The "burgers" on its menu are vegetarian, fish, or chicken.

Tuesday, May 15, 2012

It's been almost three weeks since I arrived. Time passes quickly wherever one is.

With each new experience or aha moment, I feel like a child. That is interesting because another thing my Angel Card Reader told me before I left was that I would experience India as a child, finding everything new and exciting. How wonderful to be learning all the time, even if such little things.

I discover that there are *two* electrical outlets in my room. Since the fan does not require my special India electrical adaptor as does my computer, I can plug in both the fan and my computer. Does it get any better than this?

One becomes accustomed to local customs rather quickly. First, in India, pedestrians do not have the right-of-way. *Ever.* When walking, one better get the bloody hell out of the way of any moving vehicles, and look in both directions. Drivers honk horns incessantly to alert you of their approach, but never move or slow for walkers.

Also, there will often be four or more people piled on motor scooters. The most I have seen is four rather good-sized young men, but Roger from Chennai says that he once saw five. By contrast, it amuses me thinking about our seat belt, helmet, and child seat requirements. Here one sees entire families—Mom, Dad, and two small kids zooming along on the motorbike or scooter with no helmets.

Today, I assist with the Tuesday feeding of sadhus, which is held in the open second-floor deck of the ashram next door. A lovely experience, I feel honored to serve these holy men. My sense of those present is that they are authentic characters. Twenty-one attend, all wearing some variation of saffron-colored garb, except for one in a bright yellow lungi. Also serving are Kunal's brother, Santos, and ashram employees, Leela and Siri.

Before the lunch serving commences, we four servers have tea, very hot tea. At about 11:15, Santos hops on the motor scooter, and we women walk, proceeding down the road a few minutes away to pick up the food, prepared by another lady. Santos takes the biggest one containing rice on the scooter, and we carry the others.

Already, Leela and Siri have the table—the floor—set. Seating is on bamboo mats lined up in three rows; the place setting is a folded banana leaf with stainless steel tumblers and small bowls. As to how to serve the food, Leela tries explaining where to place things on the leaf, but I suggest that perhaps instead I hand out the bananas and crispy tortilla-like bread and pour water. She agrees. The sadhus start arriving up the stairs. No one speaks. Exchanged only are namaste, prayer-clasped hands greetings, nods, and smiles.

Each sadhu, arriving in silence, takes a place. There is some confusion about where one wants to sit, and I recognize him immediately as the troublemaker from yesterday at Sir's store. Most are older, with only one or two looking younger than age fifty. Of course, living in the elements of India, many may be younger than they appear. Two look wizened with lots of markings on their foreheads and arms. It is a Kodak moment, yet it seems wholly inappropriate to ask to take photographs. A few bring hands to their heart, showing gratitude as I serve them. All are dear and sweet, except possibly Troublemaker Sadhu, who makes some complaint about his banana leaf, whereupon Leela replaces it for him.

As at the ashram, servings occur in three rounds. When we commence the first serving, one of the sadhus leads a chant; the others repeat it. Once the serving is complete, Leela and Santos perform a short ceremony at a small altar followed by another brief chant. Then eating commences, again in silence. There is a serenity of eating in silence.

During the first round, we serve water, a banana (tiny in India, approximately half the size of ours), a small spoonful of salt, a serving of one variety of vegetable, another serving of a different vegetable, rice, gravy for the rice, a crispy tortilla-like bread called papad I think, a tiny spoonful of spicy, bitter pickles, and sweets. The pickles are served each day at the ashram too, and I love them, but many of the sadhus motion, indicating not to be served those.

We watch and occasionally someone motions for something, which we immediately serve him. I keep their water tumblers filled. The second serving begins, which includes more rice and a different kind of sauce. Finally, the third serving is another milky sauce over more rice. This is served at the ashram too, but I have not eaten it. Serving them is interesting. Some make very distinct little rice bowls into which they want their gravy poured; others point to a spot on the banana leaf to place the food. And like the typical Indian diner, most spend a fair amount of time, mixing, rearranging, organizing, and molding their rice before eating.

After everyone finishes, the same sadhu leads a final chant, then all depart, again in silence. Some give gestures of thanks by bringing their hands to their hearts. I feel privileged to participate and honor them in this small way.

As for the story about Troublemaker Sadhu, yesterday while at Sir's store late in the afternoon, a loquacious Older Chap with English accent was chatting up an older woman. Suddenly, Troublemaker Sadhu comes up carrying a plate of food and starts motioning and asking him for something. Older Chap gives Troublemaker Sadhu a hard time, saying that he can usually figure out any hand signals, but doesn't know what the sadhu wants and since he has a plate full of food in his hand, he can't need money.

Unsuccessful with Older Chap, Troublemaker Sadhu turns to me. I ask if he wants a container for his food because he points to the stainless steel plates. Noting that he is wearing quite a nice watch and gold jewelry, not exactly what I would consider a typical destitute sadhu's attire, he is carrying a very large bag. It is the jewelry that I first notice today when seeing him again at lunch.

Asking Sir what he wants, Sir makes a hand gesture that I understand to be money. Then Sir gets angry and starts yelling at Troublemaker Sadhu, chasing him off. Sir comes back to us, saying, "Big problem, big problem, they always ask for money." I laugh. Older Chap says precisely what I was thinking, "Why doesn't he just eat the food?"

Yesterday, in early afternoon, I decide to try Seamstress, none of my prior *three* trips having been at that hour. Fourth time's a charm I guess for, indeed, the Sri Ramana Cotton Cloth Shop is finally open. Seamstress seems not in the least concerned that I was there yesterday, the day she told me to come. Actually, I am very happy with my $5.75 linen pants; what a great deal. They fit well, are a dark color, and should wear well here.

I read and rest for a couple of hours before returning a bit before 5:30 to see Seamstress. She is still working on my pants and says, "Ten minutes." Looking at her fabric while waiting, this is clearly going to be the "Indian ten minutes" or translated "Give it your best bloody guess of how long it may take!" Getting bored, I say that I can come back tomorrow. "No, no," she doesn't want me to come then; I learn that tomorrow she will be away shopping for fabric. So I wander to some shops, and upon returning, Seamstress has finished my pants repair and done a nice job.

Deciding to stop by Swami's Internet café to do some research about possible next stops, I ask his son if it is better to fly or take the train to Mumbai. Trent, a fellow sitting to my left says, "Fly, it's thirty-six hours by train." That's a no-brainer. Fares are reasonable enough.

The fellow and I chat a bit, and I learn that he is from the United States. Inquiring if he does any work here, he says, "A little bit, I help people get phones, find places to live and the like." When I mention that I may look for another place with air conditioning, he volunteers that he has a two-room, fully-furnished apartment to rent at a very reasonable rate of 200 rupees per night. And most importantly, it has *air conditioning*.

I like Tiruv and would stay longer if my room wasn't so bloody hot. Saying that I may call him over the weekend after returning from Pondi to look at it, he says that it is within walking distance and very quiet. Melissa says when she arrived in 2000, needing badly to find a place for a new start, everything fell effortlessly into place for her. Perhaps it is the energy of Mt. Arunachala. Happily, I too have found things to be relatively easy and smooth-sailing. Tiruvannamalai has proved a good introduction of India for me; the Westerners have given me much assistance and been terribly kind.

Pondicherry, Air Conditioning, and a Mild Case of Delhi Belly

DECIDING TO STAY overnight instead of making a long one-day journey, two days in Pondicherry has been a refreshing change of pace. Although hotter and more humid than Tiruvannamalai, it is on the Bay of Bengal, and there is something magical about the sea. I love the boardwalk, hawkers, and peaceful, blue calm. Where we spend time is rocky with no sandy beaches so people walk along the promenade.

Our driver Ravi, a lovely, gentlemanly sort, who has driven taxi cabs for thirty-three years and lived extended periods in both Chennai and Pondicherry, is a good resource. His English is quite good, and in answer to my questions, he explains that he is fifty-five years old, plans to drive for two more years, and then "sit at home." He tells us that bold headlines of today's *The Hindu*, one of the two major newspapers, and considered more intellectual than *The Times*, announce yesterday's Pondi temperature was 109 degrees F. It was a mere 105 in Tiruvannamalai. Out in the hottest part of the day playing tourist and shopping for many hours yesterday, no wonder it seemed toasty.

Depending upon traffic and the time of day, the trip to Pondi takes two and a half to three and a half hours. We make record time in even less than two and a half hours.

Our first stop in Pondi is for breakfast at Baker Street, a French pastry and delicacies shop, apparently where Tiruv residents first stop when hitting town. Not understanding why the name, logo, and silhouette of Sherlock Holmes are attached to a French joint, but it is easy to comprehend why people love the place. The food is definitely French-influenced; we eat delicious quiche. Other selections include handmade chocolates, yummy pastries, salads, sandwiches, and ice cream. The food here is worth the trip alone and so delicious that we return again for lunch.

This part of India was colonized by the French and did not obtain independence until 1954, seven years after the British, who were primarily in the north, left India. Although one feels some of that former influence, indeed, it is still India. Let's just say it is not quite the same as a charming stroll down an ancient Parisian street. Notable are the street names as Rue something, French style architecture in certain parts of the city, and some French restaurants and shops.

Our first post-breakfast stop is a trip to Auroville, a few kilometers out of town, which is the utopian living community conceptualized by The Mother, the primary disciple of Sri Aurobindo. Difficult to get a sense of the place from the visitors center there being no organized tour, my research indicates that because it is a working community, tourism is not the main focus. It is a one-kilometer walk to view, although still not to enter, the massive dome-shaped, futuristic-looking meditation structure.

Having no clue, at the time, that we are rambling around for hours in 109-degree heat, I definitely know walking that distance outdoors in mid-day holds little appeal. So what do two girls do when it is this hot? Well, shop of course. They must be commended for adopting the Western capitalist model exceedingly well from a shopping perspective for there are several little shops with nice quality merchandise.

Rather disappointed not to get a better feel of the place and see the massive meditation dome, instead, I buy postcards of the geodesic gold structure to send to people, saying, "This is what I did *not* see in Auroville." The meditation dome has been controversial in that many Aurovilleans believe resources could have been better spent elsewhere. Regarding entry into the dome, my guidebook says one thing, the rather curt employee on premises tells us another, and a sign outside instructs yet something entirely different. Welcome to India! But what is clear is that you come one day, pay your parking lot fee, get a pass, and then return or call the next day to be allowed access to the dome to meditate.

Melissa has several items on her list to purchase. Although I have no plans to shop, but I am a woman, so, of course, I buy postcards, a few gifts, some towels, food at a pretty large, modern grocery store (where everything is available from paper towels, diet Coke, Green Giant canned vegetables, Ocean Spray cranberry sauce, taco shells, Thai food spices, to all traditional Indian foods), and some purple and white fabric to have a "suit" made.

"Suits" are what the women here call the long tunic top and loose pants outfits or salwar kameez. Much of the cotton fabric is starched on the bolt and is very stiff, requiring a few washings to soften up. But in one shop, the proprietress shows us a prewashed, wonderful lightweight cotton fabric, already precut in the appropriate amounts for the tunic, top, and matching scarf with a price of about $10.

We make two final stops at a homeopathic pharmacy and a nut shop, where the shopkeeper is unable to count change. It amazes me how many shopkeepers cannot calculate change or perform simple addition and subtraction. I forget how low the literacy rate is in this country.

Before going to Auroville, we check into our hotel, with *air conditioning*. Did I mention that the hotel has air conditioning? Only one year old, it is modern and small with fifty rooms and accommodating staff. During the night, the air conditioning is actually too cold; I am freezing. We human creatures are never happy.

Unfortunately, something I eat for dinner gives me my first bout of Delhi Belly, i.e., diarrhea, today. Without thinking and being utterly thrilled to see iced tea on the menu, I order it, forgetting that ice also is not safe unless the water used is filtered. And the guidebooks warn that one should not assume water is filtered, even in good hotels, and should always inquire, which I do not. But it is a pretty mild case, subsiding so that I am able to eat lunch, our third repast at Baker Street.

We visit the Sri Aurobindo ashram, which is very beautiful and peaceful, paying homage at the samadhi sites (resting places) of him and the Mother. Both are fully covered with gorgeous fresh flowers. Well-manicured with flowered grounds, the property is small but pristine.

Pondicherry is lovely. The streets are less littered than in Tiruv. In the mornings, women sweep the streets with the inimitable straw brooms used by everyone. We see no beggars or sadhus and little evidence of Hinduism. The appeal of this little seaside oasis is obvious, but the other aspects of classic India still are prevalent. The same traffic chaos exists. Street stands, shops, and carts overflowingly crowd the streets, and despite there being a supposed horn-honking prohibition, horns blare loudly and incessantly.

Very grateful that we don't make the entire round trip in one day, I would have been exhausted. As it is, I am pretty weary upon arriving home at 2:30 p.m. today.

SATURDAY, MAY 19, 2012

No longer at the ashram guest house, this morning I decide to take the apartment at Trent's house, an approximate ten-minute walk away. I have scored; thank you, Universe. There are no accidents; I have been directed here. Trent lives downstairs in a two-bedroom apartment.

Having air conditioning is the primary selling factor. The three-room apartment has a sizeable main room/bedroom/sitting area, decent-sized kitchen with table, chairs, and gas cooktop, and a bathroom. Additionally, there is a charming, very large partially open-air outdoor space covered with a thatched roof just outside my door. With a rattan swing chair hanging from the roof rafters, a few other chairs, lots of plants, and a great view of Mount Arunachala, were it not so hot, it would be a lovely meditation spot. There are also several clotheslines, which is helpful because it is time to do laundry again.

Bathrooms here, like European ones, typically are one room with sink, toilet, and shower situated together. It has a Western toilet, with use of either toilet tissue (another bonus) or the hose rinse system, rather the Indian version of the bidet.

Walls throughout are light blue with a white sponged technique; all floors other than the bath are a white/tan/brown variegated twelve-inch marble tile. I love that floors here all seem to be tiled in marble. Bathrooms have a rougher, safer ceramic tile. Closet space is a bit lacking, consisting of some hooks on the back of the kitchen door and a rattan shelving unit in my bedroom/living room. It suffices.

Sheets and a pillowcase—Ralph Lauren no less, a pretty orange striped bedspread, and some kitchen towels are provided. My landlord mentions that the bed has a very good mattress. I make a comment about the typical Indian mattress, whereupon he quickly corrects me, saying that this is a very good one. It is very firm and about four inches thick, which apparently constitutes a "very good mattress" in India. No Beauty Rest or pillow-tops here. Fully furnished, there are plenty of chairs and tables, a two-burner propane stove, Whirlpool refrigerator, and an adequate, supply of dishes, pots and pans, and utensils.

Again, no bath towels are supplied; hence, I am grateful for buying some in Pondi. Melissa recommended not buying terry cloth, which takes longer to dry; instead, I purchased lightweight cotton ones. My bath towel is about the size of a small tablecloth, so it can pull double duty as a sheet or bedspread if needed somewhere along the way.

Since there are no washcloths, except at high-end hotels, any women traveling to India who use them should definitely bring their own supply. Melissa concurs, having brought hers from the United States. Having a few tiny disposable ones that I am hoarding, I use small cotton towels for washcloths and as a yoga towel.

My new location is a little further from the Internet café, ashram, and shopping area, which is fine in that I will get more exercise. There are a few little roadside stands, tailors, and a couple of restaurants out here.

Originally, my thought was to move on Monday, remaining tonight and tomorrow at the guest house and spend tomorrow there as my day of silence. That must have been heat-induced delirium because I realized there is absolutely no reason not to move today and spend my day of silence here tomorrow. Air conditioning and a refrigerator, that's a no-brainer. Why continue to suffocate for two more days? It takes me a few hours to organize, pack, inform Leela next door that I am leaving, take some gifts over for her and Siri, go to the ashram to chant, and have lunch there.

Quickly finding a rickshaw driver, who is pleasant and quotes me a fair price, we find the place easily because I can give him directions. If one doesn't know how to locate one's destination, good luck; may Krishna, Ganesha, or the gods be guiding him or her. What Chennai Roger told me about rickshaw drivers there is true here as well. Few know where anything is, other than the major places such as the ashram, the big temple, downtown, and the like. Even if you point to the location on the map, it is rarely helpful. I finally realize that most are illiterate.

Of course, the day I choose to move is an eight-hour power outage day. Apparently, there is one all-day blackout each month. Lovely, my first such day of joy since arriving in Tiruvannamalai. Here at least, however, there is a back-up system that allows ceiling fans, two electrical outlets, and a couple of lights to function when power is off. Not having that system at the guesthouse made power outages much more grim.

Eight hours without electricity is a long time, but how much more uncomfortable it would have been at the guest house without ceiling fans. My angels guided me here again on the right day. Even here with ceiling fans, I jump in the shower a couple of times.

While moving in, opening the gate and unloading my luggage, I have my first fall in India. Let's hope it will be my first *and* last. I am grateful that my siblings, who are amused by such ungraceful spills, are not here to witness it. Entryways to houses have two concrete inclines, used for cars or motorized scooters and bikes to drive on, along with a set of regular steps located between the two inclines. The gate lock is sticky, and while trying to open it with hands full of bags, apparently standing precariously both on the incline and the stairs, I take quite a tumble. Gratefully, I do not injure myself. Trent hears me struggling and comes out to assist.

Happily, the power comes back on a few minutes earlier than the scheduled 5:00 p.m. Most importantly, I successfully activate the air conditioning unit. These weeks *sans* air conditioning definitely make me appreciate that luxury.

A baffling aspect of Indian wiring is the configuration of multiple switches or panels situated in odd locations throughout rooms. Both here and at the guest house, there is one panel in each room, but in the Pondi hotel, there were six different electrical panels, an American journeyman electrician's nightmare. All switches, fan dials, electrical outlets are located on one panel. Nothing is labeled so I keep flipping switches until activating the right light or ceiling fan.

Bathrooms too are absolutely fascinating. Always sizeable rooms, in addition to the usual fixtures, there are multiple spigots, faucets, and buckets. There seems always to be at least four faucets or spigots. I counted five, *in addition* to the rain shower head, at our Pondi hotel. At least one spigot is located much lower on the wall, presumably for filling the bucket.

Here, there is another shower head and attached spray hose next to the toilet. The shower does have both hot and cold water, and the hot water heater, which is referred to as a geyser (pronounced "geezer"), is mounted high on the wall near the ceiling. The configuration here is better with the shower located far enough from the stool so that it isn't drenched when showering. The bathroom sink, seemingly attached to the wall with a couple of screws, is a lovely pale blue, circa 1960. But this is India, the land of color.

The actual plumbing system, such as it is, is most intriguing as well. PVC piping runs around the walls of the bathroom, all exposed and visible, from toilet to shower to sink. The sink drains from a plastic tube emptying into a floor drain. Inconveniently, the bathroom light switch is located in the kitchen, and not just outside the bathroom door. It is around the corner.

MONDAY, MAY 21, 2012

More than a year and a half ago, while still in the United States, on Valentine's Day 2010, I began spending at least one day each month in silence. It was such a gratifying experience, and I always looked forward to it. It is amazing how nice it is to cut out the chatter of television, noise of music, and interruption of telephone. Often, I spend parts of other days in silence too. Deciding to continue the practice, yesterday was my planned day of silence for this month.

It nearly is, aside from Trent coming upstairs to check on me. Responding to his knock because I am ill, unfortunately, my day of silence is not spent as planned—reading my *Monk* book, meditating, doing yoga. Instead, I experience my first bout of real TD, traveler's diarrhea, having learned from my travel health handout of its special name.

Commencing shortly upon awakening, and although the diarrhea is not too nasty, as the day progresses, I develop a headache, achiness, and a very scary forty-five minutes where my body shakes uncontrollably. But that ceases as mysteriously as it commences. Trent gives me some Chinese herbal remedy, and the shaking begins about an hour after I take it. Needless to say, that stuff is tossed out, and I vow not to simply pop in my mouth any remedy some stranger offers me.

When the shaking doesn't quit, despite trying yoga breathing, yoga postures, and walking around, I begin to imagine that I have contracted something more serious than mere diarrhea and drag out my "travel illness sheets" provided by Maricopa County Medical Services when I received my vaccinations. None of my symptoms suggest anything nastier such as malaria, dengue fever, or encephalitis.

Deciding that perhaps I have a touch of the flu as well, fortunately shortly after noon, I fall asleep. Although awakening a few times, I sleep nearly all day, and after sleeping eighteen hours, today I feel much better with only a bit of tummy queasiness. The travel materials say that TD is self-limiting and usually lasts no more than a few days. Today, I shall try to figure out what to eat, if anything.

Trying to ascertain the possible cause of my first bout of "Delhi Belly," I realize that I have violated the "if you can't boil or peel it, don't eat it" rule many times already. Not having ready access to cooked food for dinner, cooking facilities, or restaurants, I have been eating nuts, raisins, snacks, and on Friday and Saturday, cheese purchased in Pondi. But having eaten without incident everything previously except the cheese, the likely suspects are the cheese (which I ate for a couple of days without refrigerating), the water here, or residual from the iced tea in Pondicherry.

Still feeling rather low energy today, I decide to spend another day of silence and feel like napping after only being awake for a couple of hours. Hallelujah, it is blissful having air conditioning, along with a refrigerator that on its highest setting actually freezes water. If I find ice cube trays, I shall actually have ice.

Quoting someone else, in one of his tapes, Wayne Dyer, says that there are many ways to enlightenment and that one does not necessarily need to suffer to find it. I prefer that philosophy, thank you very much. Accepting that suffering indeed makes us stronger, more grateful, and probably strengthens character, and certainly expecting discomfort and challenges throughout this trip, I freely admit to not feeling the least bit guilty about taking advantage of the comfort of air conditioning.

Today, I place a note outside my door that I am observing a day of silence to discourage Trent's interruptions. It is a lovely day of reading, reflecting, meditating, and doing yoga. I cherish my days of silence.

One of the books I read today is *Arunachalam*, a history of Mount Arunachala and the major temple here, Sri Arunacheswarar. Spectacularly beautiful, apparently the temple is one of the largest in India. Not yet having been inside, I am happy to have read the book first for a bit of history about it.

In reading about the Mount Arunachala, I have a clearer understanding about what draws people here. Its energy and history are amazing. Geologically, it is considered to be as old as any place on earth, an upthrust piece of the earth's igneous crust, and far older than the Himalayas. On each monthly full moon, many, many thousands of pilgrims arrive to circumambulate it. The route around the base of the mountain is fourteen kilometers or about eight and a half miles.

About walking around the mountain, the sages say that one is supposed to walk very slowly and meditatively with thoughts of Shiva, ideally barefoot. Canadian Jerri whom I met at breakfast at the ashram does the entire thing barefoot; it takes her three and a half to four hours. Her feet must be really toughened up to do that in this heat. Also, people are to walk on the left side of the mountain because it is said that the souls of the former saints and rishis are walking on the right side.

Mount Arunachala is considered to be the embodiment of Lord Shiva himself. Multitudes of sages, saints, and rishis have spent time on and became enlightened there, and supposedly, many still live there. Ramana Maharshi, whose ashram is at the base of the mountain, spent twenty-three years in its caves, much of it in silence.

There are always fascinating stories in Hinduism about the gods. One I learn from yesterday's reading involves a tale about the three major ones, Brahma, Shiva, and Vishnu. In a spat between Brahma and Vishnu, each claimed to be the greatest god, causing Shiva to come down from the heavens to address the issue. Brahma lied to Shiva, the punishment for which was purportedly that there were to be no temples honoring him.

To this day, only very few temples to Brahma exist throughout all of India. That's some serious punishment given that there are untold thousands, perhaps millions, of temples honoring other Hindu gods throughout this country.

Unfortunately, today, I realize avoiding Trent as much as possible is necessary to maintain my own mental wellness. Having rather hoped to rent the apartment and have no further interaction, that has not been the case. If not able to avoid him, I need to find a nice way to inform him that I have no interest whatsoever in hearing about the news, government, politics, or anything in America or in the rest of the world for that matter.

During most of my adult life, the thought of not knowing what was happening in the world, especially in current affairs and politics, would have been tantamount to stringing me up by my fingernails. Being so uninformed would have been utterly shameful. Now dropping out and being thoroughly unplugged is critical. Many spiritual teachers advise people to take a break from the news and its related negativity. I have not missed one iota the absence of that information and its distraction.

TUESDAY, MAY 22, 2012

As I leave the property today, I fall again—in precisely the same place as last time—while locking the gate. Unbelievable; what a klutz. This time, I tear a hole in a pair of favorite black linen pants and skin my knee badly enough that it's quite sore. Also, my left hand is skinned a bit, and my left arm is sore. Thankfully, I don't break anything.

In a country that is so poor, at least by Western standards, I am amazed at how well-dressed and clean everyone is—the kids, the women, and the men. It is a society that obviously takes much pride in looking presentable. It is refreshing. Occasionally, one sees boys dressed in jeans, but never as on US streets with pants falling around their butts, and certainly no torn or ripped jeans.

Despite the heat, men's shirts, which are often white, are immaculately tailored and pressed.

As in Mexico, there is garbage strewn everywhere along the streets; sadly, the streets serve as the trash cans. Having noticed only two locations where there is a trash container, both are in front of little markets. Despite the trash everywhere, one of my most poignant memories of India will be of all the residents and shopkeepers out each morning sweeping the street in front of their establishments or homes with small, whisk-style straw brooms, which actually look pretty efficient. Swish, swishing away for a few minutes, and the area is clean. This ritual is performed repeatedly during the day by business owners.

Nearly everyone who travels to India comments on the overpowering smells. Possibly because I have not been to Mumbai, Delhi, or Calcutta, but thus far, my olfactory senses have not been negatively overwhelmed. I recall having more sensitivity in New York City to the pollution and stench on the streets; my eyes never stopped burning when outdoors there. Also, since arriving, I have had no allergy symptoms *whatsoever* and have stopped taking my usual allergy medicine.

It is time to exchange money again. My first exchange upon arriving was fifty two rupees to $1; today it is fifty four rupees. Kunal only takes one rupee so that means that the rate is fifty five to $1. Expats who have lived here awhile say they have never seen the exchange rate this good.

By the time I pass her little "Cotton Cloth Shop" on the way back from my daily outing, Seamstress is there. Another miracle. My ripped pants repair will cost twenty rupees, a whopping thirty seven cents, but a tailor in the hood this morning quotes me fifty rupees. So despite it being pocket change, it does pay to compare; two and a half times is quite a variation.

I inquire of Seamstress Shama's schedule for today and tomorrow. Who knows when she next will be here. Brought along is my most favorite-of-all-time dress, which in Phoenix I literally live in, and get multiple compliments whenever wearing it. All my family and friends know the dress—black rayon print, loose fitting, empire-waist, below the knee.

Before leaving, I tried without success to find fabric to have another made because the seams have been repaired three times. My plan is to have a couple made here out of cotton. If Seamstress Shama gives me a nice price, which, of course, by US standards will be nominal, and I like it, I will have several made and ship them home.

Upon my return, Trent is outside trimming trees and asks me not to leave the air conditioning running when I am out. That's a reasonable request, I guess, but since I am paying a higher tariff for an air-conditioned apartment, it seems that should be my choice. Nevertheless, I am happy to be conservation-minded and don't mention my understanding that more electricity is used to turn on and off an air conditioning system to cool overheated rooms than to leave it running at a lower level.

Grateful for whatever forces directed me here, when I left for India, my sense was that I would truly drop out and not stay in touch with people. Certainly, I never imagined keeping a journal, something never before have I managed to accomplish with any regularity, despite many attempts. Writing now has become an important part of, and special joy, my day.

All in all, life in India is good. Balmy temperatures. Sweet, kind people. Happy cows and children. Reading. Silence. Chanting. Prayer. Yoga. Meditation. Focus on a life of service, God, and love. And a consciousness about what is truly important in life. I know what is *not* important: television, newspapers, face lifts, botox, Facebook, golf (sorry sibs), cell phones, self-absorption, obsession about money, wearying concern about maintaining youthfulness, accumulation of more stuff, a closet full of clothes that one can never possibly wear, forgetting to laugh a lot every day, failing to smile at everyone you meet, missing the opportunity to be grateful for everything—the good stuff *and* the tough times.

Ifran's Amazing Cuisine, Our Temple Scam, and No Water

WEDNESDAY, MAY 23, 2012

AWAKENING AT A good hour, I decide to walk before it becomes too hot. Since I now walk a farther distance daily, I carry my backpack rather than my "wonderful bag," the small, black, multi-pocketed, zippered nylon all-weather carrier. Today, I have another India first experience, stepping in a fresh cow pie shortly after leaving the house. Welcome to India indeed! Reminder to self: look at the ground when you walk. But remarkably, twenty feet away is a water spigot. They are abundant here. People drink from them, cool themselves off; I wash cow manure off my shoes.

Not only do pedestrians *not* have the right-of-way in India, it seems that we must be exceedingly vigilant when on foot. Already

I have had two experiences, where despite a huge open road with no traffic or people other than me and the motorized vehicle, the auto rickshaw or scooter seems to aim directly for me. Habit? Bad drivers? Do I look nasty? Or is it just to scare the foreign blonde lady?

Why am I not surprised to again find Seamstress Shama's shop not open today? Multiple trips usually are required to find her door open. When last there, her door was open, and she and her small son were sound asleep on the floor.

Spending most of the day reading and doing laundry, around fiveish, I decide to walk back in to the ashram area. Going to see Seamstress Shama, miracle of miracles, only two trips to find her there. Today her gorgeous seven-year-old daughter is passed out in the sleeping space, and her precocious five-year-old son is sitting out front. Bringing a gift of multiple spools of thread and some lotions, the kid mangles the packaging with typical boyish verve. After getting permission from his mom, I give him a package of Trident gum. He is so excited that he tries desperately to awaken his sister to show her. Finally, his mother instructs him to leave her alone whereupon he then removes each piece of gum from the package and plays with those.

Selecting a gold-colored cotton fabric, Seamstress Shama will make me a copy of *my most favorite dress in the world*. If I like it, I shall have her make a few more. She tells me to return Friday at 6:00 p.m., two days away. Who knows if she will be there?

THURSDAY, MAY 24, 2012

Having arrived in India on April 24, I have been here one month—what an amazing four weeks! Not having been to the Yogi Ramsuratkumar ashram for several days, I go for breakfast. Today, they serve idlies, which are small patties of pressed rice served with a gravy or sauce, called sambar, a spicy concoction with a few veggies in it. It is delicious.

After breakfast, I do my usual rounds of chanting and tour of the Hall of Mahatmas. One sadhu, whom I see on nearly every visit, prostrates in front of the various statues, photographs, and inner temple, which is the samadhi site of Yogi Ramsuratkumar. A regular, he is not too old—in his thirties or forties perhaps—and is very thin with long hair. His orange lungi is always spotlessly clean. How can someone who likely lives on the streets be so immaculate? I like his energy; he seems to be the real deal. I am especially moved, watching him and thinking how devout are these sadhus who give up everything to spend their lives in devotion to God. That to me is real courage. He doesn't even carry a bag; most sadhus carry some belongings in a shoulder bag or pack.

Watching him and others who attended the Tuesday sadhu luncheon, I understand why Yogi Ramsuratkumar was so adamant about the import of supporting sadhus. I am unaware of any similar group of wandering holy men living in any other country, believing they are unique to India. The fact that millions of them still exist here boggles my mind. Truly in awe, the depth of commitment to their chosen vocation and lifestyle is beyond my limited Western comprehension. It is pretty hard to communicate with them because as one of my books points out, the "real ones" don't speak English. Merely being in their presence is supposed to be a blessing in and of itself.

Already past 11:00 a.m. and getting hot on my morning outing, as I near the college grounds (not college grounds as one might imagine, but acres of open fields with a couple of roads through it), my thought is that this always seems to be the toughest part of the walk. Today, I tell myself not to focus on that and to pick up my pace.

But, it is my lucky day for a minute later another motor scooter stops. Asking if I am staying down the way, I answer in the affirmative to which he tells me to hop on.

Very pleasant, Driver Ifran, of course, asks where I am from. Telling me that he runs the restaurant down the road, and passing it daily, I have wondered if it is open for business. Saying that although it is technically closed now in off-season, if I call, he will prepare food for delivery or pick-up. Not being much of a cook, he seems a godsend—a caterer a few meters away.

I continue to be amazed how these incidents keep occurring. Is it the energy of Mount Arunachala? Within minutes, we arrive at his home/place of business where several boys are playing outside. He introduces me to his son, who immediately wants to know my name, and then invites me inside. The back room of their home is the restaurant. Introducing me to his life partner and one of his daughters, they have four children. Inviting me to sit, I decline, saying that I am hot and tired and need to get home. Indians are very hospitable and especially like meeting Westerners.

Ifran gives me his business card and tells me to call any time. They all very genuinely thank me for "visiting." I shall try his cuisine soon.

Barely inside the door and into my "in the house clothes," i.e., a dress which is sleeveless and a bit too short for the street, Trent arrives at my door with a filled water container. When empty, I leave it at his door, then at some point, he fills it and brings it up to me. He always walks in and takes it to the kitchen; in the future, I need to take it from him at the door, or better yet, tell him that I am in the middle of my yoga practice and ask him to leave it outside. Despite not being invited to stay, he plops himself in a chair, telling me that I need to keep the kitchen door shut because the air conditioning unit is running too much.

Our conversation is pleasant enough, but he seems uninterested in leaving. Finally, offering to pay rent for the next week, he departs. Not appreciating my space and privacy violated, being totally left alone at the guest house was blissful. These pop-ins and lectures about air conditioning are becoming annoying.

Marking my month in India, I desire more solitude and withdrawal and decide to discontinue e-mail communications for a while.

Saturday, May 26, 2012

At least, there is water today. Yesterday morning upon awakening, there was none. Wondering if I mistakenly turned off the wrong knob in the shower, I attempt everything to no avail. About 6:45, knocking on Trent's door, a very health-conscious guy, I assume him to be an early riser. There is no answer despite my knocking for a few minutes.

Waiting until 7:00 a.m., thinking surely Trent will be up by then, there is still no answer. I begin pounding on the door and calling his name. Finally, he comes to the door. Apologizing for waking him for what I feel is a valid reason, he replies rather nonchalantly, "Oh, I should have told you about that." *You think?* He goes next door to the neighbor's house, turns on a couple of valves, and presses a red button. The water tank will be full in forty-five minutes.

Mesmerized that I am actually doing yoga in its birthplace with more than 5,000 years of history, I am inspired. Last night, I read about a chap who in either the late nineteenth or early twentieth century broke new ground by beginning to teach yoga to everyone. Prior to that, only the sannyasins knew it. My practice is lovely—nice, slow, and so long that I become hungry.

Contemplating what is available for brunch (not much), I settle for a tuna fish sandwich on whole wheat bread with diet Coke. Just yesterday, I vowed to stop drinking the stuff. I know it's poison, but I still have a can in the refrigerator so don't want to waste it—my little rationalization.

In addition to eating food that can be boiled or peeled, canned foods are safe as well. For variety, I purchase some tuna, packaged in a can with a pop-top lid. Relatively expensive here at about $1.80 per can, I want to savor it. The prices for packaged items are the same everywhere.

Eating vegetarian in India is fantastic. Vegetarian food is prevalent, of course, and delicious. So although I hadn't thought much about food before arriving, aside from the occasional tuna or some seafood in a good restaurant or hotel, I choose not to eat meat here. Even if I were not so inclined, as well as being mesmerized by the choices and flavors of vegetarian food here, the long power outages make the idea of eating meat, with questionable refrigeration, unappealing.

In one book read recently, it explains a reason for eating vegetarian is that one is only eating food that is alive, not the dead energy from animal meat. That, and the obvious health benefits of eating vegetarian, resonate more with me than the inhumanity of killing animals argument. Knowing it to be a persuasive reason for many, whose beliefs I respect, it has never been very effective for me, perhaps because of my rural roots.

Yesterday evening when walking in to pick up my dress and pants from Seamstress (that encounter in a moment), as I approach Ifran's restaurant, one of his kids shouts hello. Soon, Ifran is at the door, donning his shirt and offering me a ride into town. I decline because I want the exercise. Seeing him, however, reminds me that I should try his cuisine, so I inquire how his catering works. He provides cashew rice with a choice of vegetable for eighty rupees, and my choices are eggplant something (eggplant is called aubergine) or mixed vegetables. Eggplant not being one of my favorites, I select mixed vegetables.

Arriving last night at Seamstress Shama's at six, she is sitting on the floor doing needlework. I smile and after some miscommunication (it seeming much more common in India than actual communication) between us, I realize that *neither* my dress nor my pants are ready. Really? Two days, no customers. But why should I be surprised? I repeat my mantra: "Welcome to India, Welcome to India!"

I sew, or more accurately perhaps, I know how to sew; ergo, I know that dress should take an hour for a good seamstress to whip out, or two hours max. This is the lady's occupation for heaven's sake, she can probably complete it in less than an hour. It is becoming clear to me that this is her vacation time too. Telling me that it should be ready tomorrow, I want clarification of "should." She assures me that it *will be* ready. This is really getting old. It must be the Indian way, tomorrow.

Wanting these bloody dresses finished to send them home and not have to stay in Tiruvannamalai an additional week waiting for them to be completed, I am now on a mission. With Kjos on a mission, even in her meditating/chanting/loving/smiling India frame-of-mind, watch out!

The original plan, Plan A, is to see how the dress fits before enlisting Seamstress Shama to make more. So I pick out more fabric, but now I likely will take it instead to Melissa's tailor. His shop is very close to me as opposed to the fifteen-minute walk to Seamstress Shama, and he also is apparently very reliable. It seems wise to move on to Plan B.

Explaining to Seamstress Shama that I am leaving soon, she asks when, and I tell her next week some time. She says she can have them finished by Friday, but distrustful of her time frames, I ask if she can complete them by Wednesday. She avers. Telling her that I have been sewing since I was five years old and know this dress is not difficult to make, we agree on a price. She cuts the additional selected fabrics for more dresses, and I leave. Somewhat exasperated, but certainly not surprised, I depart with not-so-high hopes of having them soon.

Take a deep breath. Relax. You are in India. Life is good. You have no schedule, no demands, no time crunches. If the dresses aren't ready, it is the universe saying to take your time in this amazingly special place. This is one of the most sacred places in India. Drink it in. Imbibe its gifts. Relish its sanctity. Revel in its energy. Breathe. Be.

Contemplating where next to go, on my "must do in India" list is a visit to the nadi scroll readers, my main priority for coming to South India after hearing about my dear friend Mukesh's experience with one a few years ago. The most famous location to find them is not far from here. I shall go there next.

Also not far away in Kulithalai, Tamil Nadu is the Saccidananda Ashram, also known as Shantivanam. Run by Benedictine monks, it is interesting to me because they have melded both Christian and Hindu religious traditions. The monks describe themselves as "Christian sannyasis," dress in the saffron robes of Hindu holy men, eat sitting on the floor, and study Vedanta, yoga, and the Bible.

Now contemplating going to Kerala as well, I have the name of a fellow Param, originally from there, but who now lives in Tiruv and takes westerners to Kerala on trips. I plan to phone him to get some particulars, costs, and the like. Anandashram, started by Swami Papa Ramdas is also in Kerala, and it is described as truly blissful. Thereafter, I could mosey up the western coast of India, preferably by train because apparently rail travel, a holdover from the British raj, is a marvelous way to experience the country.

And although, originally, I had no interest in exploring Goa, known as a big party spot, it is on the way up the sea coast. And since this is not the season, it will be quieter. A wee state colonized by the Portuguese, it too is a unique area of India.

Coming to India without seeing the Taj Mahal would be heresy, so, of course, I shall go to Agra. And Varanasi, Delhi, and Dharamsala/McLeod Danj are serious contenders. The Dalai Lama is in residence at his home in Dharamsala in July and August. Although I heard him speak once in Arizona on the ASU campus many years ago, it would be wonderful to see him here. One certainly can never have too many experiences in his presence.

Yoga is taught in larger cities as well as in Tiruv during the season, which apparently starts in September or thereabouts. My *Nirvana* guidebook, describing ashrams, pilgrimage sites, yoga centers, and research centers, makes several references to Indian teachers being appalled at how yoga has become transmitted primarily as a mode of physical fitness. Thanks to America for that one. One can only hope that the real teachers, who have embraced *all* of yoga, continue to teach students, leaving some legacy that doesn't ignore the spiritual, philosophical, and healing aspects.

Information in my *Nirvana* guidebook is several years old, but as of its publication date, it says that Iyengar's children, Geeta and Prashant, apparently now do the actual teaching at his Pune center. It adds, however, that Iyengar often is in the back of the room, rushing in to make adjustments and shouting to rotate one's skin, or whatever.

In the neighborhood, I easily find Surat, Melissa's tailor, about a three-minute walk away. What a sweet man, and he can sew my suit as well as the dresses. This is a much more viable alternative to Seamstress Shama. Notably, while out and about, I see many women, from older to a young girl, walking along with their cows and usually a calf, carrying a large stainless steel milking pail under one arm. One lady is very friendly. Another milks her cow, leaving enough in the udder for the baby calf to be fed. Soon another woman carrying a small filled milk bottle walks by. People must come out to buy fresh milk during the milking time.

Out on the road in early evening, I see Money, Money, Money Swami ahead of me. Thinking that perhaps if I pass quickly, I can avoid the usual banter. But even in walking around him, I get the verbatim refrain. With a big, friendly smile, he calls, "Hello, hello," and my smiling response is, "Hello." Then he extends his right hand, rubbing fingers together, saying, "Money, money, money." The first couple of times I encounter him, new to the neighborhood and not recognizing him, I reply with a "no" or head shake. Today, I laughingly retort, "Money, money, money," and walk on. Unsure of his gig, but he always carries a tiffin so no doubt he makes the ashram rounds where sadhus go for food.

Meandering to Seamstress Shama's shop, I breathe a sigh of relief to see her door open and her sitting on the floor doing needlepoint. That might be a good omen; she's not working on my dress, so it may be finished. Miracle of miracles, both the pants and my dress are completed, but she needs to charge me more for the dress because it was "very much work." Fine, whatever, a few rupees, it's pennies. At least I have my dress.

Since there is no fitting room at Shama's Cotton Cloth Shop, I ask her to stand in front of me holding up a piece of fabric as a screen to allow me to try it on. It fits great, is cute, and the fabric is soft. A happy camper am I. Not trusting her business schedule, however, I decide to leave only one of the remaining four dresses for her to sew; the others will go to Tailor Surat. Leaving with both my original dress and the newly sewn one, "No, no," she tells me; I need to leave her one as a sample. Asking if she didn't make a pattern since she knew I wanted several more, "Oh, no, no, we don't make patterns, only sample," she explains.

At the agreed time of 6:30, I stop by Ifran's to pick up my dinner which is packed in a tiffin, a very handy stainless steel little bucket comprised of two containers stacked atop each other with an attached carrying handle. Not knowing if a similar item exists in the United States or not, it is an Indian version of taking one's lunch in Tupperware, the difference being that it keeps food hot.

The food is staggeringly delicious...by far *the best meal* I have eaten since arriving in India. A sufficient quantity for two people, it is so scrumptious that I overeat, inhaling all of the veggies in a curry sauce that is not hot or spicy, but delightful. All vegetables here are chopped into the tiniest of pieces. It must take forever, especially at the ashram where they serve gigantic pots of veggies at lunch. The cashew rice is yummy too.

Having overeaten, I decide to take an evening constitutional, delivering to Tailor Surat the fabric for the three dresses and the sample. Stopping by Ifran's to tell him how fabulous the dinner was and that it is the best food I have eaten since arriving in India, he is very appreciative, bringing his hands to his heart in that genuine, endearing way of saying thank you. He will prepare my dinner tomorrow night as well; I request two vegetables instead since I have lots of remaining rice. Same time, same place; a fabulous catered dinner for $2. And essentially food for two or three meals. I am over-the-moon ecstatic by this find!

SUNDAY, MAY 27, 2012

Awakening to find a similar brisk, cool breeze as yesterday, I go for a walk. Finding it a pleasant morning, I call Melissa to see if she is interested in making the auto rickshaw trip around Mount Arunachala, which we have discussed previously. Using the phone in the 'hood discovered last night, theoretically, a call costs one rupee for sixteen minutes, however, the phone keeps cutting off after a minute or two. So three calls and three rupees later, we agree that Rickshaw Driver Majinder will pick me up at the Ramana Super Market in thirty minutes.

Picking me up on schedule, we head to Melissa's, and are on our way. The paved roadway, known as Pradakshima, encircles the entire mountain. Within the town of Tiruv the normal gamut of businesses, temples, roadside shops, and stands are along the route.

Our first stop is at a huge, beautiful Shiva temple with wonderfully colored statues decorating the top of the exterior. Evidently, today is some religious festival for there is a puja in process, with lots of drumming, blessings and dissemination of vibhuti. Very tasty Prasad, like a little fruit salad, is being passed out.

First, a very pleasant man directs us to the big pail from which the Prasad is being served. Then another pleasant, gray-haired older Burgundy Sari-Clad Lady keeps directing us back to the Prasad bucket—three times until I cannot eat another morsel. Burgundy Sari-Clad Lady then leads us through the crowd to the hand-washing area and instructs me to drink some of my bottled water. Amazed at her attention, I comment to Melissa that she must be the designatee to show the white girls the ropes. She agrees.

As we exit, Melissa is taking my photo in front of the temple, when lo and behold, Burgundy Sari-Clad Lady materializes at our rickshaw for her tip. What a hoot! Asking Driver Majinder if we should tip her, he, ostensibly not wanting to get in the middle of anything, simply says, "I can't say." Giving her ten rupees, she does not seem too thrilled, apparently considering her Good Samaritan services meriting more remuneration.

Melissa and I have a good laugh about the nice lady befriending us routine. That certainly, thus far, is the best episode of being "had" here for me, and in this holy shrine to Shiva of all places. One is warned about the touts, scam artists, professional beggars, and the like, but this little con was a surprise, even to Melissa who has lived here for more than a decade. Welcome to India!

Our next stop is at another temple, the deity it honors I do not recall, where Melissa says live goat offerings are made. Thankfully there are none today. In the temple's outer courtyard are massive twenty-feet or higher playful-looking figures along with some large carousel-style horses on which kids are riding. Given that this is some Hindu festival (there are many, many festivals throughout the year, which also vary in different parts of the country), there is another puja occurring inside the temple proper.

After a few more photo stops and another for cold drinks, we head back because it is getting hot, the entire junket taking only a bit more than an hour. It is a nice way to see the entire beautiful mountain, which is quite massive.

An Elephant Blessing
and Possible Child Abuse

AWAKENING AT 6:15 to meet Melissa, we are off to the main temple, Arunacheswarar. Breathtakingly stunning, it is purportedly one of the largest temples in India. The energy is wonderful, and I feel as though I could crawl up somewhere inside and never leave.

Many of India's major temples apparently have a resident elephant. Rudu lives at this one, and she just returned from retreat. This is the first elephant I have seen here. Standing next to her, I appreciate how massive they are! She is gorgeous. With big eyes and a nice painted symbol on her forehead, she patiently blesses those who give her rupees or food. Wondering how and when elephants rest, does she stand there all day, or does she get a lunch break?

My blessing is her patting my head with her trunk, which is supposed to be very auspicious. Upon getting her rupee or food, Rudu puts it in her trunk, blesses you, and if food, she eats it. A lady feeds her a big stack of crackers, which she seems to like. Most likely, she far prefers food to rupees. If it is money, she passes it to her handler. Mesmerizing to watch, I could stand there for hours. One can understand the Indians' adoration of these magnificent creatures. And of course, Hindus love elephants also because of their sacred Ganesh.

During our time in the temple, we see statues of multiple deities and row upon row of what are apparently Shaivan saints. Watching a couple of beautiful puja ceremonies, one is rather elaborate with a lingam, several priests officiating and another group of young priests chanting in a large area where the floor is strewn with hundreds of coconuts, each decorated with fresh flowers. We also see the room where Ramana Maharshi spent many years—the period when he was so absorbed in enlightened meditation that rats were eating away at his body, and eventually, people dragged him out.

Thinking about my impending departure, after our temple outing, I visit Kunal to discuss travel ideas. He confirms that the rail runs up through Kerala, Goa, and on to Mumbai, should I opt to do that, and that getting to Kerala from Tiruchy will be easy. The only way to reach Chidambaram, Vaitheeswaran Koil, and the ashram in Tiruchy, however, other than by Indian bus—not the air-conditioned Volvo ones, but rather the Indian ones we are familiar with from movies, overloaded with people hanging out windows and riding on the roof and which takes three days, is by car. Needless to say, I'll not be taking the local bus.

Quoting me a price of 5,000 rupees, he asks if I want air conditioning—*oh my goodness yes*. Costing an additional $7.40 for air conditioning for the entire trip (an extra ten rupees or so per kilometer), somewhere between seven and nine hours' driving time depending upon traffic, conditions, stops, and the like, it is well worth it.

My plan is to leave Saturday, Sunday, or Monday, requesting the same driver I had from Chennai. Although his English is marginal, his car is new and clean with nice white towels on the seats, pillows for one's back, and cold air conditioning. Comfort of the ride is more important than talking with the driver.

On my way back home, I have no idea what motivates me—perhaps the energy of the temple makes me possessed or the elephant's blessing drives me, but I stop at two shops to do some gift shopping. Preparing a box of items to send back, it seems prudent since I will be paying for shipping anyhow to fill the box, and I now have lots of gifts purchased. When leaving for India, shopping never crossed my mind.

Most of the retail establishments currently open (the majority are closed until the season begins in the fall) are run by Kashmiris, and even my guidebook references that they are pretty intense salespeople. In one shop, Mubarak wants to show me everything in his store. All of the shopkeepers, having now been in three stores, really have the drill down. First, one is offered coffee or tea. I ask for water. Mubarak says that he will do better than that, dashing out and returning shortly with Fanta orange soda and two plastic cups. Actually preferring water, but to be polite, I drink Fanta.

Then the dance begins. He is leaving in two days, but will give me "very good prices, much better than during season." Laughingly, I respond that the last guy three weeks ago told me also that he was leaving for Kashmir the following week, and he is still here. Taking offense, Mubarak says, "I do not lie, see here is my ticket," and produces his airline ticket showing a departure on May 30. Thanks to Shilpa's good negotiating for me in the Chennai silk shop, I stick to that price for scarves at both stores and get it. I do love the silk; the colors are beautiful.

On my way home, I have my first unpleasant and disconcerting experience since arriving in India. My friend Maria suggested bringing along a whistle, which I did, and this might have been a situation for its use had it not resolved. Some young Creepy Guy, who I shortly realize is either very stoned or mentally ill, says something as I pass.

Ignoring him, he starts to follow me, calling out something. Then he walks beside me, babbling away. Telling him to leave me alone and to go away, I even shout. Nothing works; he continues to walk next to me. A short distance from the shops of Sir and Swami, I decide that I can get cover, for Sir surely will chase him off.

But coming upon the post office to my immediate left, I go inside and buy stamps, telling both the older lady and another fellow behind the counter that the kid outside is bothering me. Whether or not they comprehend what I am saying is unclear. First Creepy Guy stays outside, but then he comes in and walks up to the counter as if to transact business. Starting to walk out, he too quickly decides to exit. I return and buy stamps. By the time I leave the post office, he has disappeared; I am relieved!

Much of the fun for me after shopping, upon returning home, is looking through the purchased treasures. I decide to make a list so months from now if compelled to shop again, I'll recall what I already have purchased.

As part of my paring-down process and lightening my luggage load, I have identified some skirts, t-shirts, and a tank top to toss or give away. Since Ifran and his family have been so kind to me, I shall see if his kids might wear any of them. My plan is to drop them off on my way past his house. Approaching it, however, I hear a boy screaming and someone yelling at him.

Thinking to myself that someone is misbehaving and being yelled at by his parent, nevertheless, I walk up to the house where the door is always open. But upon getting closer, I see the seventeen-year-old daughter standing with her back to the door and someone inside swinging a cricket bat. It appears that the kid is being struck with the bat. Quickly hightailing it out of there, I instantly feel awful.

The self-chatter in my head goes like this: *Should I have gone to the door anyhow? No, it is none of my business. Why isn't it my business? Isn't that the typical excuse people use not to intercede when there is abuse going on? What right do you have to characterize abuse in your mind anyhow? Isn't a kid being beaten with a cricket bat being abused? This is not your culture. Do not bring your Western mind-set and judgment to the situation. But if I had just walked up, certainly whoever was hitting the kid (I just assumed it was Irfan but don't know for sure) would have stopped. Maybe not. Or would my showing up have made the situation worse and just have embarrassed everyone, including yourself? But is it ever okay to ignore someone being beaten? Am I complicit by my inaction? Kids can be brats, there is always drama in families; every parent in the world if not actually having hit his or her child, certainly has at least thought about it at one time or another. Kids try parents' patience to the max. Hitting a kid in India may be the normal form of discipline, even though it's not in the United States. Who are you kidding? Do you not think kids get beaten in the United States? Of course, they do...every day. You simply may not have witnessed it, so it's easy to pretend it doesn't exist in your own culture. What have you actually done yourself in terms of being involved helping abused kids or women in the United States? Certainly not enough. So don't be so bloody sanctimonious here. But you never walked away from a situation where a kid was being beaten in your presence. When we were growing up, it was still acceptable to get a spanking; I remember getting a couple of whacks and one real spanking. I deserved it and certainly wasn't scarred for life. It probably did me some good, and I didn't turn out to be a violent person. It's what parents did then, and I'm not so sure getting whopped was so bad. I'm still not entirely certain I buy into the "never spank a kid" philosophy anyhow although, of course, I could never condone serious beating. Having never been a parent, what do I know about disciplining kids anyhow? Is a slap across the butt really that bad? And certainly, I see lots of ill-behaved kids in the United States whose parents seem clueless about any form of discipline whatsoever. At least a cricket bat looks like a paddle, so maybe, it's not that painful. Are you now trying to rationalize hitting a kid as long as the instrument being used doesn't hurt so bad? I don't know the right answers. Don't second-guess yourself. You did what you did at the moment based on the information you had at the time. That has always been your guide in life. I am the guest, the outsider here. I want to respect this culture, good and bad. I don't want to be judgmental. I want to try to understand. Love is always the answer though.*

I continue to feel sad as I walk and think more about what I have just witnessed.

Stopping by the Ramana Super Market for a few things, I head home. My feet are killing me. Now the dilemma: do I drop off the clothes at Ifran's tonight or wait until tomorrow?

Since they are in my bag, I decide to drop them off, feeling somewhat guilty about not having stopped earlier. Ifran comes out. Showing him the clothes and asking if his partner (I learn later that the woman is his wife, but Indians don't refer to their spouses as husband or wife) can come out, one of his daughters comes outside instead.

Ifran mentions my coming by earlier, so obviously someone saw me outside. I pretend not to understand him, saying that I went into town. He repeats or says something else, and again, I divert the conversation, despite thinking, *Oh, you mean while you were beating your kid?* Then I tell myself to engage in no judgment, but to instead be kind and loving. I do not know their story, the facts, or circumstances.

My Final Dust-Up
with Seamstress Shama

NOT QUITE AS overloaded today as I head for home after my daily outing, carrying only one backpack, I stop at the post office to buy their largest cardboard box for my shipment later this week. Neither of the women who have assisted me in the past is there today. Two hapless chaps are behind the counter and a third is sound asleep with his head on his desk.

Telling Hapless Fellow #1 that I wish to buy the box, he indicates an inability to do that, not knowing how much it costs or having some other problem. He tries the classic Indian reply of nonaction, telling me, "Come back in a half hour." But having been here a month, it is time to become a bit assertive. Telling him that I cannot come back in an hour, that I live a long way away, and that the lady told me yesterday it costs 160 rupees, he apparently realizes I am going to be persistent. Hence, he looks at the computer and miraculously confirms the price.

After consulting with Hapless Chap #2 about the size, I keep pointing to the *sole* box on display as the one I want; a flattened box finally is brought out. Hapless Fellow and Hapless Chap consult about something, and it appears they plan to tape it. Telling them not to tape the bottom and that I will do that, he doesn't understand. After a series of hand motioning and more explanation, eventually, I depart carrying my large flat cardboard box. Every minor interaction is complicated by communication challenges.

THURSDAY, MAY 31, 2012

The Saga of Seamstress Shama continues. Of course, why wouldn't it? This is becoming an even better tale than the 24-Hour International Shipping Lady/Cow Farmer.

Having decided to take all of the dresses to Surat except the one last one, Seamstress Shama told me last week it would be ready Wednesday night. The fabric is a bit see-through so I ask her to line all but the sleeves, having purchased and prewashed an additional three meters of the same fabric for the lining.

Annoyed at getting the same runaround as last week, I explain that I am leaving town and ask why it can't be done. The same excuse "many school uniforms." Okay, I am thinking, *So why aren't you sewing them then?* When she asks, "When are you leaving?" I reply that I have to send things out on Friday. She then tells me it will be ready then tomorrow night. After more questioning, she *assures* me that the bloody dress will be ready at 6:00 p.m. on Thursday. As I leave she thanks me for all the sales, telling me that she really appreciates it. Why then aren't you fulfilling your end of this contractual arrangement and getting my clothes done on time?

During the day—*the day* the silly dress is to be completed—I walk by her shop on three occasions. Naturally, she is not open the first or second times; the third time, however, she is sitting on the stoop. No wonder nothing ever gets finished; she is never working. Perhaps it's ready? "No, tonight at 6:00 p.m.," she says.

At 5:45 p.m., with the *sole* purpose of making this jaunt again to get the dress, I hike into the ashram area. It is a very hot, humid day; after getting home earlier, I even nap for a couple of hours. As I arrive at her establishment, she is hopping on her bike to go somewhere. "Sit, sit," she says, "I will be right back." Looking around, I see no black dress. She must have it at home and is going to retrieve it.

While waiting, I take a close look at her sewing machine. There is no power connected to it; it has a treadle so perhaps it doesn't need electricity. But then the detective in me notices that on the base where one sews, there is a book and a number of other items. There is no thread on the spindle. Realizing now that there is no sewing being performed here, this explains why whenever I come by, I have yet to see her actually doing any work.

Ten minutes pass, and she finally shows up with the dress. "Where is the sample (a gold one she is using as her pattern)?" I ask. "Sample done at seven, come back in an hour," she says. "What do you mean, you've already sewn that. It's been finished for a week," I say. She replies again, "Done at seven." I have no idea what she's talking about; why isn't the dress there?

With every question, there are more and more excuses and obfuscation. "Where is it?" I finally demand. She says that it is at her house. "Fine, let's go get it," I tell her. "My house a long way," she says. I am now becoming annoyed and say, "I don't care, I will walk there; let's go." She tries again, saying, "Come back at seven." My reply is: "I am not coming back at seven. I have some-one waiting for me. I want that dress *now*. We are going to get it!" Seeing that I am determined, she finally gives up and starts pushing her bike.

Walking beside her, the "long distance to her house" is a few short blocks away, down the end of the street and around the corner, taking less than five minutes to reach. Surprise, surprise—"her house" has a sign on it, which I have noticed before when on that street. It reads: "Jeeva Tailors: Men and Women."

Still not having figured out what is going on, but I realize that this must be where she is sewing. Walking in, there is some guy sewing away with more of my same black and gray fabric as the dress she has just given me, and the gold sample dress is lying on the floor. I am now irate!

Rather strongly challenging her, "You haven't even been sewing these? This guy is sewing them? You have lied to me and cheated me!" I start grabbing all of the black material from the guy sewing it and say, "That's it, you're done; I am taking them."

Confirming that I have all of the material, along with my sample dress, I stomp out, throwing some money at her. "No, not enough. Three meters for lining," she says. Telling her I never authorized that and had already purchased three extra meters of the same black striped fabric for lining, either she misunderstood, despite our having talked about it at length more than once, or simply took it upon herself to have it lined with plain black fabric.

I throw at her a few more rupees for the unauthorized expense of the lining fabric and leave. *I am beyond furious!* What a colossal waste of time and energy this whole endeavor has become. At home, I see that the dress is very stiff and unwashed. It is awful, and it will shrink; at any rate, the lining will need to be removed and resewn.

But suddenly, at least, the explanation for all the delays, her never working, and her multitude of excuses has become abundantly clear. Why didn't she just tell me she was subcontracting it out? Or tell me she doesn't do the sewing, whoever this guy is does it? I suppose because I never asked her the precise question: "Do you actually sew these yourself?" But why would I? She must get her percentage for taking work to him so would not send me directly to him.

On the way home, I am no longer angry, just a bit annoyed and amusedly reminded of the story in *Eat, Pray, Love* where the author is trying to buy a house for the lady in Bali. I don't recall the specific details because although having read the India section of her book about a dozen times, I have only read the Bali section twice. But this fiasco reminds me of that incident. Rarely are things what they appear, and often, there is a subtext or other story.

Another lesson learned: Do not hire a tailor unless you see her or him actually sewing. It never crosses my mind that she does not actually sew the items herself. Actually, a second valuable lesson is learned: Be sure to always ask all pertinent questions as well. In my brief time in India, already there have been several instances where I failed to ask enough, or proper, questions.

I shall be most happy to have no further dealings with Seamstress Shama.

I am now off to tailor #2, Surat, who is to have the rest of my items finished tonight too—the actual second black and gray dress (having purchased enough fabric to line one dress *and* make a second), my suit, and shortening sleeves on a top. Everything is finished (well, nearly); he is very nice, takes everything out, and shows me each item. But he has forgotten to shorten the sleeves and is very apologetic. Can I come back in a half hour?

Asking Surat if anyone in the neighborhood sells bottled water, "No, no, only in town. Ramana market only," he replies. Now in India five weeks, one thing I *have* learned is not to necessarily rely on information or advice from people without verification. Walking down the street, the third little market sells chilled bottled water. Within ten minutes, I am back at Surat's tailor shop, a little metal hut, and the sleeves are finished. That is service.

Yesterday, while walking home, a lady is scooping up freshly dropped cow pies, which I believe are used for fires; it's nice that cow dung can be recycled. My only thought is that I hope she scrubs well with soap and water before preparing dinner for the family. The little hut at the end of the lane has numerous cow pies drying on the surrounding wall.

Another unusual experience was the first time I hear a car backing up. Had I not been with Melissa, I would have assumed it was a pleasant-sounding cell phone ring. But she explained to me that all of the cars here, or at least the newer models, play a very loud tune when backing up, like a song on a cell phone.

As for the street traffic in India, think New York City times ten and add constant horn honking. Maneuvering through it, one simply must be bold. Reminded of that old adage, "He who hesitates is lost," in Indian traffic, "He who hesitates is dead." One just walks into the street betwixt and amongst the jam-packed congestion of buses, rickshaws, bicycles, cars, scooters, and motorcycles and needs to pay heed. Initially, it is a rather daunting experience, but one learns to jump into the fray with courage and confidence.

Wandering to the Ramanashram and arriving just a few minutes before eight in the morning, I sit on the polished marble floor against a wall in the main room, the location of Ramana's samadhi and where a few others are sitting about as well. People come and go and walk around the samadhi, take vibhuti ashes, prostrate.

Sitting toward the back, I cannot actually see the chanting young priests-in-training, but their voices are powerful and beautiful. Mesmerized, it sounds as if there are about thirty of them. A couple of young boys, all with the same haircut shaven closely with a little ponytail in the back, continuously walk around the samadhi, a large distance of probably forty yards on each of the four sides.

Deciding to walk around the samadhi myself, I am incredibly surprised to discover that such powerful chanting is produced by only eight young boys, approximately ages five to seven, with a couple of older, adolescent-aged young men repeating the chorus repeats. They are terrific and engaging. I am moved to experience this.

Wandering about the ashram grounds, I find the ubiquitous cowsheds, which all ashrams have, and take photographs. There are lots of cows; a group of pure white, hump-backed ones have their own pasture area with brown ones in two other locations.

Scattered throughout the property are samadhi sites of other saints, including Ramana's mother, whom he credits as his guru. After he lived for several years on Mount Arunachula, she came to join him and spent the remainder of her life with him.

Having not been to the Ramsuratkumar ashram for a few days, I go, chant for a bit, and take better photographs of all the saints and holy figures, whose portraits hang in the Hall of the Mahatmas. Upon uploading to my computer those taken previously, some images were blurry, and for some reason, I feel compelled to have all of those photographs. It is nice to see again the lovely regular ashram girls who are there each day, all day long. What pure devotion they have.

Thinking that I may wish to go to Kerala after the Saccidananda ashram, I call Param, the fellow who takes people to Kerala, to see if we might meet. Meeting at the chai shop by the Ramana Super Market, he asks if I mind going to his house. I do not, so we walk the five minutes there. En route, he hands a fellow ten rupees, saying that his charity is to help feed stray dogs and that he gives twenty-five percent of his income for that purpose.

Sitting on the terrace of their modest apartment, we chat a bit, and soon, his wife joins us. They are both massage therapists, she for women, he for men. I would trust him to tour within Kerala, assuming it easier to go with a driver who knows the area than try to hire someone there. He claims to know about accommodations at all budget levels, restaurants, and the like. Famous last words or actuality? We shall see. He assures me that one can enjoy Kerala, even during the monsoon season, and that although it will be rainy, one still can get out and do things.

If I decide to go, he only needs forty-eight hours' notice and will pick me up at the ashram in the Ambassador, one of those wonderful, older big taxi sedans that I have seen and wanted to travel in. It might be a little rugged without air conditioning, however, he reassures me that a portion of the trip through the mountains will be cooler. Oh well, I need to have some real Indian travel experiences too.

We first would head to Cochin, a place that has been recommended repeatedly to me by Indians and other travelers. Getting there from the ashram would involve one long day of travel.

His rates are very reasonable, $10 per day for his tour guide services, plus gas for the car. He explains for that, "I will say good morning and good night. And if you want me not to talk, just tell me." He is pretty chatty so that loquaciousness might become tiring; however, in another sense, it is rather refreshing after being unable to communicate much with the Tamil locals. Claiming to know Kerala well, he will tailor my trip to whatever I want to do. Then if I want to go further north or south, he says that he will be at my beck and call.

Today, while walking on the main drag, Chengam Road, after returning my books to the library, I see my first goat passenger in a rickshaw...a lady and her black goat as the passengers in the back of the auto rickshaw! What a hoot; I wish I had that captured on film.

A Fender Bender, Nadi Reading, and the Beautiful Saccidananda Ashram

T HIS IS MY last day in Tiruvannamalai. The taxi comes at 6:00 a.m. tomorrow for the three and a half- to four-hour drive to Vaitheesaith Koil. Then it is on to the ashram, Saccidananda Ashram, also known as Shantivanam, about thirty kilometers from Trichy, the abbreviated name of Tiruchirapalli.

I am indeed ready to leave for my landlord who initially seemed so kind has become a royal pain. Caution to self: don't live upstairs above one's landlord. Always finding something to poke at me about: whether leaving the air conditioning on, using it improperly, drinking too much water, not taking clothes down, and on and on, it has become very tedious. Perhaps, those dealings with him, however, are the universe's direction that it is time to move on.

This morning *the most* hideous creature that I have ever seen in my entire life, which crawled on me a couple of days ago, is in the sink. Not sure what it is, but it is the ilk of creepy crawler that could induce nightmares. At least today, it is in a controlled space, which means that it no longer lives. Not usually afraid of bugs and insects, this one is a major exception. Cleaning and scrubbing the kitchen counters, I thought an earlier infestation of hundreds of miniature ants was under control. But forgetting about the ghee container on the kitchen counter, its oil a magnet for the little buggers, a couple of days ago, another detachment of ants surrounded it.

Reaching for the jar to wash and toss it, the same nasty, dark brown three-inch varmint crawls onto my arm. Whatever *the thing* is apparently was into the ghee as well. Screaming, I flick it off my arm and then, of course, never see it again. Until today that is.

Today, Melissa and I go to the main commercial town area, a few minutes from the ashram, where we have a delicious meal at Hotel Hanna. Our last stop is the vegetable market. It is glorious. Aisles and aisles of merchants, a few old ladies but mostly men, hawk their products—veggies, fruits, spices, dried tobacco leaves—shouting loudly what I assume to be announcements of their wares and prices. It is like a circus of produce sellers or the equivalent of a very large, boisterous farmers market.

We have a nice afternoon together, and this is the last time that I will see Melissa before departing. I am so grateful for her kindness and friendship. Her suggestions, advice, and direction have been invaluable for this newbie to India.

My final dinner at Ifran's little outdoor bistro is also delightful. His daughter sets up a wee metal table outside, with burgundy linen tablecloth, salt and pepper shakers, a little vase of flowers, and napkins. Paper napkins are another rarity here; although there are napkins on tables in some restaurants, they essentially are not used, even in the Westerners' homes.

Indians wash their hands before eating, eat with their hands, then wash their hands, and rinse out their mouths after meals. Bringing small gifts for everyone, we take photographs. The food is delicious. I will miss Ifran's cooking.

Sunday, June 3, 2012

Driver Rajesh, the same one I had from Chennai to Tiruv, arrives a few minutes late, but we are on the road by 6:10 a.m. He is such a nice guy, and his car is spotless, which I love. I actually take a couple wee naps during our approximate nine-hour trip, which based upon the condition of India's roads and the nonstop horn honking, is a major feat. All of Kunal's drivers wear white shirts and pants, are very professional, and most pleasant.

Our drive takes us through myriad, typical little villages and completely agrarian areas. Struck by how this part of India looks, at various times, it appears to be plains of midwestern United States with sparse trees, lots of grass, and farmland. Then it quickly changes to a tropical topography with large stands of palm trees, bananas, and impressive massive greenery. Speaking of bananas, I did not know until learning recently, that a banana tree bears one harvest of bananas and then dies. That seems very sad.

Rolling along the Indian roads and highways, I am reminded again that it really is Darwin's survival of the fittest out here. Rajesh honks his horn continuously, the universal warning to everyone—cyclists, pedestrians, scooters, other motor vehicles. Many auto rickshaws and trucks have large "Sound Horn" notices painted across the backs of the vehicles. Whenever possible, he moves at a pretty good clip, driving a white Tata. The Tata family conglomerate is one of the billionaire groups of India, and the Tata is by far the most common vehicle although I also see

Toyotas, Suzukis, a couple of Chevrolets, a BMW, and various other models.

The Tata is Indian-made, relatively small, and must get amazing gas mileage because when we arrive after some 650-700 kilometers, I notice that he still has nearly a half tank of gas. Asking Rajesh what kind of mileage he gets, trying to explain kilometers per liter, he does not understand what I am talking about. That must be my inability to communicate because I would assume that a taxi driver is well aware of his gas mileage. By the last leg of our trip, we are traveling on four-lane paved freeways, a welcome change from the bumpy, potholed roads earlier.

Driving along, one notices almost exclusively tiny little huts, constructed of concrete or stucco, bricks or wood, with pointed, thatched roofs. Then, plopped amidst them is a three- or four-story, gated multicolored house, a mansion by comparison, with a satellite dish on the roof. Driving today, I notice laundry hanging on old-fashioned jute rope clotheslines; in my neighborhood in Tiruv, everyone's clothing, including the women's colorful saris, was draped to dry over barbed wire fences.

Cruising through one little berg, out of nowhere from a side street zooms a small red scooter that T-bones us, ramming into my passenger door. The driver is pretty elderly. Sitting by that door, I see the impact clearly. Rajesh immediately jumps out, and having heard horror stories about accidents in India (that people go crazy, beat people up, and the like), I immediately lock the door, thinking, *Oh, great, I am about to have another authentic Indian experience.*

Apparently, the impact is minor and the fellow not hurt because soon Rajesh returns and off we drive. At a later stop, when examining the door's exterior, there is visible damage. Since Rajesh is pretty nonplussed by the whole situation, as a taxi driver in India, accidents and dings and dents likely come with the territory. I am grateful that it is minor, that the fellow is not injured, and that no police are involved.

Arriving in Vaitheeswaran Koil in record time about 9:30, I think that we are in Chidambaram. "No, no, back there," Rajesh says pointing behind us. Looking for the nadi reader that my friend Manesh had used, I have the name of the business and the scroll reader.

After my reading, however, I am pretty convinced that mine was not the same guy. In asking if that is the fellow's name, of course, he says that is him. The odds of the first place we stop upon hitting town and finding "the guy" are pretty low. Furthermore, Manesh's reading was seven or eight years ago, so the place and fellow may no longer even be here. The locals in Tiruv all advise not to go to these people and that they are scams; however, I already pretty much had decided, "Hey, you worship gods represented by giant monkeys (Hanuman) and a half elephant/half man (Ganesh), don't tell me this is bunk!"

Less than overwhelmed by my reading, *miraculously,* my scroll is there. That is the first question—if one's scroll exists. I doubt that they ever fail to find one's scroll because the price is substantially less if one's scroll is not located. The theory, as I understand it, is if one is destined to come to India for a reading, the person's scroll will be found. Sensing that my reading is not from one of the "golden nuggets," i.e., real deals, among the charlatans, a skinny old curmudgeon translates while a younger guy reads the scrolls. Having been told by my friend that it could take up to three hours, mine lasts about an hour.

Interestingly, however, he gets right a few of pieces of information. One is that I am a lawyer, which is the most surprising because I have told no one that. Another is that I teach yoga and meditation, which would be a pretty easy guess given that I am wearing "om" jewelry and have come from Tiruv, a yoga and meditation mecca.

Supposedly, in a prior life, I was born in Sri Lanka, the former Ceylon, where my father was a Brahmin priest in a temple. Of course, one likely would always be of the upper caste, not from a lower one, right? Going into a long convoluted tale about my sins in that life, including stealing money from the temple until I repented and found the error of my ways, overall, I was pretty underwhelmed by the entire experience. Feeling similar to the corner psychic with crystal ball, I don't bother to ask about other past lives.

Taking notes, my reading also is recorded and transferred to a CD. As for my future acts in this life, the predictions are pretty outlandish. I, of course, am going to do wonderful and altruistic things, including start an ashram and help children. And I am to have a long, happy, and healthy life, the standard drivel everyone is likely told. But my favorite is that I am to return to India at age seventy-five for another reading about the rest of my life.

There is lots of fortune teller happy-upbeat-prediction-kind-of-stuff, that this will be good and that is very aspicious, yada, yada, yada. My Hindu god is supposedly Hanuman, which is fine. Although never particularly drawn to him in the past, he seems to be an all right kind of dude.

In addition to seeing the Taj Mahal, this is the only "must" on my India to-do list. So although disappointing and certainly not enlightening as was my friend's reading, I came, I saw, I got my reading, and had another classic Indian experience, all for the cost of less than a facial. I have no regrets. Recalling what my friend Manesh told me—that in India one finds the authentic, the frauds, the real, and the scam artists—and "that it's all good," this is the advice guiding my attitude here.

It doesn't take us long to reach the ashram. Noticing off to the right amazingly gorgeous tropical foliage, thick with banana and palm trees, thinking it could be some Asian jungle on a seacoast somewhere, voila, Rajesh turns onto a little dirt road. Wondering if the ashram is in this area and how cool that would be, suddenly less than 100 meters ahead of us, is our destination. Set amidst a lush forest, the name Shantivanam means "Forest of Peace." It is beautiful and feels a bit cooler. Pia, the nice lady who meets us, asks if I want a room or a hut. I say that it matters not, whichever is cooler.

It's a short trek to my room located at the back of the property in a one-story structure housing several rooms. Gratefully, Rajesh carries most of my luggage for despite trying to downsize, in addition to my original two backpacks, day handbag, and wheeled suitcase, I also have one cloth bag of powdered Gatorade, nuts, and raisins and a second with bottles of water.

Both my room and building exterior are painted a soothing pale blue. The little housing compound is comprised of four separate, low-slung buildings around a center courtyard replete with coconut palms and bananas trees.

My *Nirvana* guidebook says that the rooms are sparse but adequate. Actually, mine is better than anticipated. The place is run by monks so I am not expecting it to be posh. There are two twin-size beds with colorful Indian cotton bedspreads and pillowcases, mosquito nets, a desk, a bookshelf, two plastic chairs, and a bathroom with shower and again a Western toilet. Hallelujah! I am lucking out on the bathrooms thus far in India.

Pia advises me that tea at the tea circle is at 3:30. Wandering down, which takes only a couple of minutes, thinking that I may meet someone, I am the only person there, and despite the temperature probably being 100 degrees, I have a cup of tea. To reach my room, I walk past the cow barns; ergo, depending upon the wind direction permitting a strong whiff of the sacred creatures, a couple minutes of mouth breathing may be required.

After tea, I meander. The grounds are very pretty, heavily wooded, and peaceful, with small buildings and residential huts tucked here and there. The property doesn't seem too large, about eight acres I think, but it is definitely larger than the Yogi Ramsuratkumar and Ramanashram properties. In the directions and information pamphlet in my room, it requests that guests honor the silence of the property, which I love. The temple or church is very pretty, and because of the Christian aspect it is much different than other ashrams, with both Hindu deities and

Christian iconography. On the ashram grounds are samadhi sites of past sannyasins.

Mentioning to Pia, whose English is quite good, that the water in my bathroom sink doesn't seem to work, she immediately comes with me. Rattling the faucet, it still is not functioning so she moves me to another room across the courtyard. Actually, I like the layout of my second room a bit better. The configuration of the beds makes it feel more spacious, and there is room to do my yoga. And the sink works, despite the entire faucet mechanism hanging loosely from the sink. What is it about plumbing in India anyhow?

But it gets better. The toilet sits only eight to ten inches off the floor, about the height of a toddler's potty chair. Having short legs so I manage, but I envision a six-foot tall person having to adopt a Lazy Boy reclining position. The ceiling fan—thank the gods that there is one—rattles continuously, but it will provide white noise for falling asleep. Obviously, I shall be back to taking daily showers to cool off and using my cooling ties again.

It is so humid that perspiration pours off me while merely sitting still. Or is it glistening? What's the old saw: horses sweat, men perspire, and women glisten? I don't feel like I'm glistening, that's for sure. The minute I enter my room, I rip off my clothes. Drinking liter after liter of water, I rarely have to urinate.

The printed schedule posted in my room indicates something at 6:00 p.m. Heading to the church, there is only one priest meditating, and it is stiflingly hot in the room. Leaving, back in my room, I tear off my clothes *once again*, wishing that I were wearing a floor-length sack held together by Velcro. Looking at the schedule again, it appears that 6:00 p.m. is private meditation, silence, and angelus (whatever that is). Evening prayers and supper are at 7:00 p.m.

Thinking possibly that prayers are before the meal, I go to the dining hall a bit before seven, but it is dark with no one around. Then hearing a bell, I realize the action must be in the church.

Rushing to the temple, several priests, a couple of sisters, and about three of us lay folk are present. The service has not yet begun, and a nice, adolescent-aged kid brings me the psalm and prayer books. During the brief service, he shows me the appropriate pages in the books. What a thoughtful young man, but then, why should I be surprised, all of the Indians have been so very kind and helpful.

It is a brief service—a prayer, reading of two psalms and a Bible passage, chanting, arati, and receipt of vibhuti on our third eye. After prayers, we exit quietly although a couple of people speak to me, and I join everyone in the dining hall. Sitting on the floor, a brief prayer is offered by a priest whereupon everyone goes to the counter window where pots of food are set out for self-service. Much preferring this approach to being served, it is easier to limit portions, eating more veggies and less rice.

We sit on bamboo floor mats and eat with our hands. The food is good—chapatis (essentially grilled whole wheat tortillas, rather a cross between lefse and tortillas), rice, a couple of sambars, and bananas. After eating in silence, another brief prayer is offered, and we wash our plates and cups at four rinsing and washing stations, including one with soap and a final rinsing in hot water.

After supper, I meet a few more people, including Sister Catherine (at least three renunciates are women) and Brother or Father Paul. As we are finishing, Father George with whom I spoke by phone comes in. Very kind, he informs me that the power will be off shortly, but for less than an hour, and again for three hours tomorrow morning commencing at 9:00 a.m.

The little tract in my room, in addition to explaining the ashram's origins and development, describes many traditions and ceremonies, the elucidation of which I am grateful. It explains that at Mass an offering of the four elements—water, earth, air, and fire—is made, and that every Hindu puja consists of the same offering of these elements to God.

It also describes sandal paste made from sandalwood, which is considered the most precious of all woods. Having a sweet fragrance, it is viewed as a symbol of divine grace and unconditional love of God. It is placed on the forehead or hands as a way of consecrating the body and its members to God. Sandal paste is used here at morning prayers.

The purple powder, known as kumkumum, symbolizes the third eye and is placed there, located between the eyebrows. The explanation is that our two eyes are the eyes of duality viewing the outer world and outer self, whereas the third eye is considered the inner eye seeing the inner light. The pamphlet further explains that according to the Gospel: "If thine eye be single, thy whole body shall be full of light." The third eye was often marked on Greek icons of Christ and considered a universal symbol. In India, the red color is considered feminine, the mark of mother goddess, representing feminine wisdom. Kumkumum is used during midday prayers at the ashram. Vibhuti, or ashes, placed on the forehead represent that our sins and impurities have been burned away, and the ashes signify the purified self. Vibhuti is used at evening prayers.

Arati, common in all Hindu temples, consists of waving lights or incense as a sign of honor or worship and occurs at the completion of all prayers. The pamphlet explains that the inner sanctuary of the temple is always kept dark to signify that God dwells in the cave of the heart. Lights waved before the shrine reveal the hidden God.

Deciding to go to bed early to awaken for 6:30 prayers, my room is hot even with the fan running at full pitch. I shower and crawl into my mosquito-netted bed, another first for me. Having seen only one mosquito and assuming it's too hot for them yet, nevertheless, out of an abundance of caution, I zip myself into the pink tent.

Sweating It Out
at Shantivanam

MONDAY, JUNE 4, 2012

A FITFUL NIGHT, I recall awakening three times and jumping in the shower, then covering myself with a wet towel. I am getting the message about traveling in Tamil Nadu in May and June. Before retiring, I debate leaving the windows open, deciding against it because they aren't screened. It might have helped cool the room, however.

When the alarm goes off at 6:00 a.m., I cannot believe it is already morning and decide to sleep a bit longer, taking about one millisecond to decide to blow off morning prayers. I easily rationalize that attending two times daily is twice more than I usually attend church. Amazingly, I sleep for another couple of hours, missing prayers and breakfast. Never interested in eating at 7:00 a.m. anyhow, that is fine with me.

Some ashrams are very strict about requiring participation in all scheduled activities; others take the approach that you are there to work on whatever you need to and are more flexible about guests' participation. Having seen nothing in the printed materials that this place follows the more strict protocol, I assume participation is optional.

My bed frame is a wooden platform on legs; the mattress is firm and only about three inches thick, but I haven't found the Indian beds to be uncomfortable. There are no marble floors here though; instead, I have terra cotta cement floors and a rather slippery tile bathroom floor. I try to be very careful to avoid falling.

The noon prayer service is nice; it's an interesting mix of Christian and Hindu with some chanting in Sanskrit or Tamil, reading of Bible scriptures and Psalms, and reciting the Lord's Prayer and Christian liturgy. Unaware that there were Christian ashrams in India until preparing for my trip when I discovered a few, I decided it would be interesting to visit one. Saccidananda is the first and most prominent.

According to published materials, the temple is in the South Indian style with an inner sanctum that is kept dark. Simple, but pretty, and light pink in color with stark white trim, various figures decorate the exterior of the temple. All windows have images of Christ with an Indian flair. Although there are some benches and small chairs along the back and sides of the temple, most renunciates sit on the floor.

Gracing the walls of the dining hall, an open-air pavilion, are pictures of the Last Supper, the Virgin Mary and Christ Child, Jesus Christ, Mother Theresa, Ramana Maharshi, Sri Aurobindo, Bede Griffiths, who was the spiritual guru and last head monk who died in the 1990s, and various other priests, whom I assume to be the two original monks and founders. Lunch is very tasty, including bananas and mangoes. My friend Connie just e-mailed me, from China no less where she is traveling, having read in the *New York Times* that it is mango season in India. There are something like 500 varieties, and apparently, India supplies sixty percent of the world's mangoes. It is considered the fruit of kings.

Also served at lunch is a delicious mildly sweet concoction, the consistency reminding me of the homemade cottage cheese Mother made when I was a kid. Asking Father Paul what it is, he doesn't know the name but says it is made from the milk of the cow immediately after the birth of a calf, to which sugar is added. It is considered a celebration of the birth.

Sugar is added of course. Melissa told me that the rate of diabetes in India is staggeringly high. Indians do put lots of sugar in coffee, tea, juice, and pretty much everything. Additionally, they have their "sweets" as they call their sugary pastry concoctions. Happily, the few sweets sampled here I find as though sucking on a sugar cube and don't care for them. Lots of milk and buttermilk are also drunk. Interestingly, I was surprised to learn recently that milk has a high sugar content, something astonishing like twenty-five grams per cup. Hence, India probably competes with the United States for sugar consumption and incidence of diabetes.

Chatting briefly with Father George regarding my seva, my service in contribution while here, the ashram rules/schedule lists various tasks to be done by guests, a common requirement when staying at ashrams. He says that I should chop vegetables after breakfast, and then adds, "But you weren't here this morning." I guess my absence was noted, which is not surprising given that I am the only guest.

Asking Father George about access to a telephone, he wonders if tonight after supper would be all right. Whether I call tonight or tomorrow, my current thinking is to contact Param about heading to Kerala, and inquiring if he can obtain an air-conditioned car instead of the Ambassador sedan. This heat is pretty grim; I can "experience" an Ambassador during cooler climes. When arriving, I had no idea how the place would resonate with me and how long I might want to stay. A few nights will probably be enough, particularly if I am unable to sleep due to the heat.

The name of the ashram, Saccidananda, means "Being Consciousness Bliss." A descriptive pamphlet also calls it "Shantivanam, A Christian Ashram"; hence, its two names. Originally founded in 1950 by two French priests, one died in 1957 and the other became a hermit in the Himalayas. It was later taken over by Father Bede Griffiths from the Kurisumala Ashram in Kerala, and since 1980 has been part of the Benedictine Order. Father Bede Griffiths passed away in 1993, and I am not sure who is in charge now.

In explaining its mission, the pamphlet says this:

> Among the gifts given by God to India, the greatest was seen to be that of interiority, the awareness of the presence of God dwelling in the heart of every human person and of every creature, which is fostered by prayer and meditation, by contemplative silence and the practice of yoga...
>
> "These values," it was said belong to Christ and are a positive help to an authentic Christian life." Consequently, it was said: "Ashrams, where authentic incarnational Christian spirituality is lived, should be established, which should be open to non-Christians so they may experience genuine Christian fellowship." The aim of our ashram, therefore,...is to bring into our Christian life the riches of Indian spirituality, to share in that profound experience of God which originated in the Vedas, was developed in the Upanishads and the Bhagavad-Gita, and has come down to us today through a continual succession of sages and holy men and women.

Doing my morning yoga practice with no electricity, i.e., *sans* ceiling fan, is rather like being in a Bikram studio; sweat pours off. Then I am off to noon prayers and lunch. Both are nice. Back to my room for more sweating; oh my heavens, it is definitely hot, and the power cuts out at three and doesn't come back on till after six. This is going to be fun...or not.

Not too excited about hot tea, neverthess, I wander to the tea circle a few minutes before four. Father George and Brother Martin are chatting. Brother Martin, the fellow who responded to my e-mail inquiry about staying here, introduces himself and pours me tea—steaming hot with milk and sugar—before I can object. To be polite, I try to drink the stuff when it cools down.

Not liking milk or sweet tea (India's chai), it is an effort to gag it down. The two continue to chat as I sit quietly wondering when the Four O'Clock Talk is getting under way. After fifteen minutes or so, Father Martin asks if I've finished my tea whereupon I advise that it's still too hot for me. "Okay, bring it with you," he says, and I follow him to a nearby, little round building, the meditation hall. There are no fans, but there is some air circulating. Offering me a stool, I choose the floor.

During his Four O'Clock Talk, he explains the history of the ashram, the founders' backgrounds, its development and purpose, and asks if I have questions. "Is there a Coke machine on premises?" Just kidding; I do have a few. "What is angelus on the schedule?" It means ringing of the bell.

Then I inquire about the Hindu religion and its traditions. Very scholarly, he has written several books, teaches throughout Europe in the summers, and is a strong proponent of interdialogue among all religions and inclusivity versus exclusivity.

Wishing I had a notebook and pen, it is as if I am back in college taking a religion course. Making notes on a crude blackboard of black painted wood, he explains the development of Hinduism and that there are many forms—advaita as well as many others.

In its earliest stages (some claim 25,000 years ago, but more likely about 3,000 BC, he says), the worship was of nature—the sun, sky, and water. Later, it evolved to a level known as polytheism, then henotheism, next monotheism, then pantheism, and finally in about 500 BC to monoism, which is belief in one God.

Unlike most of the other major religions, there is not a founder or originating spiritual head. I had not really thought about that difference, there being Christ, Buddha, and Mohammed, and of course, Buddhism differs also in that it is not monotheistic.

Explaining the differences between the beliefs about creation in the Christian and Hindu religions, he explains that in Hinduism, Brahma was the creator. There is only one God in Hinduism, referred to as Brahman or Atman.

The other many manifestations are representations or characteristics of God, whether it be Vishnu, Shiva, or Ganesh. Analogizing to God in the Christian tradition, he explains that God is compassionate, loving, forgiving, and kind. Then laughingly (he has a good sense of humor), Father Martin says that after Brahma created the universe, there wasn't much left for him to do. Hence, he created Vishnu to protect it, and Shiva to handle destruction and death, which is why Shiva lives in cemeteries.

Of all the manifestations that Hindus can choose to worship, I wonder why so many choose Shiva, the destroyer who spreads cremation ashes on his body. It seems rather morbid to me. I should have asked him that question; perhaps I am missing some important piece. For example, the majority of sadhus in the North are followers of Shiva. Were I Hindu, I definitely would select a happier, more upbeat god; actually, I probably would choose one of the feminine representative energies.

If I understand correctly, there are four main groups worshipped in today's Hindu religion, although he also explains that during the evolution of Hinduism through thousands of years, not necessarily all of the nature-worshipping, pantheistic rituals ceased. Hence, those components still exist also.

No wonder the Hindu religion seems so complicated. The four are: Vaishnaism, the worship of Vishnu; Shaivism, the worship of Shiva; Shaktism, the worship of the feminine forms of the gods, Lakshmi and Parvati; and Ganeshans, who worship Ganesh.

Brother Martin further explains, however, that Ganesh, the remover of obstacles, is worshipped by all of the groups, is very important to everyone in the Hindu tradition, and is found at the entrance to every Hindu temple. He tells me the story of the creation of Ganesh, portions of which I have forgotten, for example, why he has an elephant head. After Shiva chopped off his head, Parvati, Shiva's consort, instructed Shiva to go out and bring back the first head he found, which happened to be an elephant.

I learn too that Hanuman is not really a god, but rather a representation of a characteristic of God, that of strength and power. Having now a wee understanding of this fascinating religion, what a bonus to have the benefit of this religious scholar's teaching. Tomorrow, I shall take notes.

Regarding my questions about the ashram, he explains that the sisters are not part of their order; they attend prayers here, but have their own order and nearby ashram. Later in the evening, I learn from Sister Catherine that their order was started as an adjunct to this group of Benedictine monks. The founding sister is elderly, but lives in their ashram, and there are only five of them. She invites me to come visit them, perhaps tomorrow after tea.

Forgetting that I have Brother Martin's lecture at four, perhaps I can go after his talk. But what is this scheduling business? I am trying to avoid any schedules and go with the flow; however, discipline is an important attribute, one which I have become lackadaisical about. Ergo, perhaps developing better discipline is one lesson that I am to learn in India.

The Benedictines, as were the original French priests who started the ashram, are Catholic. Neither having been raised Catholic nor ever studying the religion, I am pretty ignorant about even the basics not even knowing, for example, the difference between a monk and a priest. Brother Martin explains that they are all monks, i.e., renunciates, but some choose to become priests as well allowing them to offer the sacraments. The fathers are the priests, the brothers are the monks.

TUESDAY, JUNE 5, 2012

Leaving the windows open last night cooled off the room, and pleasantly, I awaken only once during the night. Nevertheless, when my alarm goes off at 6:00 a.m. to make it to 6:30 morning prayers, again, I again am not compelled.

Uncertain why, but my most favorite sleep seems to be those extra minutes or hours when I successfully fall back asleep in the morning after first awakening. It seems like a special gift. Is it because it feels like forbidden, stolen time? Resetting my alarm to make it to the kitchen by seven to chop vegetables, after awakening and showering, I arrive, but no one is there yet, and I hear service still in session on the temple. Kitchen Girl tells me to come back at 7:30 after breakfast.

On my second trip to the dining hall at 7:30, most are finished eating. Going to the kitchen for my assignment, and after some sign language and pointing, I sit outside to chop my vegetables. And what am I chopping? Onions, of course, five of them. Why wouldn't she give me the task of cutting the one and only vegetable that makes people cry? Why wouldn't I be given the chore of cutting up the *only* vegetable on the planet that I honestly don't care for? We have eaten carrots, beets, tomatoes, peppers, potatoes, okra, and lord knows what else, but, *noooo*, I get the dreaded onion. Another test or lesson from the universe. Thank you, God.

Still having the smell of onions on my hands seven hours later, despite multiple hand-washing attempts, I try to channel Sister Sherryle, who loves onions and whom I have watched efficiently chop many an onion for potato salad, burgers, tacos, and other yummy dishes. Not minding the flavor of cooked onion, it's just the texture, smell, and taste of raw onions that are unappealing, along with wearing their odor all day.

Completing my little job in probably thrice the time it should take, but never claiming any culinary skills (besides, everyone in India moves at a slow pace), I manage not to slice myself and am proud of my first veggie-cutting episode at an ashram. When I take them to the kitchen, the Kitchen Lady is cutting okra (and why couldn't I have been given *that* vegetable?), and I ask if she wants me to do anything else. "No, no," she motions me out. So the question is, will I be the onion girl every day, relegated to smelling like one for the rest of my days here?

While chopping away, Father Paul wanders in for his breakfast, sitting outside eating instead on the usual mat on the dining hall floor. Occasionally, the monks arrive later, wearing street clothes as he is today, instead of their saffron garb. Obviously, aside from their official duties, they wear street clothes when on the outside. Father John was hanging out yesterday back where we both stay, wearing no shirt and khaki shorts; later, I saw him leaving wearing blue jeans and a red polo shirt.

Knowing that breakfast is to be in silence, I wait until he first speaks to me. Asking his original home, it's Kerala again. Half of Indian's population seems to be from that state. Of course, given that this ashram is now affiliated with one in Kerala, it is not surprising that so many of the monks resided there. We chat a bit about Kerala, its history, the Communist party, and its educational system. Interestingly, I learned from my guidebook that it was the first country/state/area anywhere to adopt a communist form of government in 1957. It has been very successful and, apparently, is more communist-capitalist.

Curious about who the head domo is since Bede Griffiths' passing in 1993, Father Paul, explains that Griffiths was a true guru who can't be replaced by someone simply being pronounced as a guru. Father George is currently the Father Superior in charge. All of the monks are engaging, well-spoken, bright, and speak multiple languages, including pretty understandable English. Asking Father Paul if he is a monk or priest, he considers himself a monk, having been drawn to the monastic life, but is also a priest.

Inquiring if he prefers to be called Father or Brother, he says, "Just Paul." Then he tells me an amusing story of someone once asking the same question. Thereafter, the person called him "Just Paul." We laugh. When I next see him, I shall jokingly say, "Hello, Just Paul, how are you?"

Father John, following me out of prayers, asks what time of day I do yoga. Telling him that it varies, I wonder how he knows that I am doing yoga at all. Because I wear little clothing doing my practice, I keep the lower shutters closed; ergo, he should not have been able to actually see me doing my practice in my room.

Then, however, he offers to teach me yoga, pranayama, and meditation, advising that he has training and offers lessons for guests. Despite wanting to decline, I do not quickly enough find a gracious way to say, "No, thank you," so instead reply, "Of course." Is it because I am the only guest here that everyone feels a need to entertain me or is that the way of this place? More importantly, should I not just consider it service from the monks and be grateful?

So today at six p.m., I have a meditation lesson from Father John. Then tomorrow, I have 7:30 a.m. veggie chopping, 10:30 yoga lesson, 12:15 prayers, 4:00 p.m. Brother Martin lecture, 6:00 p.m. meditation, and 7:00 p.m. evening prayers. That is way more "scheduled time" than I desire. Is this my lesson to develop more discipline?

Washing my hands for the tenth time, unsuccessful at removing the smell of onions in preparation for my asana practice and then off to Brother Martin's lecture, the day is a wastin'. I am so thrilled that there is both electricity *and* a breeze today. Struck again by how my allergies are nonexistent here, with similar winds in Phoenix, they would be stirred up. Either it is the result of more humidity or different pollens.

Brother Martin's Four O'Clock Talk interferes with my asana practice. Not yet finished when it is time to go, I feel irritated. Walking over, I realize, "Hey, this is not the monks' journey, it is *my* journey. Take control of it." More silence and isolation is what I am craving.

Since the power is out, I spend some time before my meditation session in one of my all-time favorite poses, legs up the wall. Now also dreading my meditation appointment, I dutifully get out of my yoga pose, put clothes on again—at least the fourth or fifth change today (when in my room, I wear my loosest sundress), and head to the designated meeting place that I left but only an hour ago. At least, the breeze is delightful and *almost* cool. One appreciates the little things here.

Arriving a few minutes after six p.m., no Father John is to be found. Sitting on the front steps for ten to fifteen minutes, I conclude that he must have forgotten or gotten waylaid. Walking to the dining hall to fill my water bottle, happy to have escaped my session, alas, as I walk away, who should pull up on a motor scooter but Father John, dressed in blue jeans and a casual shirt.

Asking if I am ready, he says he'll be back in five minutes. Actually, I think everyone just universally says, "Five minutes," which may mean five or fifteen or fifty minutes. But I enjoy the cool breeze, realizing it is more pleasant than sitting in that stuffy room trying to meditate. Finally, he arrives; we go in; I decide to sit against the wall. At least, it's a bit cooler, and he turns on the ceiling fan.

Having taught meditation using various techniques, his is a new one for me. Going through a complete body inventory relaxation, as one typically would do for a relaxation in savasana, there is no focus on breath, no om chanting, no mantra. We sit, then come out of meditation, taking three full breaths while noticing the sounds from outdoors and moving the body, then opening eyes and observing things in the room. Then we chant, "Om shanti." It is pleasant enough.

Realizing on my way to meditation the reason I feel irritated is that because suddenly there are these men, and Indian monks no less, trying to dictate my life. Historically, I have not been assertive in taking care of my own needs, instead being more concerned about tending to others. While recognizing that is not necessarily a bad trait, and clearly, believing it better than being selfish and self-absorbed, nevertheless, it is an issue I need to address. One can learn self-attention and self-care without being selfish.

I think about Mother, one of the most selfless women I have ever known, who always tended to everyone else first with her family always taking priority over herself. Having incredible respect and adoration for that quality, I want to emulate her care for others without overlooking tending to my own needs.

Ergo, after our session, I thank him, and he mentions tomorrow's yoga. Knowing that the Indian culture focuses on service and not wanting to insult or offend him, I thank him so very much for the offer of a lesson, but explain that my yoga practice is sacred to me.

Explaining that it is my sadhana, my time with God, and that sometimes I want to practice two or three hours and find if I have other things scheduled, it interferes with my practice and my desire to be in silence, he seems to understand and accept my explanation, saying that they are all here to give guidance as people want it. Hopefully, I have handled a delicate situation acceptably.

More Onions and Withering in the Tamil Heat

THIS IS MY third full day at Shantivanam. Although there is another lovely breeze today, I am tired both yesterday and today. I try my friend Suzanne's recommended Gatorade remedy again, hoping it will perk me up.

Sleeping pretty well, I awaken once scratching itches, thinking, *Probably bedbug bites.* Whatever, I'm in India, hence, I probably will get them at some time. Considering that four- and five-star hotels in the United States have had problems with them, the likelihood is pretty good. Reading somewhere that you are supposed to check the sheets to see if there is blood on them, which purportedly indicates the presence of bedbugs, I have not even looked at the sheets, sleeping on top of the bedspread.

But if one does suspect there are bedbugs, what is one to do, simply not go to sleep? Sleep on the floor? Wash the sheets? If one washes the sheets, that probably doesn't matter, aren't the little buggers in the mattress and pillow and everywhere?

I'm not going to worry about it. I fall back asleep, remembering the childhood bedtime rhyme, "Good night, sleep tight, don't let the bedbugs bite." I purchased bedbug spray, but when my bag exceeded the weight limit at the Phoenix airport, it was an item discarded, probably a mistake. Oh well, as Mother would say, "There is no use crying over spilled milk."

Continuing to sleep until some unknown time when the peacocks start wailing, it is a night without awakening to take cool showers. I rejoice over the wee comforts. Even earplugs don't drown the piercing screeches of the peacocks.

People traveling to India often talk or write about the dramatic, powerful smells of India. For me, the cacophony of sounds is more intense, perhaps because I so cherish silence or possibly my aural sensitivity is more prominent than the olfactory. Sounds of birds chirping, crows cawing, peacocks screeching, dogs howling and barking, horns honking, people shouting and talking rapidly, whirring ceiling fans, wafting music from the open doors of homes, kids yelling while playing cricket, chanting from temples and ashrams, music playing as cars back up, cows bellowing, men next door spitting, coughing, and belching.

Resetting my alarm to the last possible time, allowing me to quickly get ready and dash to the dining hall, about a minute walk, for vegetable duty, people are still eating breakfast when I arrive.

Onions again it is today, but of course, why not give the smelly, tear-provoking veggies to the guest? These are little purplish-colored ones and only a small bowl full. She shows me how to cut them up, telling me, "Small." I am guessing that yesterday's batch was not sufficiently finely chopped. Today, I am clever enough to touch them only with my left hand to limit the overpowering smell. Having tried regular soap, my facial cleanser, and dish-washing liquid, nothing successfully removes the odor.

Neither variety of onion either day makes me cry though, which Father Paul notices and comments that perhaps it is because I am wearing specs (what eyeglasses are called). Or sometimes, he says if they are soaked in water, they won't be as powerful. I thought it might be because I am outdoors.

When I see Father Paul, I greet him, "Good morning, Just Paul, how are you today?" He laughs and has a terrific sense of humor. I like him a lot. As we chat, I ask about the tall, silent monk. He explains that the only language he speaks is Malayalam, the offi-cial language of Kerala. Question answered; mystery solved. The tall monk always sits on a stool at the back of the temple, so today when I walk in, I just smile and bring my hands to a Namaste greeting. He returns my smile.

One thing many extended-time travelers to India might miss is diversity of food. George, the owner of my storage unit facil-ity, who has been to India several times, and his wife warned me about the lack of a variety of foods, which I pooh-poohed at the time because I love eating vegetarian. But thus far, at least in South India, the meals are essentially the same at breakfast, lunch, and dinner.

Hence, in comparing meals in the United States with myriad selections of meats and seafood, eggs, Chinese, Japanese, Thai, Italian, Mexican, Vietnamese, Korean, Cambodian, Indian, and more, along with salads, burgers, and fast food, it is pretty restric-tive. In South India, at least, it is pretty much the same meal of rice, chapatis or the other crispy bread, sambar (sauce/gravy with veggies in it), one or two side vegetables, pickles (a very spicy concoction of something, here it's mango with various spices, which I love), and usually something sweet.

I suspect upon departing India, one of the things on my mind will be what food I shall most want to eat when back home. After five months, what will I be craving most? When my feet hit US soil, which restaurant will I want to head to first? Today, my thinking is that it will be for a really spectacular salad. Or to Sweet Tomatoes for its salad bar.

After supper, Father George takes me to the office to copy my visa and passport. He is so dear; he looks at my passport photo, then at me, and says, "Oh, very beautiful." I tell him that he is too kind while thinking perhaps it is time for a prescription change for his glasses. Using his cell phone to call Prasam in Tiruvannamalai, who was much easier to communicate with in person than via telephone, we agree that he will drive here, arriving Sunday night, allowing us to get an early start on Monday for Cochin, Kerala. He will sleep in the car.

Claiming that if we leave early in the morning, I will manage fine in the non-air conditioned Ambassador sedan because we will be in the mountains where it is cooler and he will stop for needed breaks, I decide, "Okay, I'm up for this."

A lovely evening, we sit in the tea circle chatting after my telephone call. Also, with us is a priest-in-training, who agrees I may call him Dora as a shortened name since I cannot pronounce his full moniker. They are both lovely guys.

Father George tells me that the elderly, tall thin priest is Brother George and is seventy-eight years old. Never having guessed him to be that old, sixty-five would be my estimate perhaps, the monastic life must be good for one's health. He suffers from arthritis, which explains why he never sits on the floor, and has been here for thirty-five years, the longest of any of the priests. Nine monks live in the community, but three are currently away.

Father George asks about my family and whether I teach yoga. I am very grateful that he and pretty much everyone have not asked me what I do in America. Not interested in explaining my life story while here and deciding that if anyone asks questions, my reply will be that like a sadhu, whose past life ceases to exist when he becomes a sadhu: "I have no past."

It is fun to hear that several are reading and enjoying my ramblings, and it is special to share this amazing experience with those interested in it. Not surprisingly, many are lawyers, who are always voracious readers. And even though now others are reading them, I am committed to continue writing whatever I choose, being careful not to sanitize or edit. Undoubtedly, many will know more about my personal foibles than they might care about.

Los Angeles Barb writes that she reads them with her morning tea. Kara in Phoenix writes that she prints them and reads them in bed at night (sweet dreams). California Suzanne is saving them in a computer folder. Sister Sherryle is printing them and placing in a binder as a book. Jack says he prints them to read with a glass of wine because he likes to hold pages in his hands. Colleen saves them to read on weekends as does Phoenix John who reads them while smoking a cigar. I am touched to hear from them all.

THURSDAY, JUNE 7, 2012

Morning vegetable duty...more onions, of course. I am resigned to being the Onion Girl. Today's are the wee ones again. Kitchen Lady demonstrates what I am to do: peel the onions, and cut only one time in half. Wondering if perhaps I forgot to peel them yesterday, I really have no memory whatsoever.

Peeling and chopping, I regret not having watched more television cooking shows. Visions of Wolfgang Puck with his impressive knives, cutting boards, tools and gadgets, chop, chop, slice, dice, wam-bam, touch my consciousness. Perhaps this is why cooking has held limited appeal for me; like anything else, practice, of which admittedly I have not had much, improves one's skill level.

Nephew Nathan, who has spent much time in restaurants and around chefs and is a very good cook himself, is most adept at the impressive chef's maneuvers with knives and culinary gadgetry. Even the girls, Maddy and Meemo, who like to cook, probably would handle this onion chopping detail better than I.

Determined still to only touch the onions with my left hand, I methodically cut, peel, cut, peel, cut, peel, cut. I start to develop a rhythm. Saying to myself, "You are a bright woman, certainly, you can figure out a system for expediting this little job." Systems, repetition, processes. Discovering that by slicing off the little bristly ends first, then cutting the onion in half while pressing on the skin with the knife, the outside layer slips off easier, my skill improves.

Upon finishing, I cull carefully through my plate of beautiful little purplish onions. Proud of my achievement, I check for lurking skins and arrange them for a pretty presentation to Kitchen Lady. A little work of art, I should have my camera. Immediately, I wash my hands twice with two different dish detergents, hoping to mask the pungent aroma.

Who would have imagined that this little onion chopping assignment would be another gift that I would receive in India? Doing something one doesn't enjoy is my seva. I gain a greater appreciation for those who prepare my food, whether it be the kitchen staff here, my family members, restaurant cooks, or friends.

Reflecting more seriously on my chore and the Buddhist approach to living a meditation in all actions of one's daily life, for many, cooking *is* a form of meditation. My onion chopping, in a way, has become a morning meditation. I can learn to do it joyfully and selflessly. Others, who have come here before me, have written about finding more growth and understanding from experiencing everyday life in India than in meditation rooms, temples, and with gurus.

An interesting new dessert item is introduced at dinner. It takes me awhile to ascertain what it is—small hard nuts wrapped inside bananas. Enjoying the prayers more now that I am able to follow along, the chanting in Tamil remains a bit of a stretch, but I manage the Sanskrit ones. The ritual is soothing. And I love that the entire session is relatively short; with prayers and dinner, I am back in my room in less than one hour. Father John often leads the chants. He has an amazing voice, and I love listening to him.

People with whom I have spoken who were in India for extended times talk about the difficulty of reentry back to the United States. Anticipating that also will be an issue for me after five months, it is too early for me to think much about it yet. Susan from Sedona told me that it is difficult to easily return to the United States after six months in India; she went to a convent and taught English to nuns. My kind friend Suzanne has offered to let me decompress at her home in California for as long as I need.

Spending some time with my *Lonely Planet* guidebook and contemplating where I may want to travel, I realize this definitely is the ideal way to make this journey, allowing it to evolve as opposed to having a predetermined, planned schedule. It is delightful to get a sense of the culture, finding what resonates with me and the direction I feel compelled to take.

Having thought a bit about it previously, there are a few "must go to" places on my itinerary—Delhi, Varanasi, Agra, and most likely Haridwar and Rishikesh. Just having completed the second little *Monk* book, which is very dear, the story ends at the Taj Mahal, representative of the great love Shah Jahan had for his wife. Leaving that amazing edifice as his legacy to her, one of the Seven Wonders of the World, it is visited each year by two to four million people.

The author's message is that "it is important that we contribute, make a difference, and leave a legacy." Making the Taj my last stop would be a poignant punctuation mark for my India exploration, and a nice initiation for what is next to come.

Initially, Kerala was not on my considered itinerary, despite knowing that it is beautiful. But now, I am happy to have decided to go there because everyone raves about Kerala, "God's Own Country." Monsoons will have commenced.

I remind myself that intrepid travelers cannot fear the less pleasant moments, and perhaps only the hearty, or is it the foolhardy, make their Indian journey in the heat of summer anyhow? Who knows, the rains may be a delightful variation. If nothing else, it will give me something else to carp about besides the heat. That's something else I realize—that we Americans like to complain.

By comparison, Indians seem not to complain about anything, being a far more accepting lot. As an example, one day walking to the temple with Paul, I comment how nice it is that the power had not gone out yet. His reply was, "On, off, all good," or something to that effect. It reminded me of years ago when I told myself in Phoenix to quit complaining about the heat and instead just to embrace it. That's a good philosophy to adopt here as well.

The hill stations sound charming as well, but less appealing destinations during monsoons. Originally established under British rule in the early nineteenth century as cooler locations for government officials during the summers, apparently, April to June are the busiest times when people make a mass exodus there.

The most famous hill station in Tamil Nadu is referred to as Ooty, an understandably abbreviated name for Udhagamandalam. That's quite the mouthful. In trying to master Indian names, I still chuckle thinking about Sherryle's e-mail to me before I left, responding to mine that set out some tentative travel plans. Bar none, it was the best reply I received. She wrote, "I hope there's not going to be a spelling test!" The pronunciations are what

I struggle with most. I try to pronounce names of people and towns, but usually murder them.

FRIDAY, JUNE 8, 2012

Getting a relatively decent night's sleep, I awaken only twice, but again itching crazily. So there must be some critters in my bed. Immediately upon turning on the light in the evening, many more bugs materialize. They love my LED light spelunker headlamp too. Arriving at the kitchen at 7:45 for my onion duty, Kitchen Lady has nothing for me today. Feeling tired, I decide to return to my room, and amazingly, sleep another couple of hours. A lovely unexpected gift.

The whole modesty thing here for women becomes a bit tedious. Although guys run around in essentially loincloths or just a bit more cloth, often with holes in the rear end, wearing no shirts, heaven forbid if women show any leg above the ankle. Is some guy really going to hyperventilate if he sees a woman's calf? There must be something psychological about a woman's leg though.

On that subject, while lying in jet-lagged stupor on my Chennai hotel room bed, determined not to fall asleep, I watched whatever non-sport, English programming was on television. In one interesting program about the evolution of fashion, apparently, when women flappers in the 1920s began wearing dresses revealing their calves, they were considered to be utterly scandalous—wild, daring feminists of the time. Why though is it acceptable for women to show midriffs, necks, upper chests, backs, and lower arms when wearing saris? The distinction is lost on me, but I obviously am the product of a Western culture.

Once in a conversation with an Australian woman about the issue of modesty and need to cover up, she understood the reason is that men are unable to control their urges; hence, women must not tempt them. She queried, "Why is it that Western men are able to control theirs then?" I laughed. It takes a long time for cultures to change. In Mumbai and Delhi, one assumes that all manner of dress are worn.

Certainly, there is advertising, on billboards and television showing women wearing shorter dresses. And India women commentators conducting interviews on some television programs are in Western attire, wearing sleeveless, knee-length sheath dresses.

Never having been much of a shawl wearer, I constantly fuss with how to wear the bloody thing, readjusting it to cover my chest and struggling with techniques to keep it in place. Really, is it necessary? I wear underwear, no see-through clothing, proper dresses or long tops, *and* long pants. Isn't the shawl/scarf thing overkill? When I remember it, I wear one to the temple; however, when walking into the village or around the grounds, I don't bother. Somehow, the sisters' shawls always seem to be in place though; it must be practice of many years of wearing them.

After prayer and supper, Father George tells me that Param phoned earlier, instructing me to wait because he is to call again in twenty to thirty minutes. We sit in the tea circle and chat; evenings outdoors are very pleasant. Soon, the phone rings. The purpose of his call is to inform me that he has secured an air-conditioned car—by "God's grace" he tells me. His favorite expression, everything is by "God's grace" with him. He's very funny. Currently in Kerala, he apparently took the bus there, got the car, and will see me Sunday night. Since there is air conditioning, we don't have to leave at the crack of dawn, which is fine with me.

SATURDAY, JUNE 9, 2012

For the first time, I awaken hungry, so I go to breakfast. Sometimes, breakfast items are different than lunch and dinner, but not today. Breakfast is a repeat of last night's dinner: chapatis, the same sambar with lots of garbanzo beans, canned green peas, and *my* chopped onions.

Noticing lots of food remaining after meals, I wondered if perhaps such large quantities were made to serve ashram employees. But the only person I ever see go into the dining room is the front gate security guard. Now, I understand the drill—the sambar and vegetables are recycled as leftovers until gone. Other than the milk and buttermilk though, there is nothing that I don't like or eat. Buttermilk is served at pretty much every meal; ick! Never in my life having drunk it, I pass on it here as well.

Checking in to see if there is any veggie-chopping duty for me, Kitchen Lady gives me large clusters of an unknown green vegetable, similar to cilantro or parsley. Asking what it is, she tells me, and naturally, I still have no clue. She gives me a quick tutorial, and I am off to the races. This is a much easier and a more familiar task than chopping onions.

Finishing my task, she thanks me, and in response to where to dispose of the refuse, she tosses it over the fence for the cows. Requesting if I may take photographs of the two kitchen ladies, they happily agree and, in typical fashion, laugh when they see their picture on my camera.

Essentially, I am cut off from cell phones, Internet, television, and newspapers, all by choice—if I use the Internet, I must go to another location to seek it out. Without those distractions, I have a greater appreciation for things I once loved but that have received short shrift in my life. Elimination of that clutter allows one to focus on quiet and going inward. I remember one spiritual teacher once saying that God can't speak to you if you are not in silence. That has become abundantly clear to me.

Other things now important to me are, obviously, writing, and thinking without noise of a stereo, radio, or television. Listening to the sounds of the birds. Reading more books. Going for walks. Being. Doing nothing.

My intuition is amazing here, even about insignificant things. At least three times recently, *vis a vis'* the power outage, the very moment when thinking about it, the electricity goes out. Today I decide to pop in the shower for a rinse-off, contemplating that the power will likely go out soon. Immediately, as I exit the shower, it surges. Many times, something else materializes as I think about it, another aspect of magical, mystical India.

Certainly neither dehydrated nor suffering heat stroke, nevertheless, I feel as though I am withering on the vine. This is how Arizona would feel without air conditioning *and* electricity. It is too hot to read or to nap. Finally, about five o'clock, I decide to wander outside, hoping to find air movement somewhere.

Meandering, but unsuccessful in finding much relief or any breeze, I see guys cutting fruits from trees. Assuming they are mangoes, I call to Sister Catherine, who is leaving the library, and ask her. They are mangoes indeed. Now I know what a mango tree looks like; the place is filled with them. It surprises me that we are not served mangoes at every meal. Sister Catherine explains that they are picked green, then ripened in sacks of hay; some likely will be sold. She also answers my question: bananas are plants, not trees.

We chat a good long while. Originally of the Carmelite order, she has been a nun for some forty years since about age fifteen. Apparently, the Carmelites' focus is education, and she spent more than a decade teaching in Gary, Indiana, and Chicago where at the time there was a dearth of educators. She is a lovely woman.

I wonder what monks do during the day between prayers and eating. Do they pray, meditate, study? Nap or play video games perhaps? I notice that they clean their rooms and do laundry. Since it is really none of my business, I certainly will not ask, but I am curious about the contemplative life. Spending one's time in spiritual pursuits in contemplation and communing with God is very appealing to me at this last stage of my life. Many Indian householders, for example, traditionally would spend their last years in such a manner.

Tomorrow is my last day here. Although I am ready to move on, leaving will be bittersweet for I have really come to love these monks, and the ashram is truly special. Speaking of ashrams, when chatting this afternoon with Sister Catherine about my plans to head to Kerala and Anandashram, she tells me that it is a wonderful place where she has visited three times.

On to Kerala, Another Expensive Lesson, and Fender Bender # 2

MY LAST DAY at Shantivanam. Awakening at 6:30, it is too late to make it to prayers. Deciding since it is my last day, I also am not checking in for vegetable duty. None of the other guests have done it anyhow, so I can blow off one day.

Returning to my room after lunch, I am very weary. Lying down for a while, I doze a bit. At lunch, Sister Catherine suggests visiting their ashram at five; she will meet me at the gate. The power goes out at 3:30, and with little breeze, it's another toasty day. Sitting typing, the sweat pours onto the keyboard. I wonder how far it is to Antarctica from India? Actually, I have always been intrigued with and would love to go there. Fantasizing, what would it feel like to actually be cold?

Even a short asana practice doesn't pep me up. Today is chalked off to a quiet, lazy Sunday. Off to meet Sister Catherine, she gives me a delightful tour of their ashram, comprised of eight acres, which is more land than held by Shantivanam. The sisters each have a hut; there are cows—also more than the monks have she claims—and a nice main building with a small kitchen, dining room, and parlor. She says that each day, the cows are taken down to the river for baths. They do take *very* good care of their cows here.

From a wonderful light blue painted deck above the main building, the views are breathtaking; it would be a lovely place to meditate. She shows me the tank where gas, used for cooking fuel, is made from cow manure and urine. The same process is performed over at Shantivanam as well. Sister Superior, whom they call Ama, is still in the hospital; she is eighty years old.

Guests are allowed to stay there, but she says Ama is very particular about whom she allows. Ama has been at that location for thirty-five years, and until sometime in the 1990s, she was there alone with only ashram staff. There still are only six in their community, the Sister Superior and five other nuns.

Asking me if I have seen the river, I tell her, "Yes, just today." Informing me that it is the Kaveri River and that it is as sacred in south India as the Ganga is in the north, I am flabbergasted to be staying next to a major sacred river and not have known it. It rather explains also the visits from sadhus since pilgrimages to sacred sites, including rivers, is part of their lifestyle. Maybe that little nugget would have been worth mentioning in the little ashram pamphlet or in my *Nirvana* book? Note to self to be more diligent in my research, adding to my questions list: Are there any sacred sites or rivers in the area?

Upon returning from my visit with Sister Catherine, Father George informs me that Param has arrived, but has gone off somewhere, probably to the village. Materializing a bit before prayers, we talk about possible itineraries and look at some maps now that I have done a little more research. Explaining that, "Oh yes, the air conditioned car is an additional 1,000 rupees per day," great, the price for this little Kerala junket has just tripled, which I am not too happy about it.

Falling asleep, I decide to have a "come to Jesus talk" with him before leaving in the morning, explaining that he should have given me the option of the air conditioned car and the rates for both. But the broader issue is communication, some of it stemming from the Indian culture of wanting to please and a portion simply that of viewing foreigners as money pits. Most likely, when asking in our telephone conversation about the availability of an air conditioned car, Param interpreted that as a request whereas I merely was inquiring about it as an option to consider. Another lesson learned. Welcome to India!

THURSDAY, JUNE 14, 2012

Feeling withdrawal symptoms from not having written in my journal for three days, there is lots to catch up on.

At about 7:00 a.m. on Monday, the eleventh, we leave Shantivanam. In my "come to Jesus talk," I tell Param that he should have talked with me before renting the car because now, the trip is suddenly triple the cost originally discussed. He replies, "Oh, Madam, Madam, do not worry about money. I only came here with the car to discuss with you your options. If you want, I can go back now. I will not charge you for yesterday," referring to his trip to the ashram. I agree to go on, but reiterate that he should have talked with me about it. The other thing I *should* have made clear to him that morning—hindsight indeed being 20-20—although I am not sure it would have mattered was: "Do not make any plan or decision *without* first discussing it with me."

Something becoming abundantly clear to me, which is a difficult adjustment and remains to be seen if I ever truly "get," is how one deals with people here. At least from a business perspective, it is entirely different than in the United States. Whereas we pretty much can rely on the price someone quotes or services to be received, that is not necessarily the case in India. Of course, there are scam artists and dishonest people everywhere, but for the most part, if dealing with reputable businesses, the terms of a transaction are clear. Contrarily, in India, a wiser mind-set is to expect to be taken advantage of or misled or have additional fees tacked on along the way. The way one needs to approach commercial transactions is *caveat emptor* magnified tenfold!

First, haggling about price is a given, except in better establishments which have fixed prices. Even then, however, I suspect that the "fixed price" may vary depending upon many factors, such as whether it is high season or if the customer is a local or a tourist. Never enjoying that process of negotiating in Mexico or elsewhere, I prefer knowing the price and paying it. But in India, that approach simply is not possible in most situations. Guidebooks recommend negotiating as a standard practice because locals automatically inflate prices, assuming that bargaining will occur.

Second, what one is initially told is likely partially true or only half the story. There probably will be another variation or explanation down road. Or a deviation of some sort will occur. Or less than complete information will be provided.

The car rental rate that Param quotes me seems rather high for India, given that I can rent a car for that amount at Enterprise in the United States. Undoubtedly, he is getting a commission from the rental car agency. It's just part of the standard drill, I guess. The trip takes fifteen hours from Shantivanam to Cochin in central Kerala. We stop many times for bathroom breaks and food; nevertheless, it is an arduous trip. Happy to have air conditioning for the beginning of the trip, but by the time we hit the mountains, the Western Ghats, it is blissfully cool. Driving with windows open, after a time, it becomes too chilly, requiring me to roll up mine. Oh my heavens, "chilly," a sensation foreign to me since arriving in India on April 25. And one neither my family nor friends in Arizona will experience again for many months either.

Driver Param is a colorful character, pretty much talking nonstop all about himself, his wife, his family, his education, his various jobs, his experiences, India, whatever. Rarely is any of the conversation initiated by questions from me. His blathering begins the moment the trip starts, and unless I pretend to be napping, it is incessant. At least because he is totally self-absorbed, there are no prying questions of me.

Well-educated with at least a bachelor's degree in commerce, I am able to converse with and usually understand him. He even knows colloquialisms and little adages. While his father was assigned to a government post in Africa, Param attended an international boarding school for two years, which is where he learned English. That explains why his English is far better than most Indian-taught speakers.

Amazingly, Param eats nonstop the entire trip. There is always something in his mouth, and each time we stop, he buys some snack. A bit into the trip, he confesses to being a smoker, which explains the constant noshing and oral addiction. So whenever we stop for my bathroom breaks, food, or whatever, he grabs a cigarette. Single cigarettes are sold for five rupees apiece at little roadside shops. His food purchases include a big bag of bananas, another large bag of grapes, jackfruit, chips, and various sodas. Skinny as a rail, obviously with a metabolism like those of my nephew and niece, Zach and Haley, he reminds me of an Indian version of Jeff Goldblum.

Our car is a Suzuki. It is acceptable, but less comfortable and with inferior air conditioning than the Tata. It takes many hours before we arrive in Kerala from Tamil Nadu. But immediately upon entering, it is as if we have arrived in an entirely different country, not merely a new state. I understand immediately why everyone raves about Kerala, referred to as "God's Country" or "God's Own Country."

Not only is it cleaner and magnificently green, but in addition to the usual plethora of ramshackle roadside shops, there are bigger and much nicer tea shops, Ayurveda shops, nurseries, fresh flower stands, and spice shops. There are scads of spice shops, all bearing signs in English. Driving through one fair-sized town, at an intersection, there is massive, many-stories tall white statue of Mary with Jesus in her lap. Kerala is primarily Christian, having originally been colonized by the Portuguese.

At one little road side market, I taste jackfruit, which is quite tasty. Lime green in color and the size of massive watermelons, they hang in clusters on trees. Sliced open down the middle, the fruit is cut into chunks. There is a hard nut inside, which can be cooked and eaten. In explaining the dessert recently eaten at the ashram with a hard nut inside the banana, which I had assumed was a coconut, Param says that it was a jackfruit nut.

In this same area are the tea plantations. Hills are blanketed with the most exquisite, lush forest green imaginable, appearing as if covered by vibrant sculptured carpeting. Continuing as far as the eye can see, I learn that tea is picked by hand.

Other differences that I notice are that the auto rickshaws are black (I have become rather fond of the bright gold ones in Tamil, like yellow cabs), and in the larger towns through which we drive, billboard after billboard after billboard advertises gold jewelry featuring beautiful women. The models are definitely not South Indian because they have much lighter skin. Posed in rather fetching poses, some display navels while another wears a sundress with spaghetti straps. The environment is clearly more liberal down here. Even Param comments how distracting the huge billboards, featuring beautiful scantily clad women, are for him and other male drivers.

About skin color, I learned early about the light/dark skin issue upon seeing a skin lightening kit in the Le Meridien hotel gift shop in Chennai. Apparently, it is a popular technique, and lighter skin is considered more desirable. The clothing that women are wearing here, however, for the most part is the same, although a few younger women wear jeans or long pants.

The Western Ghats is a mountain range that runs from somewhere in the north through Kerala. Not Rocky Mountain or Alaska mountain caliber, they resemble northern Arizona desert mountains or tamer California ones. Our travel is on winding roads that are not too treacherous other than the normal craziness of Indian driving. Indeed, however, our travel speed slows considerably. The drive is very pretty, and mostly, it is wonderfully refreshing to have cooler temperatures. Not haven't checked a Web site, I estimate the temperature is twenty degrees cooler here than in Tamil Nadu.

Along the way, I am amused seeing a classic Indian bus so overloaded that it lists badly to one side. Another bus with signage designating it as a "Luxury Coach" is a wickedly beat-up relic. In a couple of areas, a sign reads: "Accident Zone. Go Slow." No kidding, the whole roadway system of India is one giant accident zone. As we arrive in a few little villages, suddenly one entire lane of traffic is blocked by a big metal barrier. Param says that the purpose is to reduce speed, but it seems rather dangerous to me.

After multiple bathroom stops, I confer the "Best Gas Station Bathrooms in India Award" to Indian Oil. Although there are some smaller petrol stations, the two majors are Indian Oil and Bharat Petroleum. Perhaps I shall experience much worse elsewhere, but the bad rap that Indian bathrooms get in writings seems grossly overexaggerated; I have been in much more disgusting bathrooms in US gas stations. Or perhaps, I just have had good bathroom karma. Whatever the reason, I am most grateful.

Learning en route that Param also has taken it upon himself to book me into some resort in Cochin, with a rate of 1,250 rupees per night, I explain that I am not interested in staying there. His stated reason for booking it is that he wants me to be "very comfortable." Beginning to understand why his tour guide rate is so low, he likely is expecting nice commissions from the hotel guy, the car guy, the tour people, and the like.

Elaborating that I may wish to stay in Cochin for a few nights, do not need such an expensive hotel, and do not want to pack and unpack and move to another property, he responds with, "Oh, yes, of course, madam, I just wanted to have something booked so you had a hotel." Uh-huh; this is now the second unauthorized arrangement.

Pulling out my *Lonely Planet* guidebook and finding two acceptable-sounding hotels in the budget section, we stop, and he telephones for me. The first is fully booked, but the second Sapphire Tourist Home has availability for one-third the cost of his luxury property. As it turns out, the two hotels are directly across the street from each other. Located close to the boat ferries, it is an older hotel, however, it is clean with a powerful ceiling fan, hot water, and great old pink/gray/beige marble tiles similar to those I saw throughout Greece, which I think provide character. Air conditioned rooms are available for a higher tariff, but ceiling fans are adequate here. The staff is very kind, so I am a happy camper.

After making my hotel reservation for that evening, Param calls his "professional friend" to say I will not be staying at the resort. I still have no idea where this place is. He advises that his friend says that "it will be risky, and that because of the price, there will be Indians staying there." Really? Imagine that. I am in India; there may be Indians staying at the hotel. And why exactly is that such an abomination I wonder to myself.

Tonight will be my fourth night here, and I plan to stay another three. Today, I book a train, which will be my first train ride in India, up north to go to Anandashram. Not having received a response from the ashram regarding availability yet, I have a sense that there will be room since this is low season. I was willing to leave a day or two earlier, but no train seats are available in any reserved seat/air-conditioned sections. Apparently, one does not want to travel in the general ticket section where there are hoards of people on floors, lots of unticketed passengers, beggars, and unsavory characters.

Param is planning to stay at a friend's house, this after telling me from the get-go that he would sleep in the car. We agree that he will pick me up at 11:00 a.m. the next morning, the first day after arriving. In my hyper-exhausted state, I barely remember going to bed and sleep like a corpse. He insists on giving me one of his mobile phones to call him if I need anything. Awakening and still feeling tired, I call and change our meeting time until noon.

Arriving promptly at noon, now he is accompanied by his childhood friend, Kiran. Rather annoyed, I inquire why he is along to which Param replies, "Oh, he knows the city very well. I have friends in every city to help me." So I am wondering, then why did I bother to hire him as my guide who knows "everything about Kerala," which was his sales pitch. It has started to rain pretty hard, and is pleasantly refreshing, lasting only a couple of hours.

Param also advises me that he has purchased tickets for me to go on the afternoon boat cruise. *What?* We never discussed this. What about my discussion with him about not making any plans or decisions without consulting me? Is he deaf or does he think I am a moron? What if I wanted to stay in my room and write or shop or wander around or do whatever today? Or just recover from riding fifteen bloody hours in the car? So now, I am even more annoyed. But I concede and agree to take the boat trip.

By the time of the 2:30 p.m. tour, the rain has ceased. When I give him the 150 rupees for the ticket, he says, "Mine too." Telling him that there is no need for him to accompany me and that I do not need a babysitter, I refuse to pay for his ticket. The last thing I want is him hanging around, yakking nonstop anyhow. Even though it is only a few dollars, I want him to get the message about making these decisions without consulting me. And, I am already thinking, *Why am I paying for you as my guide? I found my own hotel room. I could have figured out how to arrange a boat tour. And your friend is here to help you around town.* Oh, brother—Welcome to India!

Param also decides—*again* without consulting me—that I ought to take the all-day backwaters cruise the subsequent day. Relenting and agreeing, although later I regret it because I am so incredibly exhausted afterward. Perhaps *eventually* I shall learn to simply say no or be less complacent...probably about the time I depart India.

We go together to the travel place to purchase my ticket for the next day. Another childhood friend, this time of his sister, works at the agency. Later, when contemplating his making all of these decisions without consulting me, I conclude that it may partially be attributable to the patriarchal culture where men most likely make all of the decisions for their womenfolk. And likely, he assumes that this foreign older woman needs his direction. He does comment later, however, that he can tell I am capable of taking care of myself.

Ready for some food, I ask about restaurants. His friend suggests the Greenhouse. Neither of them sees it as we drive right past it. Telling them that we have just missed it back at the corner, Param promptly stops the car in the middle of the street and begins backing up, running smack dab into a car behind us. Great, another accident...that's two and counting. Not wanting to deal with whatever repercussions may result, I exit the car and head to the restaurant. Apparently, it is only a tap, and there is no damage; later, Param claims that it was the other driver's fault for proceeding while he was backing up. Really? Interesting driving rules.

My lunch of vegetable biryani is adequate. Although not the most interesting Indian dish, because my waiter's English is poor, it seems easier to order something I know than expend the necessary effort trying to negotiate other choices on the menu. It's time to familiarize myself with a few other common Indian foods. There are actually two other women lunching at a nearby table, ladies who shop and lunch or possibly work in the area I wonder? I have not seen that yet in India. There is an excessive amount of food, so I ask if they can prepare a to-go bag for the excess. "Package?" he asks. There is an additional five rupees or ten cents for a package.

Calling Param on his mobile upon finishing lunch, we leave for the boat jetty. He has no idea how to get to that either. Geez Louise, could he perhaps have asked his friend who lives here for the directions if he didn't know where it was? And just why is it again that am I paying him to be my guide anyhow? Thank goodness, it's not much. The concept of "guide" must have a different connotation in India. After stopping six times to ask for directions (at least Indian men *do* ask for directions), he finally parks the car. However, it is still at least a half-mile walk to the dock. I suspect that there is a parking lot much closer to the boat dock since my hotel is essentially across the street from the boat ferry. Or I wonder why we didn't just *walk* across the street?

With my cruise departure time fast approaching, we are literally running down Marine Drive, the promenade adjacent to the water, then up one full flight of stairs and down the other side, and up and down another set of stairs. Param, who is tall and lanky, is charging ahead of me. Hoping that if he arrives as the boat is departing, he will manage to delay it until I make it, amazingly, my angels again must be watching out for me because we arrive five minutes before the boat takes off. At least I get exercise running down the way.

By this point, I am *beyond* thrilled that Param is not joining me on the cruise. Most likely, he has never been on one himself and was looking forward to his free ride. It is becoming more and more clear that at least thus far, I could have managed *this well* on my own for I am perfectly capable of asking ten people for directions and wandering around lost. My first guided tour in India has been at best comical, if not pathetic.

But the "Param Encounter" is to get even better. Of course, it does; after all, this is India.

The cruise actually is relaxing and pretty, and the rain has ceased. Cochin, or Cochi as it is also known, is comprised of the area on land, Ernakulam, where I am staying, and several islands, one of which is Fort Cochin and Mattancherry, located in the Lakshadweep Sea. It is a similar configuration as San Diego. The guide's English is quite good, and amusingly, he refers to me, the only non-Indian passenger, as "Foreign Madam." Where are all of the foreign tourists, I wonder? Out ahead is the Arabian Sea, and in transit are many large fishing vessels, oil tankers, and magnificent Chinese fishing nets, huge exquisite-looking cantilevered nets introduced by the Chinese in the fourteenth or fifteenth century. They are now used only for catching small fish during high tides because newer, better technology exists.

We boat over to Fort Cochin, but our stay is brief. The shops look cute and quaint, and I would enjoy rambling around here. We visit St. Francis Church, the first purported European church built in India and where Vasco da Gama was originally buried before his son removed his remains to Portugal, and the home where Vasco da Gama lived.

Heading to another part of the island, Mattancherry, with an area referred to as Jew Town that originally was populated by a fairly large Jewish population, supposedly only nine families remain. Their original homes are now shops and businesses. The Jewish synagogue is beautiful, but unfortunately, no photographs are allowed inside. Our tour guide must get his commissions here because he directs me to a shop with his friends with "very good prices." Not finding the prices so very good, I shop instead across the street, buying a sundress and beautiful green sari as a gift for Olivia.

Calling Param to meet in the same parking lot where he dropped me off, I mistakenly walk past the agreed spot, and it takes thirty minutes of calling back and forth on the mobile phones for him to find me. So having his cell phone proves beneficial today. Back in the car, I explain that it makes no sense for him to stay and me to pay for his services and the car another day, especially since I am spending the next day on the backwaters cruise. I also am thinking that he has provided very minimal value to this junket anyhow aside from driving the car. He agrees and says he will leave tonight.

By the time we finish dinner, I learn that he is not leaving tonight after all, now claiming that to avoid me paying another day, the car had to be returned by 8:00 p.m. Wondering why he didn't mention that to me an hour ago when I specifically said, "It makes no sense for me to pay for another day of your services and the car," I now am stuck paying another day. Sadly, and I feel badly thinking this way, I consider this may be another scam, whereby he calls his pal back in his home town and they concoct this means of charging me another day's rental. Although it's only $20, it becomes principle for me.

And I am now getting the picture of transactions in India. Never expect full disclosure. Do not assume anything. Nothing is likely to be what it appears from the get go. The guidebooks and Web sites warn about myriad travel scams, deals, and unhappy travelers with people ending up paying more than they agreed to, cautioning people to get everything in writing and clearly understood upfront as to what is and is not included.

Rather oddly, he immediately wants to settle up in the car in the parking lot after dinner before leaving for my hotel. After repeatedly telling me for two days to "not worry about the money," suddenly, he has become very concerned about it. And, in calculating the number of days for the car rental, he tries to charge me for an extra day. I remind him that he was not charging me for Sunday, his travel day to the ashram. "Oh, yes, yes," he says as if he's forgotten.

So now, I have the pleasure of paying the petrol back to deliver the car, which I volunteered to pay before realizing I was getting stuck for another day's car rental, an additional car rental day, *and* his fee for today for essentially no services since I was in his company for less than an hour. I probably could protest, but it simply isn't worth it to me at this point. I am just happy to be finished with him.

Owing him 4,500 rupees, he counts it twice and doesn't say anything. He likely is expecting a nice tip, which he would receive had I not felt taken advantage of and that he provided any real service. This is one Western goose *not* laying golden eggs. Having no idea if I could have flown here or not from Trichy, but if so, it probably would have cost less than this car trip. Another lesson learned, although I did enjoy the scenery of the drive.

The End of the Param Saga. Hallelujah!

Feeling disturbed by the entire experience with Param, I contemplate what lesson I am to learn from it. How to remain loving and nonjudgmental and open-spirited? What is the ultimate purpose in my having made this trip with him? Clarification about that may come later. He did constantly refer to his life as being in God's hands, always saying "by God's grace," so perhaps that connection is part of the explanation. If nothing else, I certainly learn the importance of vigilance and to ask more questions before engaging services here.

My backwaters cruise leaves at 8:00 a.m. the next day. Param has both shown me the way and drawn me a map so that I can walk from the hotel, but as I leave my hotel, it is raining so I hire an auto rickshaw, arriving thirty minutes early. Another young Indian woman and her mother from Gurujat also are early so we gab away while waiting for the office to open.

To arrive at the starting location for the cruise, we have an hour's bus ride. The time passes quickly because we yammer the whole way; our cruise gang is comprised of we three women and three of the nicest young men I have ever met. Two kids from

Germany, Franz and Helmut, have just finished high school. One is off to university to study environmental engineering, the other chemistry. Both are so very polite, bright, and kind. The third is Manuel from Brazil, who has finished his university studies and has been working for a time. He too is an absolute sweetheart. What gems all three of these young men are. Despite our age differences, we all have a great time together.

Manuel spent his first two months in India studying English, attended a Vipassana meditation program for eight days, and leaves in a couple of days to spend two months in Europe before returning to Brazil. All three of the guys describe their time in India as "just amazing!" I am incredibly impressed by all of them. Not only do they have interested, adventurous spirits, but kind hearts and souls as well. They met each other backpacking in Goa and began traveling together then.

The young Indian woman Priti is full of questions for us all. Her mother Neha understands English, but speaks little. The most interesting is asking what religion we all are. I tell her that in the West, religion is very different than in India, in terms of its intertwinement with the culture. Trying in a nice way to explain, I answer that we don't typically ask what religion a person might subscribe to, and that we usually have no idea what religion, if any, someone might follow. Manuel and I try to clarify the concepts of "spirituality" versus "religion," explaining that we both are more spiritually inclined than religious. Agreeing that it is the same in Germany, Franz asks if she knows what an atheist is.

Later in the trip, Neha has her daughter ask Manuel what he likes most about India. Describing many things that he likes, he says that because his time here has been so "amazing," an adjective he uses repeatedly, it is hard to identify only a few things. Something poignant for him, however, is that despite how chaotic it might be wherever he has been in India, he always feels peaceful here.

His response is interesting to me because I realize, in thinking about it, that I feel the same way. Despite challenges with language, heat, or dealing with a Trent or a Param, I nevertheless feel very content here, a kind of serenity. There is an indescribable energy about India, perhaps it's the thousands of years of sacred rishis, sages, and deep spiritualism entrenched in its soul.

The mom then wants to know what Manuel doesn't like about India. In a very thoughtful response, he says that it is the paradoxes of life—things he doesn't understand, such as if the Ganges is so sacred, why do people continue to pollute it so badly? Priti heartily agrees with him.

Saying what I most like about India thus far are the people, Priti asks, "Even though you've been cheated?" This morning when waiting for the tour company to open, somehow our conversation got round to subjects of how to bargain, hiring rickshaws, my having felt taken advantage of by my last guide, and the like. Priti cautioned me, "Everyone will try to cheat you here. When we are here as tourists, they try to cheat us too." My response was, "Yes, and I think I am beginning to understand the culture better," analogizing to a tradition of the Navajo culture in America. A woman I once worked with had spent quite a lot of time teaching on the reservation, and she told me that in the Navajo culture, if one liked some item that another person owned, the person would take it. It was not considered stealing there, but was simply part of their tradition.

India seems a bit like that. Because everyone struggles to survive and merely get by, figuring out ways to make extra money in whatever manner possible is simply part of life, scratching however one can. Where the vast majority of the population lives in poverty, earning 100 rupees per day (less than $2), it is more understandable. Trying to comprehend and accept that aspect of this culture will help me be less critical and upset when circumstances impact me personally. And it is important to continually remind myself not to use my Western filter in judging people or this country.

The first half of our trip is on a rice boat, cruising the backwaters of Kerala. "Backwaters" simply refers to the lake region into which the sea spills. Our travel is during low tide, but our guide says that there also is a high tide. A leisurely, pretty cruise, we stop in a couple of wee villages. We wander around a bit, and our guide points out various indigenous plants. There's not much to see—all wooded areas, some dogs, occasionally a human being or two. I learn that a pineapple grows on a plant and see taro, tapioca, cinnamon, pepper, and cardamom plants.

The villages seem to be comprised of about four houses; nevertheless, at one of the houses, a lady is selling snacks. Most likely these tours, which run each and every day, drop a fair number of visitors at her doorstep, so this is probably her occupation. I buy a bag of tasty crispy, spicy snacks which we all nosh on.

Another major attraction is seeing fellows climbing up huge coconut palms, a goodly sixty to eighty feet, to collect toddy. Toddy is palm beer with a very low alcohol content (two percent or so) produced from coconut palms. Collecting toddy requires a license, which is granted by the owners of the grove. Coconut palms either are used for toddy or for coconuts, but not both.

A barefoot toddy collector, with simian ease, scampers up the tree trunk, with a big hatchet, knife, rope, large sharpening flint, and metal bucket strapped around his waist. Nearing the top, he balances precariously on the trunk and branches, slashes the "flower" (what the guide calls it; it looks like a green branch), collects milky liquid in his bucket, and slithers back down. This procedure is performed twice daily. Asking if anyone ever falls, I am told that it occurs. Since there is a guy up the tree as we speak, I decide not to make the obvious follow-up inquiry.

Our guide says we may buy a bottle of toddy for fifty or seventy-five rupees. The guys buy some and offer us a taste. Not an imbiber of alcohol, I decide, nevertheless, that I should sample a wee bit. It has an odd flavor, not really alcohol-tasting, neither particularly good nor especially bad. The guide, pointing to one older toddy collector's belly that we meet along the path, jokingly says, "He drinks toddy." Then he points to his own tummy, saying, "I drink toddy." Laughing, I mention the term "beer belly" in America, explaining that it is like a "toddy belly" here.

Earlier in the trip, our guide tells us that freshly caught mussels are available for purchase, saying they are delicious and pushing the sale, again probably because these tours provide income for the locals. Franz and Manuel order some, but not being too keen on mussels, I pass. Later, when they are served after we return to the boat from one of our village outings, the guide advises that he has an extra package of the cooked mussels wrapped in a taro leaf. The guys offer me a taste of theirs.

Amazingly delicious, I buy the extra serving and offer to share it with Helmut since the Indian women are pure veg. Very sweetly, he says, "But I didn't order it." I tell him it's fine, that I have purchased it, and will share with him. We scarf it down. Chopped ever so very finely and prepared with a variety of spices and garlic, they are utterly delectable—well worth $1.50. Aside from Ifran's gourmet food in Tiruvannamalai, this is the second most tasty cuisine I have eaten in India.

This portion of the cruise ends where it commenced. Lunch is included, so we leave the boat for a few minutes while the meal is set out. Several of us are doing stretches (the chairs weren't the most comfortable), so I show them a few yoga poses, which we do in the sand, including supported wheel where one person lies back across the hands of two others; the guys get a kick out of that pose. Lunch is tasty: a couple of vegetables, sambar, and rice, which is a different larger grain variety.

After lunch, Guide #1 bids us adieu whereupon we again are picked up by our bus driver and taken a short distance to another small village, where we are met by Guide #2. Next to our meeting spot are two elephants. I love these massive creatures; getting so close to them is fantastic! Tied up in the grassy area, their handler lives there. One is sick and very agitated, moving constantly. After the obligatory photographs of the magnificent beasts, we follow our guide down a circuitous pathway behind people's homes to our canoe, which is rowed by an older fellow standing barefoot at the back using one very large pole.

Cruising down a canal, it is essentially silent aside from the two Indian women chattering away. Very peaceful and lovely, we see a variety of birds, a couple of water snakes, and much foliage. It is quite charming. We boat for an hour or so, then turn around and stop at some chap's house for tea, who brings out the requisite sales items all made of coconut shells. I rather like the wine bottle, but it's too heavy to schlep around India. Reeking of alcohol—toddy perhaps, I realize that he is hammered. In addition to having the highest education rate, Kerala also has the highest alcoholism rate.

Replying to a question about who lives along the canal, our guide claims that everyone in Kerala owns a house. He is very proud to tell us that the government gives everyone houses. There are a couple of beautiful, sizeable ones, but most are modest. There are "no slumdogs and no millionaires," he tells us. The communist system at work.

Finally, I do glimpse an indicia of the Communist party here—a couple of red flags with hammer and sickle on Cochin street corners and one rickshaw with a picture of Che on it. But thus far, that is the only evidence seen of this being a communist state. It certainly feels nothing like Russia did in the late '80s.

The last to be dropped off at our original starting point, the travel company, I am certain of the way back to my hotel since Param has both shown me the way *and* drawn me a map. However, I do not even look at his map because *I know* the way back. Famous last thoughts. It should be a ten- to fifteen-minute walk, but fifty minutes later, I am lost walking around in circles, recognizing places I have passed earlier.

Asking several people for directions, I still cannot find my way. So utterly fatigued that I feel faint, and for the first time since arriving in India, near tears, primarily from exhaustion, I finally stop a rickshaw driver and ask the tariff to my hotel. An honest fellow, he quotes me fifteen rupees, although by that point I would have paid any amount. Knowing it isn't far, I haven't paid enough attention to landmarks when riding in the car, and since there are *no street signs*, my map is useless.

Back in my hotel, I feel ill. Unsure if it is just my fibro stuff from exhaustion or if I am coming down with something, out of an abundance of caution, I pop extra vitamin C, my homeopathic osoccocsomething flu remedy, Airborne, Tylenol 3 for pain, and two aspirins for my throbbing headache. Pretty much covering the entire gamut from my medicine repository, by morning, I should know if I am ill or just whipped.

One of the reasons my luggage is so heavy is the amount of meds, vitamins, and remedies brought along. People counseled me to bring those things, and I am happy to have them because once one feels sick, it is a colossal hassle to track down medicine. The biggest challenge is to locate them. It is not like running to the corner Walgreens that's for sure.

There may be dozens of tiny chemist or pharmacy shops in a town, but it is hit-or-miss with some carrying drugs that others do not. Some are allopathic, but here, there are also ayurvedic medicine shops as there were in Pondicherry, but not in Tiruvannamalai. Some places have homeopathic stores, others do not.

As one example, while searching for cranberry tablets one day, I stop at four establishments. The men at the first three shops have no idea what I am even asking for; finally, one run by a woman has a few capsules. Also, unlike in the West, drugs are not sold in bottles of twenty to a hundred or more tablets or capsules. Instead, they are sold individually in little tin foil packages for a few rupees apiece. It seems like one is not paying much for medicine, however, if calculating the per tablet cost, compared to prices at Costco or Walgreens, where we purchase a substantially larger quanitity, I suspect our drug costs in the United States are less.

Sleeping for more than twelve hours, I awaken Wednesday, still not feeling particularly perky, but clearly not sick. That's a relief. Realizing my body cannot do so many consecutive long days of partying (haha), I vow in the future only to do half-day sightseeing junkets. Yesterday was another eleven-hour day by the time I collapsed back at the hotel.

My lunch experience is hysterical; I love these little Indian incidents. Entering a vegetarian restaurant, I ask to see the menu, and Front Counter Fellow points to it posted on the wall. Recognizing the names of a few items, I sit down, ordering my usual bottle of refreshing chilled water. Unable to understand anything my waiter says, after multiple attempts, he finally motions over Front Counter Fellow.

Unsure what he is telling me either, it appears that only a few items are available. This is pretty typical in Indian restaurants, unlike American ones where if something is listed on the menu, one can order it. Various things seem to be available at certain times—lunch or dinner being the main meal times. I, of course, have no clue when those intervals are, and they most likely vary from establishment to establishment anyhow.

Front Counter Fellow mentions item # 17, which is masala dosa. Not knowing whether this is the only selection available or if that is what he decides I should eat, and noticing another fellow nearby eating it, I conclude, "fine, that is what I shall eat." And, at least I know what it is—a dosa is a large crepe and masala is the potato mixture inside. Served with a variety of sauces, pieces of the dosa are pulled off and dunked in the sauces. Tasty enough, I finish my meal; the price is very reasonable.

Toast and Eggs
and the Nose Picker

FRIDAY, JUNE 15, 2012

SLEEPING WELL, I awaken early, unable to fall back asleep. Still feeling tired, however, I do my asana practice, shower, and dress. It is nice to do yoga after a few days' hiatus. While on the mat, I decide to eat when leaving the hotel, not having been hungry for dinner. I fantasize about eggs and whole wheat toast, and then laugh. But hey, one can dream, right?

Hiring a rickshaw, I head to the sari shop, which overcharged me for my purchases a few days ago. Thinking that a massage might be nice, I walk across the street to a pricey hotel, Avenue Regent. It is immediately apparent that it is a very nice property—all uniformed staff, nice lobby, and the like. Room tariffs start at ten times the rate at my hotel. There is an ayurvedic spa on the property, but their only female therapist has just gone home ill. Ayurvedic massage is not my first choice having had them previously, but being in the state known for Ayurveda, I might try one here.

Asking if they have a restaurant, the concierge says that they have a breakfast buffet, but that it has ended. "But let me see if they can make you anything," and he runs up a flight of stairs. Returning, he apologizes that they cannot but tells me that possibly the hotel next door can make me some fried eggs. *What? Eggs?* Only an hour ago, I was thinking of eggs. Talk about synchronicity; I am now totally blown away. This indeed *is* India!

Walking literally only a couple of doors away to the Hotel Excellency, I enter the restaurant and ask if I can order breakfast. Yes, and yes, they can make me scrambled eggs. *I am about to have scrambled eggs and dry toast with jam and freshly squeezed lime juice in India!* There is no whole wheat bread, which is called brown bread here, but I am ecstatic nevertheless. Truly feeling as if I have found nirvana, it takes a long time for them to arrive. But the wait only makes me savor the anticipated flavor of food I've not eaten in nearly two months that much more.

When they arrive, the eggs are served on a separate small plate, shaped in a little mound by a mold or cup. Having never seen eggs presented that way, it is very charming; what a cute idea for serving eggs at a brunch. And, interestingly, there is a marinated cherry on top. Three pieces of toast are unbuttered; the jam is strawberry. In heaven, I eat some of the toast and all of the eggs, which are delicious.

Asking their hours for breakfast, perhaps I shall come again tomorrow. What a treat for one who loves eggs for breakfast *and* at my favorite breakfast time of late morning. It is about 11 a.m.; breakfast ends at 10:00 or 10:30 my waiter tells me, but they have cooked these especially for me. These are the things one loves in India. A happy camper, I leave, walk back through the first hotel to get to the street, and thank them profusely, telling them that my breakfast was great.

Checking my e-mail, Anandashram in north Kerala near Kanhangad kindly has welcomed me to stay there on the eighteenth. Ergo, the next piece of my journey is set. Ram has welcomed me; my *Nirvana* guidebook says that the ashram treats everyone arriving as if he or she is Ram; how very lovely.

The ashram was started by devotees of Swami Papa Ramdas, an Indian mystic, and his spiritual partner, Mother Krishnabai. Papa is the last of three teachers that Yogi Ramsuratkumar credited as his gurus, claiming Ramdas killed "this beggar," referring to the ego of his former life.

Not only have innumerable people told me it is an idyllic place, I love the fact that the Ram Nam chant goes on all day long. *Om Sri Ram Jai Ram Jai Jai Ram.* It sometimes was chanted at the Yogi Ramsuratkumar ashram, and I chant it a lot, often silently. It is very beautiful and powerful. In fact, it is what puts me to sleep each night. Both Papa Ramdas and Mother Krishnabai attained God-realization simply by chanting this mantra in praise of Ram.

For some reason today, I am even more weary than usual answering the same question: "Where are you from?" from everyone on the street. Others call out as I pass, "Where are you going?" I must appear an alien, although during season, certainly there must be more Westerners and the odd blonde around. Wishing I were a brunette, maybe I will dye my hair brown or black. Or perhaps I could wear a burka. I start ignoring people, simply smiling as if I don't understand the question.

As Franz pointed out, when discussing this issue on our cruise, people ask the rote questions, "Where are you from?" or "Which country?" for really no reason and without any intent to follow up with a meaningful conversation. I hadn't thought about that, but he is right. Occasionally, someone, such as the hotel concierge today, strikes up a conversation about family living in a city in the United States or having traveled there, but that is exceedingly rare.

But since arriving in Kerala and answering "the United States," the standard response from locals has been, "Oh, Obama." That is interesting because no one in Tamil Nadu ever said that. This is a much more educated populace. Franz says that when answering they are from Germany, many say, "Oh, Hitler." Understandably, it upsets him. I told him when people say that, he should respond, "No, Merkel."

An interesting local piece of information mentioned in guidebooks is that Indians, although very kind and service-oriented, do not necessarily have the best manners or etiquette. For example, even if you have been standing in a queue for some time, a person will cut right in front of you. It has happened to me several times, which in the past I just ignored.

But today at the post office, waiting at least ten minutes behind several gentlemen, I am next in line when a lady marches up to the counter ahead of me. When the postal clerk finishes with the chap, I simply say, "Excuse me, I was here first."

So one learns quickly that one cannot be timid in India. That reminds me of an interaction I had chatting on New Year's Day in Sedona with the Buddhist nun, who had been to India a few times. Telling her that I planned to come here, she told me that one has to become aggressive in India. Thinking that a rather odd comment at the time, from a Buddhist nun no less, I now understand what she meant.

Spitting is common too. Men spit anywhere apparently; I haven't really noticed it much, and gratefully, have not been spat upon. Many chew some red gunk and then spit it out regularly all day long. This was something that the Indian ladies on the cruise mentioned as being particularly offensive to them. Along the hallways in my hotel are signs that say, "Please do not spit outside," meaning from the windows to the ground below.

My favorite thus far though, bar none, has to be the "Nose Picker." This may be my all-time top India tale thus far! My early encounter with the International Shipping Clerk/ Cloth Wrapping/Cow Tending Lady in Tiruv is in the running, probably because it was my very *first* Indian experience of near-exasperation.

The Nose Picker, a thirty-something aged Indian male, is sitting directly in front of me as I use one of the two hotel lobby computer terminals. In my line of vision, the only way to avoid the show is to leave because his chair is less than a foot away from me.

First, he begins picking his nose. But then, it continues and continues and continues, serious digging and searching and exploring. I try to ignore him, but it is impossible. It is as if he is engaging in a nose-picking performance for me—"hey, lady, look at how expert I am at the art of nose picking." This *literally* goes on for a good five minutes, really intensely and spirited. It is gross!

Clearly, picking one's nose in public is not considered bad manners in India. I ponder, *If there are nose picking competitions in this country, this guy would definitely win a prize.* And I am reminded of that *Seinfeld* episode. Even in India, experiences remind me of those iconic, great episodes and the timeless humor of that sitcom.

When booking my train ticket, I don't have my guidebook with me, so mistakenly my destination is to Kasaragod instead of Kanhangad (where the ashram is located). When booking it, I remember only the town's name is "Ka" something. After discovering the error, I return to the travel agency and am relieved to learn the stop is only one beyond that for the ashram; ergo, I merely disembark early.

Not actually calculating the price, when the travel agent quotes 341 rupees, it seems most reasonable. For a seven plus-hour ride in an air-conditioned train (rates are even less on non-air conditioned cars), my ticket, *including* the 100-rupee commission for booking it, costs a mere $6.30. No wonder everyone travels by train. How can they charge such low tariffs? They must be heavily government-subsidized.

America should take lessons from India in running passenger trains. The much smaller size of the country (India being approximately the size of Europe) and long-standing, existing infrastructure must contribute to its efficiency and low costs. My guidebook says that 14 million Indian passengers travel daily by train, and that Indian Railways is the second largest employer in the *world* with 1.6 million employees. And my guidebook is a few years old so that number is likely greater by now. I wonder who the largest employer is.

Guidebooks always highly recommend train travel here, saying the trains are a wonderful remaining vestige of the British Raj. The system runs throughout the country, except up north in the state of Jammu and Kashmir. I am excited to experience my first ride, but need to research and understand the system better. There are various classes, coaches, and speeds, with reserved and unreserved seating.

My guidebook recommends single women on long, overnight journeys travel in 2AC, which are sleeper cars that one sits in during the day. There are only four people in 2AC compared to six in a 3AC. My first trip will not be an overnight one; I depart at about 8:00 a.m. and arrive at approximately 4:00 p.m.

Sending e-mails to the guys from the backwaters trip to tell them how delightful they are, how much I enjoyed traveling with them, and to contact me if they ever come to Arizona, Manuel from Brazil has responded. This is his e-mail to me:

> Victoria,
>
> You made me so happy with all these beautiful words! Thanks for each of them!
>
> I am glad the destiny put us together on that boat! Enjoy the max your trip! Let India come inside you and feel it to the bones!
>
> When you decide (if you decide) have facebook acount, dont forget add me!

Hug and kisses!

How precious is that? Another treasured experience, his e-mail brings tears to my eyes.

Sari Shopping Extravaganza, My First Train Trip, and My First Community Bathroom

SATURDAY, JUNE 16, 2012

HAVING SLEPT WELL, I awaken feeling rested and ready to hit the streets, deciding to do my asana practice later. Although having contemplated it, I decide not to visit the elephant farm up north. I enjoy being unscheduled, writing (which is becoming an enormously important aspect of my sadhana), wandering around, meditating, and simply being.

This is a good day for a long walk. Feeling energized and knowing that the amazing, massive sari shop is in one of two directions, I stop and ask a fellow. Going inside, he brings out a young kid (verifying my theory about the preference of getting directions from the youth), who points the way. Just down the street, the store is Kalyan Silks. Its ad declares it, "The world's largest silk saree showroom." The building is six stories high with huge, beautiful advertising billboards covering its exterior. Looking as if it could be in New York City, I take a couple of photographs before entering.

The staff is magnificent, very friendly, service-oriented, and proper. No hucksterism or pushiness exists here whatsoever. Instead of "this is a very beautiful one," "this is very special silk," "very special price" or whatever pitches one hears from sales people in other stores, there is no salesmanship. It is as though I am in the Saks Fifth Avenue of the sari world where they know they are the best game in town, so there is no need to sell the product.

It is a most refreshing change from the typical sellers, and I might add, an effective approach, at least for me, and I suspect for most Westerners. It's too bad the street vendors don't understand that many folks are more likely to buy something if *not* harassed, but are treated instead with polite courtesy.

I am amused by the feature that escalators go "up" to each floor, but once finished shopping, there are only stairs in the "down" direction. Entering the open six-storied lobby, beautiful saris hang from above over the railings of each floor below. In all Indian offices, hotels, and stores, the first floor is not the first floor, but rather the ground floor.

Door Man tells me that saris are upstairs. Up I go. If I were a wearer of saris, this would be like the proverbial kid in a candy store. Actually, the experience is so darned enjoyable that I rather become one anyhow. Having already purchased some saris as gifts, I am interested in this place simply because of its impressive inventory, the uniqueness, and quality of saris. Param says the store is like an "ocean of saris," but it's more like seven oceans, with different kinds and fabrics on various floors.

Someone greets me on the next floor, and I say that a particular black one hanging over a railing has caught my eye, it being unusual in that most saris are bright-colored. Soon, there are two young women to assist me, removing the black one and an adjacent orange one. "Oh, you have such good taste," one says, "these are very beautiful." I do like them both, but having just arrived, I plan to look around more.

Telling the women that I wish to look more, I head to the next floor where I am immediately assisted by a nice man and three young girls, my Sales Clerks. The saris are stacked high on rows of shelves behind the counter; hence, a clerk has to pull them out for you. They start indiscriminately pulling out sari after sari after sari, trying to sense what I like. After about twenty are laid on the counter, I point to those that appeal to me, whereupon one of the Sales Clerks removes them from the plastic bags and opens them on the counter. Soon, the thirty-foot length of counter space is covered with gorgeous fabrics.

Facing the long banks of counters, which surround the entire floor in front of each wall are dozens of arm chairs. "Sit, sit," they tell me, but I can see better standing. I love the fabrics, especially the silk ones, and the choices of colors, patterns, and textures are staggering. Each one is like a separate piece of art. Being intrigued by saris immediately upon arriving in India, this is incredibly fun! Never did I imagine myself shopping for saris while here.

This process of pulling out saris will continue as long as one wants, hour upon hour upon hour if desired. Thinking what a nightmare it must be to fold them all up again, I ask one of the girls, but she says it's not difficult at all. I suppose if that is what one does all day long, it becomes second nature.

After about twenty or thirty are on the counter, I ask if they have any with elephants or peacocks. One Sales Clerk disappears and promptly returns with a collection of both. Now there is a huge pile of opened saris on the counter. I ask them to open and sort them, coordinating by colors: oranges in one section, pinks in another, and so on. Then the elephant and peacock ones are separated. This sorting helps me determine which I like best.

The next culling process is separating the saris into the "maybe" pile (the fellow calls them the pending group) and the "no" group. These are definitely more expensive than the others I purchased, but every price range is available, from a few hundred rupees to several lakh (a lakh is 100,000 rupees or about $1,850). The most expensive are the bridal saris, which may be sewn with gold thread and covered in jewels.

Speaking of the monetary system, whereas the US system is in tens, hundreds, thousands, millions, and billions, the Indian system counts in tens, hundreds, thousands, hundred thousands, and ten millions. It is confusing to me, but since I shall not be spending in the lakh or crore range, I do not concern myself with understanding it.

Now I eliminate several more. I am becoming fast friends with the Second Floor Manager Samar and his Sales Clerks, Amyra, Sonali, Sasheh, and Hanni. One of the saris is approximately three to four times the price of the others; it is a magnificent teal silk with peacocks.

Telling myself that I shall buy three or four...what I will do with them, I am unsure, but my inner voice is saying, "If you leave India and don't buy these, some day you will look back and say, 'Why didn't you spend a few hundred dollars for these gorgeous mementos? You may never have that chance again and will regret it.'" I rarely have an inner voice telling me something like this, certainly not about shopping, so I am listening. My intuition and creative juices in India have been indescribably powerful.

After perhaps an hour or so, a stunning sari-clad woman walks up. Wearing unusual jewelry—not the standard gold necklace, bracelets, and earrings of most Indian women—with heavy makeup, she has a presence about her. Assuming that she is a wealthy customer, Second Floor Manager Samar introduces me to Mrs. Someone, the Store Manager. Most pleasant, she welcomes me, poses for a couple of photographs, and serves as the model for a wrapping of the peacock sari. Earlier, they wrap the same sari around me.

The sari-trying-on routine goes like this: the customer stands on a round, raised pedestal, and a couple of Sales Clerks begin wrapping, tucking, and folding the sari around her. Another Sales Clerk brings out a full-length mirror for the customer to view herself. It's easier, and quicker, than going into dressing rooms, taking off one's clothes, and trying on multiple selections. Also, wearing only saris is extremely economical for some cost as little as a couple of dollars, perhaps another reason for their continuing popularity.

Fascinatingly, shopping nearby is an entire family—a mom with husband, a few daughters and sons, seven people. They go through the pulling-out-saris routine for a while, and Mom tries on two different ones. She is wrapped first in one, then a second; the husband and children all watch intently. Asking my Sales Clerks if it is typical for the whole family to come to shop, I am told that is normal.

I learn that the lady is buying a sari to attend a nephew's wedding and that ultimately, the husband will choose which to purchase. I giggle to myself envisioning an American man, his wife, and five teenaged children shopping together for four or more hours for a dress for Mom. Obviously a serious endeavor, everyone is very involved in the process; no one is on a cell phone or texting.

Mom tries on two, but apparently, the husband isn't keen on either because soon, the entire family is back at the counter looking at more selections. I find this widely charming. The kids are wearing blue jeans and tennis shoes or sandals. Mom wears a sari, and Dad is in slacks and a knit shirt.

Mesmerized by this entire experience, I still have at least fifteen or so in my "possibles" pile. Now, *this* would have been fun to have shared with someone who likes to shop—a girlfriend, niece, or sister. Not so much into the modeling/wrapping routine, with a shopping companion, I can imagine it being a blast. I especially think of Mother and all the great things we sewed together. She could be looking at these confirming that one would work for a jacket, a skirt, or pair of pants. She was the *best*!

There are a couple of definites; I must have the hot pink with green elephants and black silk spotted upon first entering the store. Rather like ordering the first item one considers on a menu as ultimately being the best choice, so is the black sari. It is unusual—a raw silk with bright colored stripes along the bottom.

Having Samar tally my damages, which I also confirm on my own calculator, I inquire whether prices are fixed or if he can offer me any discount, suggesting that might impact my purchase. He leaves a few times, probably checking at one point with Store Manager, and advises that although their prices are fixed, "because he wants me to come back if I am ever in Kerala," he can offer me a five percent discount. He whispers this quietly to indicate he doesn't want other customers to hear.

Considering the peacock sari, it is the most expensive one, *of course,* but hands down, it also is the most exquisite. But do I want to spend that much on it? Others are moved to the no pile; there remain a few possibles. Very adept, Samar recommends removing one of the others and buying the peacock one because "it is so much better." Seeming a good idea, ultimately, I follow his suggestion.

So there are four saris on my pile: the peacock silk, another vibrant pink and purple silk, an elephant one, and the black one. It is an interesting assortment. Perhaps this year, instead of my Women's Christmas Party, if back in Arizona, I can have a sari viewing, and if able to figure out the knack, a wrapping party.

Realizing that saris are heavy, each a minimum of three meters, and that I am not interested in schlepping them around India for three and a half months, I ask Samar whether they can ship them. Apparently, no one has asked him to do this previously, and he has to check for me.

Returning, he says that the store cannot ship them. But he has the name of a courier service that the store uses, suggesting it rather than the post office because delivery can be insured. That is another story, but I digress. He has the courier's telephone number and the cost.

Having no idea the time or how long I have been shopping, it is time to finish this process and be on my way. The experience has been fun, fun. My lead Sales Clerk Amyra hands me a small piece of cardboard with her name on it, saying she will be on the second floor when I return. On my way back down to find her, I notice a gorgeous turquoise with gold trim sari hanging on the railing. Loving it, I decide if Samar gives me the same discount, it will be added to my pile. He agrees.

The next steps of checking out, paying the bill, and wrapping the parcel are most time-consuming. But of course, this *is* India. Although far more pleasant than standing in a checkout line, the process goes like this. When indicating that I am finished shopping, they ask, "No more?" Then while I sit, they prepare the bill. Many times while in the store today I am told, "Sit, sit."

Next, we walk together, with Samar carrying the bill, to the cashier station, located behind a counter with terminals, cash boxes, and the like. Cashier Man does more calculations whereupon the bill is presented to me for review and payment. But no, I am *nowhere* near yet having my parcel to depart the store. This is not Macy's; several more steps remain to complete my transaction.

No one should go to India without either having patience or accepting that it must be learned while here. Despite knowing this and constantly reminding myself of it, I still occasionally feel exasperated that everything takes at least twice as long as seemingly it should. Patience indeed is a wonderful lesson, and one that I especially need to learn. Thankfully, during the day, I am served tea, and additionally, pop in to an upper-floor cafeteria for a bit of sustenance.

Now, we move on to the wrapping section. Samar accompanies me. Not paying much attention, but I think my saris are kept in a holding section en route, where Samar presents the paid bill and retrieves my saris. In the wrapping section, several people review the bill and check it against the number of items presented. Those saris that are individually wrapped in plastic are placed in another large red and white plastic Kalyan Silks logo bag. A couple of my saris, however, are not encased in plastic. These are first wrapped individually in green paper bags bearing the logo, which bags are *both* scotch taped *and* stapled shut. Then *finally*, those bags are placed in the larger store logo shopping bag. It is quite the production!

On our way to the wrapping section, I tell Samar that I first want to speak with the courier. We call Courier Jamal, but his English isn't great. Samar jabbers away with him in Malayam, but I want to know what is being said. Courier Jamal is to come over—in the usual "five minutes." I suggest waiting to package things until Courier Jamal arrives, but Samar assures me it will be fine. Listening to yet another Indian male's advice, what are the chances?

My saris are now packaged in two boxes, taped carefully with packing tape (but with my instructions how to do it neatly, sometimes my Virgo genes kick in), then wrapped in paper, and taped *yet again* with scotch tape. I write my mailing address, return address, and hotel address on a piece of paper, which is taped to the outside of the box. The bill compilation/payment/collection/wrapping process has taken at least another hour.

About thirty minutes later (far longer than five), the most pleasant Courier Jamal shows up, and I am to leave with him to ship the parcel. Good-byes are said all around; Samar gives me a business card and requests I sign a guestbook and include comments about my shopping experience. I write that he and the women sales clerks have been phenomenal.

Courier Jamal, who has ridden his bike, advises that he will leave it, and we will walk, and that, *of course*, it is only a five-minute walk. Amazingly, it actually is only five minutes until we are down the street and up a couple of flights of stairs to the courier office. In the office are a few gentlemen and a young woman. "Sit, sit," I am again directed for the tenth time today.

Upon arriving, Courier Jamal disappears for a goodly length of time with my receipt. Returning with another gent, Boss Man perhaps, he is a nice guy who says that they cannot ship the items with this invoice because the amount is too much. Not understanding the issue but thinking it has something to do with customs and paying duty, I ask several questions. It sounds as though Boss Man needs a receipt for six items, reflecting a total purchase price of much less.

Boss Man explains that they do *not* provide insurance (contrary to what Saram told me) and that none of the couriers do. But they provide tracking like UPS, which he claims is more secure than using the post office. Discussing options, I comment that I may as well just send via the post office. "Oh no, you will have the same problem there," he tells me, "they will need the receipt." *Really?* I think. Let's see, since arriving in India, I now have sent seven or eight parcels to the United States, one as recently as yesterday from here, and not once, has any post office asked for a sales receipt. Of course, none has had a stated value of this amount either.

This is becoming complicated...of course, "Welcome to India!" Later, I come to understand they are saying that the declared value must not exceed 1,500 rupees, otherwise a customs duty will be assessed in the United States. I won't be there to receive this parcel so how can I be assessed a duty? Can my friend to whose home I am shipping it to myself receive it on my behalf? Will she have to pay duty? I have no answers to these questions. Clearly, he wants me to ship the parcel with them. And I am happy to do that, having already made that decision many hours, and seemingly several galaxies, ago.

Suddenly Boss Man cries, "Wait, wait," as if he has had an ephiphany, and makes a telephone call to someone. After the call, he reports that they can send the parcel, without the receipt, removing price tags, and stating a lower value for each item on the customs form. Asking at least twice if this is problematic, if the items be seized and the like, he reassures me, "No problem." Great, suddenly an entirely different answer materializes, just as I am possibly about to depart the building. And now, am I participating in fraud? Oh, this makes me feel soft and gooey inside—not. But by this juncture, I decide why not, if the parcel doesn't arrive, so what? It's only stuff. I decide to keep the most expensive peacock one, however, which I will carry or ship later.

And *naturally*, the boxes that have just been carefully packed and taped at the sari store indeed must be opened. The courier explains they are required to open anything before they accept it for shipping. That makes perfect sense, but it certainly would have been nice if Second Floor Manager Saram knew that *or* if I would have trusted my own instinct and insisted that the boxes not be packed until Courier Jamal arrived at the store. Another valuable lesson learned.

So this process takes another hour; there are at least five forms to fill out in addition to the unpacking and repacking. Sending through the post office would probably have been lots easier.

My passion in India has become writing. When describing what I do or what I am, I wish to say, "I am a writer." It has become the most wonderful outlet for me. I want to develop, nurture, and continue it. I lose time when I write, similar to when painting pottery. It is therapy; yesterday when feeling grumpy, after writing a few hours, the feeling evaporated.

Sunday, June 17, 2012

Today is both Father's Day and Dad's birthday so I think about him a lot and what an important influence he was in my life. I learned so much from him, values that I cherish hard work, honesty, integrity, and generosity. What a good and decent man he was, always there to help out a neighbor, family member, or friend. To this day, I cannot think about either him or Mother without becoming teary-eyed.

Sister Sherryle, the family historian, who has amazing recall for everyone's birthdates, marriages, ages, dates of death, and the like, e-mails me that he would have been 106 years old today. If he were alive, I think he would get a kick out of his youngest daughter's India adventures. A man of few words, he never told me directly, but I think he was proud of me and respected my choices in life. I suspect that both he and Mother serve as guardian angels watching over me here. I honor them both, feeling privileged to have had their direction, love, and guidance.

Finally, I see the petticoats that are worn under saris, having both seen them in a store in Kanhangad, as well as drying on clotheslines or on the ground. Fascinatingly, after being laundered, often the clothes are laid on the rocky ground to dry as opposed to hanging them on clotheslines. This seems rather counterproductive—after beating the living daylights when washing clothes to remove dirt (the reason given me for throttling clothes against rocks)—to then throw them on the ground. But hey, I wasn't raised here, what do I know?

The "petticoats," and when is the last time I have even heard that word (as a kid from the television show *Petticoat Junction*), are cotton, have a small ruffle at the bottom and a drawstring waist, and come in a variety of colors. Having seen white, pink, green, yellow, and orange ones, it appears that the color is selected to match the sari. Before I leave, I definitely shall try one on. I even would wear one as a skirt in the US. Guidebooks, however, advise Westerners not to make the mistake of wearing petticoats and blouses, the short-sleeved midriff tops worn with the sari, on the streets here as outerwear.

MONDAY, JUNE 18, 2012

More "firsts" in India; today's is my first train trip on India Railways. I anticipate that most of my remaining travel time here will consist of them.

My train departure is at 8:10 a.m.; however, since this is a new experience for me, I allow plenty of time for Plans B and C, getting lost, and the like. Ergo, even though the train depot is only ten minutes from the hotel, not taking any chances, Rickshaw Driver Barab is to pick me up at 7:15. No Barab arrives by 7:15; I wait five minutes and then ask Front Desk Fellow to phone him. There is no answer on his mobile.

Not too concerned because there is sufficient time, I ask Front Desk Fellow about getting another rickshaw. Having given him a tip last night, he is friendlier today and actually walks outside with me to see if there are any about. Within minutes, up pulls a rickshaw driven by Amit, advising me that Barab is sick and sent him in his stead. Whew; having used Barab a few times, I knew that I liked him. Thank you, Barab. Amit is a friend of Barab, and he is just as nice. I pay him well for the trip.

There is only one glitch en route. About a block from the hotel, checking my bags, I note that my little camera bag is missing. Oh great, I have no memory of packing it or even seeing it last night. What is it with my camera karma anyhow? Having just replaced here in Kochin the one I lost in Tiruvannamalai, this is absolutely bizarre. Telling Amit, he promptly turns around. My last memory of the glitzy little bag with elephant, my camera bag, is having it with me at the computer terminal in the lobby last evening. Distinctly remembering taking it off my neck, placing it atop my regular bag, and saying to myself, *Now don't forget this here*, clearly, that is precisely what I have done.

Dashing in, I ask Front Desk Fellow if the bag is at the front desk. He says it is not. I run upstairs, even though knowing it is not in the room for I checked the room thoroughly before departing. Nevertheless, I engage in the drill of checking under the bed, in the wardrobe, and on the tables. The phone in the room rings, and Front Desk Fellow tells me that he has it. On our way, Amit lectures me about being careful. I laugh...if he only knew my penchant for losing and misplacing things.

A wonderful porter meets us at the train depot, how lucky is this? He schleps all of my bags, not even allowing me to carry a backpack. Am I ready yet to accept that I can dump most everything and reduce the amount of luggage? Probably not as long as I keep finding nice porters. Also, having read in my guidebook that Indians travel with a huge amount of luggage, I figure, whatever, after all, I am here for five months. I fear that as soon as I discard more medicine or something else, naturally that will be what I shall need.

Porter looks at my ticket, tells me the train name and number, walks me to the right platform, and announces in Schwarzenegger fashion, "I'll be back." Listening carefully, I finally can interpret the automated announcements (English as spoken by Indians is brutally difficult to understand) and hear my train number. 16606 or something like that.

Absolutely on key, Porter reappears as the train pulls to a stop, grabs my bags, boards the train a few people ahead of me, and neatly stows them for me. Tipping him well, I am off. Fortunate to have a seat by the window in the rear of the car, I have only one seatmate on the aisle, a nice guy who speaks only in response to my questions and doesn't ask where I am from until many hours into our trip. One side of the car has two seats, the other three; this is air conditioned Class 2, referred to as "2 AC." At some times, it is even a little too cool—just like in US restaurants, theatres, and airplanes. So I shall wear something long-sleeved next time.

I see why everyone loves the trains! There must be an Indian equivalent of Mussolini because they do run on time, and they are delightfully pleasant. The seats aren't the most comfortable, but I have my great little multipurpose REI pillow. And, the ability to get up and walk around well compensates for that wee inconvenience. I move often, do yoga stretches, stand by the door outside the car watching the scenery from the open door—which is my favorite vantage point actually—and disembark at a few stops.

If train travel were a viable option in the United States, I would never fly again. Everything about this train is more pleasant than air travel, unless perhaps one flies only first class or on private planes. There is plenty of room for luggage, which is easily stowed; the motion of the train is very soothing, and there are no annoying announcements or flight attendants bumping carts into seats.

Early in the trip, a kid comes through selling little doughnut-like things with a sauce. Already up for several hours and having read that the food is often good on trains, I decide to try them. Very tasty and not greasy, I can only eat two of the three. Offering the remaining one to my neighboring travelers, all decline. Shortly after eating though, I experience stomach cramping. The self-talk begins immediately: "Wonderful. You ate unfamiliar train food on your first train trip, and you may end up sick the whole trip. How brilliant is that? You couldn't have just eaten the almonds and raisins in your bag? Or brought some fruit with you? Oh, well, too late now."

So, my first trip to the bathroom on a train is pretty foul-smelling, but I am prepared, having been warned about train toilets. But after the fourth or fifth visit during the journey, I become accustomed to it, or if necessary, hold my nose. If this is my "worst bathroom experience" here, however, I have little concern.

The most challenging aspect in the loo of a swift-moving train, however, is maneuvering with clothes, toilet paper, and handbag. After practice in my multiple trips, I develop skills of how to roll up pants legs so as not to get them wet and to throw my long top over my shoulder or tuck it in my money belt, holding on to the grab bar while squatting. Just lovely, these long Indian dresses and tops drag on the floor toilets when squatting! How do the Muslim ladies wearing their flowing robes manage? Or women in saris? I suppose with lots of practice anything becomes second nature.

Any travelers to India, unless their travel is all first-class with Western toilets guaranteed, should be practicing their yoga squats a couple of months before departure. I definitely am grateful to be a yogini today. Signs on the bathroom door advise not to use the facilities when stopped at train stations, which is understandable.

The one good thing about any Indian bathroom is that there is plenty of water everywhere, including all over the floor. Here, also there is usual array of faucet, buckets, hose spray, and sink. The toilet is rather a combination: squatting over the toilet on the floor, but flushing water down it as well. Worried about being sick from this food, my fish curry last night at dinner was pretty greasy, most of which I did not eat, so that too may be a contributor. I finally just tell myself, "You might have a stomach ache or cramps in the United States too. Do you freak out about it there? No. So get over it. Just relax." Actually, after that little self-lecture, I am fine for the remainder of the trip with no stomach discomfort whatsoever.

Directly in front of me is a young Muslim couple in their twenties, and both are incredibly good looking. They seem very much in love; he often turns and gazes longingly into her eyes like a scene from an old movie. At one point, he puts his arm around her as she rests her head on his shoulder. They are very sweet, and it is unusual because one rarely sees public displays of affection in India, other than boys or young men holding hands. I compliment the young woman on the beautiful beading on her scarf and robe.

Having been referring to the Muslim women's black robes as burkas, I know that it is not the correct term, except for the head-to-toe coverage where only the woman's eyes are visible. So I need to learn the proper name. In seeing other women out and about, never have I noticed this exquisite beading; it is most likely an indication of being more financially well off. Also, she wears the same gold jewelry that Hindu Indian women wear.

We speak a bit, and I learn that they are from Mangalore. Later, when they buy some fried bananas from the roving train Food Chap, I ask what they are, and they kindly offer me a taste. Another first; they are interesting. Thus far, my experience is that Muslims do not engage me in conversation (no "where are you from?" questions); I always first initiate conversations with them. Everyone is very pleasant.

Knowing little about the Muslim culture, I hope to gain more exposure to it here as well as the Hindu one. Deciding to be a good ambassador representing America and be kind and friendly to everyone, I want to make a special attempt to connect with Muslim women. Whenever I make eye contact or smile, they are very responsive, as, of course, are the children.

Throughout the trip, various Food Chaps walk the aisles at stops shouting their offerings, from the unknown doughnut-like food I ate to candy bars and snacks to chai to fried bananas to other complete meals. There is no dearth of sustenance on Indian trains that's for sure. At one stop, many people rush out to buy their lunch from a street vendor. My guidebook says that the locals know what food is sold at each particular station along the way. The young couple in front of me buys some rice and fish curry.

Looking at my watch for the first time, I am flabbergasted that five hours have already passed, guessing it to be only about three. Train travel is so much more pleasant and comfortable than flying. Although I must reiterate how wonderful my Air India flight was from the United States, which is interesting because all of the Westerners in Tiruv said that it is a terrible airline and reported awful experiences. I have been blessed and guided by my angels thus far on this entire trip.

At the prior stop, Train Employee comes back to inform me that mine is the next one. Seeing people moving toward the doors with their bags, it is my tip to do the same. Arriving at Kanhangad about 4:00 p.m., it is raining. Train Employee is standing at the door as I exit, but doesn't assist me getting my bags off, so likely he is prohibited from doing that. But a kind passerby sees me struggling with the large one and helps me get it down onto the platform.

Seeing lots of rickshaws on the street below, I ask a fellow how one gets to them. He is a rickshaw driver and quotes me sixty rupees to the ashram. He grabs my wheeled bag; I jump down the couple of feet from the platform to the street with my other bags, and we are off.

For some reason, from my research, I thought Kanhangad might be a mere hamlet. A fair-sized town of 100,000+ population, the traffic is heavy as we leave the rail station, and the road leaving the train station is treacherously uneven and rugged. Raining heavily as we travel to the ashram, either the monsoons are more intense up here or they vary from day to day, week to week.

Dropping me at the gate with my bags, I am referred across the driveway to "Reception," where Reception Man has me enter my name and address in a register book. He also gives me my room key, another form to bring back tomorrow with my passport, and a tiny piece of paper encased in plastic bearing my name and room number, which I am to show at the dining hall. Then I go back to Gate Guy, who grabs my wheeled bag and his umbrella and takes me to Room 83. It is just up a small hill not far away.

Bucket Bathing, Blissful Chanting, and Noisy Neighbors

I AM AT ANANDASHRAM, "The Abode of Bliss." The ashram grounds are gorgeous, lush, and green, spectacularly magnified by the rain. The property, seemingly quite large, was built in 1931 and obviously has expanded and developed over the years.

Now this is more what I anticipated from ashram accommodations. My room is in a dormitory building. Five rooms line one hallway that is partially enclosed by a concrete wall, with an upper grated portion open to the outdoors. My room furnishings consist of a single bed, an ancient metal shelving unit with four shelves, and a rustic wooden table with table covering. The window to the outside doesn't fully close, and notably absent is a bathroom.

My neighbor's window on the hallway side features a large hole as if someone has thrown a rock through it. Perhaps it is the Indian version of ashram air conditioning? The official ashram paint color must be light blue because again that is my wall color. Floors are a brick red painted concrete, with badly peeling paint. My door is tin or aluminum, and the walls are paper-thin.

Reminiscent of my first year of dorm life in college, the bathroom is a community one, albeit this one is a bit more Spartan. Located at the end of the hallway (my room is in the middle), it consists of three toilet rooms: one with Western toilet, two with Indian toilets, all with the usual conglomeration of spigots, hoses, and buckets. Separate shower stalls are the Indian type as well—buckets.

This is a bit more rustic; that's fine, and it is certainly what I was anticipating at Indian ashrams. I'm here for the chanting and the spiritual juice. It also will be my first Indian bucket shower experience; Indians refer to showers as baths. Actually, Indians seem to be very cleanliness-oriented, with baths in the morning and laundered clothing always hanging or lying around to dry, which in this wet weather will take a while.

Lots of people are hanging out in the room at the entrance to the building, and they are very noisy. That's somewhat disturbing at the ashram of universal love and bliss. But I tell myself not to rush to judgment yet. Perhaps I can move to another room, or this group may only be there at the moment; it may not always be this noisy.

Finding my way to a building where I hear the Ram Nam chant, "Om Sri Ram Jai Ram Jai Jai Ram," I stop and peer in through the window. One of the men motions me to come in and where to sit on a low bench or bamboo mat on the floor. It is the samadhi site of Mother. It is a serene, wonderful experience, and I stay a good while. It is a favorite, and powerful, chant.

People, alternating one-half hour times between gents and ladies, either sit in the back or walk continuously around her samadhi site. This chanting is on rotating days among the three samadhi sites of Swami Papa Ramdas, Mother Krishnabai, and Swami Satchidananda, who was the prior resident Swamiji and successor to Papa. It continues from 6:00 a.m. to 6:30 p.m. After chanting, I head the direction someone tells me is the dining hall location. Dinner is at 7:00 p.m., breakfast is at 7:45 a.m., and lunch is at 12:45 p.m.

En route, I ask the way of Bhanu, a lady from Chennai, who immediately takes me under her wing. A regular, she and her beautiful nineteen-year-old daughter, Jalaj, an IT engineering student in Chennai, are both devotees and come at least twice annually.

Bhanu invites me to join her and Jalaj for dinner. The food is good, although more basic than the food at both Yogi Ramsuratkumar ashram and Shantivanam. A first here, bread—white, soft doughy pull-apart rolls—is available. Not particularly appealing to me, it reminds me of bread possibly eaten in my childhood, but as a departure from rice, I may sample it at a future meal.

The two serving lines, separated for men and women, move quickly, and my quick head count estimates more than 100 people being fed, including many sadhus. Food selections are rice, chapatis, and or/bread, and sambar. At lunch, the spicy pickles, which I adore, are served. Men sit on one side of the room, women on the other. Instead of floor seating though, there are tables with marble slab tops and benches. And, we do not eat in silence.

Bhanu asks lots of questions about me. Not having any interest *whatsoever* in talking about myself or my life, I haven't found a good way to avoid or answer questions. Most people haven't asked any so that has been nice. Finally, I tell her that I consider myself here rather like an American sadhu, who has no past. "Oh," she says, "then I shouldn't ask you questions." I smile.

If pushed, I acknowledge teaching yoga, but that's the extent of my history and resume I choose to share. Since I am trying to burn my ego here, not expand it, talking about me is not part of the program. Earlier, an older chap standing outside on the grounds asks where I am from. Experimenting with a new answer, I reply, "I am of the universe, like all of you." "Oh, yes, yes," he says, immediately querying, "What is your profession?" I respond, "None." The guidebooks state that Indians are very inquisitive, and my experience certainly confirms that.

Later in town, when answering the "where from" question, I try the answer, "Phoenix." That ends the conversation; no one knows what that means. Aha, I have my idyllic answer. Also, I develop a better sense of when to simply ignore comments and questions from passers-by and when to respond, for example, when I am in a shop or actually interacting with someone. To those who have never been here, this all might seem a silly exercise, but after answering that question hundreds of times, one simply wearies of it.

Bhanu is a retired government employee; her husband, age sixty, is also retired, but was a private employee and still does some consulting in labor matters. She is very helpful and maternal, filling me in on all of the ropes, worrying that I am not eating enough, urging me to go back for more food, and showing me the plate-washing routine. Asking about the showers, she informs me that there is hot water available (yippee) for baths and that I should ask someone where I am staying how to access it because it is different in various rooms. In motherly fashion, she also tells me that it is not healthy to take cold showers. Upon returning to my building, I notice a faucet in the bathroom entryway that has painted above it on the wall "Hot Water."

Finally falling asleep, I awaken at 4:00 a.m., itching myself crazily. What is the deal with ashram beds? Bedbugs, ants, mosquitoes? Bhanu has told me to apply mosquito repellent at night, but I dislike the smell of the stuff, instead taking my chances with the mosquitoes. Actually, though, I have only seen a few mosquitoes despite all of the rain and standing water.

Awakened by my shouting neighbors about 6:00 a.m., literally, they all scream down the hall at each other; this whole group must be traveling together. Throwing a long shirt over my nightgown, I wander to the door to find that it is bright and sunny with no rain. That's nice because yesterday the rains were pretty much torrential downpours most of the day. People are standing in the hallway, waiting for bathrooms. Still tired, I go back to bed, hoping to catch a few more winks. Eventually, the crowd leaves, and I fall back asleep until about eight when they return again, most likely after breakfast. Figuring that at some point, they will leave again whereupon I will take my bucket shower/bath, I decide to read and contemplate my next destination.

After the lovely chanting and various pujas, the noise is disconcerting. Shantivanam was blissfully silent, which I adored. Deciding to inquire if there are any other rooms available, I decide the worst that can happen is that Reception Man will say sorry. In first contemplating that action, I tell myself that perhaps this is a "lesson" and just to suck it up. After all, there are 1.25 billion people in this country; hence, it is bound to be noisy somewhere that I stay. But on further reflection, I conclude that it is a needless sacrifice given my objective here is to experience its bliss. And it ain't feeling very blissful over here.

When no longer hearing noise from my neighbors, I peek into the hallway and see no shoes at the doorways. Everyone is gone. Gathering myself together to shower, I need to develop a procedure. Do I take my clothes to the bathroom and dress there? No, I decide to towel dry there, put my nightgown and shirt back on, and return to my room to dress. That works fine, but I should have a dop kit. One of the ubiquitous Indian cloth bags for toiletries suffices instead. Feeling absolutely gluttonous, I fill a very large bucket with two smaller buckets of hot water. It has been a long time since I have had hot water for a shower.

Much cooler and very damp from high humidity and rains, the hot water feels absolutely divine! I revel in sudsing my hair with shampoo, rinsing with hot water, basking in its warmth, and remembering what a hot shower feels like, using every drop of my big bucket of hot water. Okay, so it's not a real shower, but it is glorious.

Each day, I better refine my technique—drizzling with a small bucket from the very top of my head allowing the water to softly pour across my body, then emptying it a little more quickly, then swishing water from side-to-side, then gently over my back. Ah, the joys of the simple things in life. India helps us remember them.

Having no bathroom in one's room, it is amazing to realize how frequently one uses water, whether from the kitchen or bathroom sink, during the day. That convenience is not at my immediate fingertips; instead, there is one very small bathroom sink for us all to share, located outside very near my room. Not surprisingly, the faucet is loose, and by this morning, I cannot get the water to turn on at all! So I now resort to using buckets from the bathroom to wash my hands. And the one Western toilet no longer flushes either, so Indian toilets it is. Actually, that's fine for at least one doesn't sit down on a wet toilet seat, which probably isn't that sanitary anyhow.

About 10:30 with my morning ritual finished, I decide to drop in at Reception with my passport. When I gingerly inquire about the possibility of another room being available, explaining the noisy crowd in my building, Reception Man immediately assigns me to a different building, assuring me that it will be quiet there. How very, very kind.

This building, not a dormitory, is *much* quieter. Even though next door to me is a family with two little boys, no one is shouting. There are ten rooms laid out in an L-shaped configuration. The bathroom, unfortunately, is quite a way from my room—down two hallways. Finding my way in the middle of the night should be fun. The bathroom area consists of three separate commode areas, where all of the toilet seats have fallen off, but are propped up against the wall, and four separate bathing rooms.

My new room in the Vridaran building is essentially the same, with the exception that I have two single beds instead of one, and in lieu of a metal shelving unit, there is a four-shelf wooden medicine style cabinet built into one wall. The window is larger here, so the light is better, and nicely, it closes tightly as well.

My "mattress," if one wishes to stretch one's imagination to characterize it as such, is a half-inch thick pad that has definitely seen better days. The bed that I select is the cushier of the two, the "mattress" on the other bed consisting of two thick woolen blankets atop the wooden bed frame. I remind myself that Master Hong always says that sleeping on a hard bed is better for one's body than a soft one.

Dropping off my bags, I do not unpack; leaving things in my suitcase is simpler since there is no closet or wardrobe anyhow. And because it is so damp, everything feels wet in the room. Something I discover accidentally is that clothes zipped inside my suitcase remain drier. Also, since I am unsure if ants will crawl into my suitcase (why wouldn't they?), I keep my main wheeled bag zipped up, serving as my nightstand. I rather like the creative ingenuity of living simply like this, *almost* camping but with the comforts of a bed, electricity, and a bathroom.

Wandering over to the Information Centre, I inquire if there is a dhobi. There is; I am told to have clothes there before 10:00 a.m., and they will be ready the next day. How on earth in this rain and humidity do they launder clothes? My shirt lying on the bed feels wet simply from being in this damp weather. Somehow, I doubt that there is a clothes dryer on the premises, but perhaps an iron?

At the Information Centre, there is no printed ashram schedule to give me, but several are posted around the premises. About
to depart, another woman arrives to watch the ashram introduc-
tory video. Asking to stay, by its completion after twenty or thirty
minutes, several others have wandered in. Very well-done, the
video summarizes Papa Ramdas' life, the ashram's founding, its
mission and objective, and has lovely photography. It is low-key,
which I like.

The ashram schedule is also summarized on the video. There
is pretty much chanting of some form or another continuously
from 5:30 a.m. until 9:30 p.m. and a meditation hall and library
are available as well. This entire place is very mellow and serene.

Still having seen nary a mention about donations, I have
no idea what their recommended daily donation fee is. Asking
Bhanu, she says that there is no suggested donation; one can give
nothing or whatever one chooses. She explains that when I meet
with Swamaji before I leave and receive his blessing and Prasad,
if I wish to make a donation, which, of course, I will, it is given to
him at that time. It is interesting how the ashrams vary in their
policies about donations. Shantivanam clearly stated its suggested
donation amounts, which varied for Indians and foreigners, with
the level for foreigners being more than ten times higher.

Arriving for lunch, Bhanu and her daughter Jalaj are seated
and invite me to join them. The amount of food is plentiful, but
Bhanu is again concerned that I haven't had enough to eat, especially since I didn't take breakfast. Today, she is pushing buttermilk. Just the thought of it makes me gag; I tell her that I don't
drink milk or buttermilk and that I am allergic to milk. Who
knows, I well may be. This routine continues at every meal. She
is a riot. I explain to her what a "Jewish mother" is, telling her
that she reminds me of one with her instructions to eat, eat, eat. I
don't know if she understands my attempt at humor or not.

A Local Bus Ride, Ashram Critters, and Getting Thrown Out of Another Ashram Dining Room

ON THE SECOND night after the move to my quiet room, I return weary from chanting and arati at about 9:30 p.m., planning to fall asleep early and arise for the 6:30 a.m. darshan with Swamaji. I want to make it at least once. But soon after retiring a bit after ten, the group next door (at least six of which two are cute little boys) all are talking exceedingly loudly, and simultaneously. At one point, a kid starts crying, but the incessant chatter continues at a louder level. Indian ashram walls aren't constructed with any insulation.

Next, the power goes out, so now *sans* ceiling fan, there is no noise muting at all. Welcome to India! Finally desperate, I take half of an ambien (which I do not like taking, but sleep is critical for me), and the power comes back on. With earplugs in, I do manage to drift off, awakening a couple of times to more itching. I conclude that they are most likely ants.

That's it, I decide; tomorrow I am getting myself to town to buy a train ticket out of here. A day later, I have mellowed, realizing that I experienced these same feelings at both of the last ashrams too. Note to self: when you get to a new place, allow yourself a couple of days to acclimate and settle in. Relax.

A delightful, kind ashram employee Udaar arrives at the linen storage closet across from my room each morning. Staff bring dirty linens, counting them out to him, and he provides fresh ones. He is very nice, speaks good English, and I ask him several questions.

Udaar shows me where the dhobi is, so I drop off my clothes before 10:00 a.m. The dhobi service is free, but it is not the typical dhobi who takes your clothes, launders, irons, and returns them pressed and folded. Here, washerwomen launder the clothes, which entails beating the living daylights out of them on rocks, and then hang them on the line for guests to retrieve. The ladies warn me to watch for rain and remove my clothes. And they will not wash women's panties (men's, I think, they tell me along with bras yes). Dhobis are from the lowest caste, and they still won't launder my underwear. Actually, I like that; I can wash my own just like at home.

Just before it starts to drizzle, I manage to grab my clothes off the line. A few are actually dry; most are damp, and I hang them in my room to finish drying. Fortunately there is a long pipe running the entire length of my room, which serves nicely as a clothes drying rack.

Udaar gives me the name of a travel agency in town, and calls Manoj, a rickshaw driver who previously worked at the ashram. He also informs me that his wife Soni works in the office, that there is a sister ashram in Rishikesh, and that she will send an e-mail there for a reservation for me. That is fantastic. Later, when I meet Soni, she tells me that she will need a precise date.

When my travel plans are more firmed up, I shall e-mail her whereupon she will e-mail the ashram and copy me. She handles communications here for the ashram and seems very organized. Their sister ashram is the famous Sivananda ashram, which is a very difficult place to obtain accommodations. So I am even more thrilled to learn that little detail.

Rickshaw Driver Manoj arrives promptly yesterday at the agreed 2:30 p.m. time to take me into town. His English is good also. I have two errands—to find an Internet café and the travel agency.

In the Internet Café, the computers all have little curtains around them. That's a first, but not that it matters for on three occasions, people open my curtain. Once it is a guy, possibly the owner/manager, on the phone for several minutes standing right beside me apparently quoting prices for photographs on a sheet at my station. Clearly, he is looking at my screen, which makes me most uncomfortable, so I minimize it. A second time, it is the guy who sits down next to me. And the third is while I am on Google where the language is non-English. Trying to find English, the girl who works there pops in to help me. Obviously, the way the curtain closes, she too can observe my screen.

Very unhappy, I draw the curtain tightly and noisily shut, deciding not to access bank or credit card accounts in this place. Actually, I regret having accessed my e-mail account; just to be safe, I may change my password again. Reading somewhere that there are programs that can read each keystroke entered on a computer in public places, including one's password, and this being a Communist state, it may be prudent. This is the first time that I have felt uncomfortable using computers in India.

Deleting my browsing history and cookies, as I leave and pay my twenty rupees, the same fellow, who earlier hovers by my computer, asks if I am leaving Kerala. No doubt, he saw me researching Goa locations. Answering in the negative, clearly, I need to find a different Internet café to use.

Wandering down the street, I find the travel agency in a small two-story mall where there are many shops catering to Muslims, including a shop selling the women's black robes. Stopping to chat with the friendly Shopkeeper, he tells me that they are called pardas, which I am happy to know. Curious about the prices, a pretty one trimmed with beadwork worn by a mannequin sells for 4,000 rupees or about $72.

In answer to my question, Shopkeeper tells me that women wear them only in public, and that underneath, they wear street clothes. Thereafter, looking carefully, I notice women's pants. Some women's hair is completely covered by their scarves; the hair of others hangs outside the scarf down their backs. Sometimes, the scarves cover hair starting at the crown, others have forehead hair showing.

Watching Muslim women walk down the street, I think how interesting it would be to hear their views about wearing the robes. Do they resent them? Do they believe they are an important part of their religious tradition and, therefore, have no issue with wearing them? Do they find them restrictive? How about the younger girls? Will they wear them as they get older? Do they have choices about wearing them or not? Are certain sects more restrictive than others? For example, I think that the Wahabis are the most conservative group.

Walking into the travel agency and money exchange shop, its primary business is changing money, I later learn. A rarity to see a woman in such shops, I head to the sole female employee, asking a couple of questions. But working with a woman clearly is not to be for soon a pleasant fellow wearing a bright pink shirt whisks me to his computer. Finally, I ask his name and position. He is Sanjay, the store manager; his business card identifies his title as "Business Head."

Explaining some of my thoughts about onward (the term used here) travel, I ask for any suggestions, thinking that since this is a travel agency, he might provide some input. He has none, but says that perhaps he can look at some things, and I can come back tomorrow. No, I do not want to return tomorrow. "Tomorrow" is another standard, frequently-used Indian answer.

Now learning that travel agencies in India are different than in the United States, pretty much the function here is to book tickets, not to provide travel assistance or suggestions about itineraries. It quickly becomes clear that I know more about the location of places in Goa than he does; thankfully, I have my guidebook and show him places on the map. Great; I begin to fear another memorable travel experience with an Indian man at the helm. At least, I am not getting in a car with this one.

Business Head Sanjay's English is passable, and after many backs and forths and multiple queries, I learn that he can book a train ticket, and although they only book three-, four-, and five-star hotels, he can call other hotels for me. Regarding hotel ratings in India, my research indicates that they bear no resemblance to the same ratings in the United States or Europe. As one example, when cruising the harbor off Cochin, on one of the islands we passed, our tour guide pointed out a high-end resort under construction, informing us that it was to be a "seven-star" hotel. Gotta love the Indian penchant for hyperbole.

Business Head Sanjay is very pleasant and not in the least pushy. We make some progress. I have a list of three potential hotels in Palolem, located in southern Goa, planning to stop there first and then decide where next to travel within the state. It is tiny and about the size of Rhode Island.

The first hotel he calls has availability on the day I contemplate leaving, the twenty-sixth. But in trying to book the train, unfortunately, the Indian Railway computer system is down. Apparently, that is a common problem. He offers to do research tomorrow and come out to the ashram. Realizing from a communication perspective—at least, I am beginning to learn a *few* things—it is probably wiser to be together in front of the computer to book this, I say that I will return the next day.

Wandering somewhat aimlessly back down the street yesterday looking at shops, out of curiosity, since the purchase and ownership of gold is such a major part of the Indian culture, I visit one of the plethora of jewelry stores lining the streets. From what I can tell, only the poorest Indians do not wear gold. In discussing this with Param, he told me, "Yes, everyone has to have gold, they will go without food, but not gold."

Essentially, the women I see on the streets wearing gold have a necklace, earrings (possibly with some fake stones), and two or more bracelets. Identical bracelets are worn on each arm, with one or two or more on each wrist. And if a woman is not wearing gold bracelets, but instead other colored ones, she still wears identical ones on both wrists.

Currently, the price is 2,795 rupees or about $50 per gram. A sign with the current price is posted in the jewelry stores. The price for eight grams is also posted; I don't calculate to ascertain if that rate per gram is less, assuming it is not because rates likely are based on the international gold market.

As in all Indian commercial establishments, immediately, three people are waiting on me. For fun, I try on a few little rings and look at some pretty om pendants to ascertain prices. The procedure goes like this—the item is placed on a scale identifying the weight to the customer, whereupon the gold price is calculated and an additional sum is added, presumably for the manufacturing/setting/sales costs. This amount varies with different items. Presumably, this latter add-on amount is the only negotiable item.

Easily finding a rickshaw, as we arrive back at the ashram, it is raining cats and dogs. Where on earth did that saying come from, I wonder? Happily, my driver takes me directly up to my room. The weather here is fascinating. One moment, there is not a drop of rain falling, although it is always overcast and rarely sunny; then instantly, a torrential downpour explodes as if a gigantic showerhead is turned on at full force. An umbrella is my constant companion.

Today's little junket to town takes a few hours. Arriving back at my room, I notice that the big group in the adjacent room has left. Yippee, sleep tonight. Doing some yoga in my room and while in savasana at the end of my practice, I hear something on the rafters above me. The peaked interior roof of my room is thirty or more feet high, comprised of wooden slats and rafters.

Looking up, I see something scampering on one of the beams from my room to the next. Not having my glasses on, I cannot see clearly, which is probably for the best. I decide that it must be a squirrel. Realizing that squirrels are rodents too, somehow the furry tail makes them seem cuter than rats or mice.

Indians also have no compunction about asking one's age. Why not tell them the truth, I decide. Especially if a reason for being here is to burn my ego, my chronological age should matter not in the least. When Bhanu asks me at dinner how old I am, I ask her to guess my age. She estimates that I am thirty-five or thirty-six. Gotta love this lady. Most likely, it's just a cultural thing for I could never pull that off in the United States. For example, I am hopeless at ascertaining ages of women of African or Asian descent. She is genuinely surprised when I tell her my age; she is only one year older than I.

Bhanu's in-laws live here at the ashram, and her mother-in-law will celebrate her eightieth birthday this year. She explains that their meals are delivered to them because they are no longer able to go to the canteen. Also, her mother-in-law goes to the 6:30 a.m. chanting and her father-in-law, who is in a wheelchair, sits outside the samadhi and listens to chants from 3:30 to 5:30 p.m. It seems a lovely way to spend one's golden years.

Udaar says that thirty-five or forty people live here full-time and those who are able, perform some seva, but most are older and cannot. Bhanu's in-laws bought their apartment long ago and will live in it until they die, whereupon it reverts to the ashram. Prior to moving here permanently, they stayed in the unit whenever they wished, and when not occupied, the ashram used it for guests.

Last night leaving dinner with Bhanu, ever the mom, she asks if I have on my mosquito repellent. Having concluded that Indian mosquitoes must not like my American blood since I have not been bitten, I tell her that and, therefore, have not been using repellent. Famous last words. Awakening in the middle of the night, itching crazily all over my body and having no clue what is gnawing at me, but wondering if it might be mosquitoes, I dazedly open my suitcase. I find a packet of the Ben's mosquito repellent, and apply it on all exposed body parts, except my face, deciding to pull the covers over my head instead.

Then awake, I go to the bathroom. Turning on the light to enter one stall, I see another creature scampering off. Assuming it to be a mouse, it is another "Indian first." I won't really mind if there is *not* a "second." First, there is the scurrying creature on the beams, and now a mouse. This is *real* ashram living. Returning to my room, I find a huge sewer roach, but accustomed to having those charming creatures in Phoenix, that doesn't freak me out.

It's quite the animal farm around this place today. But it is not surprising given that there are sizeable openings in the rooms and hallways everywhere, and doors to the outside are kept wide open. There are still lots of ants around as well, wee ones and the bigger red ones. Happily though, I don't see many in my room, and I am fanatical to keep any food in my room in ziplock bags inside yet another bag high on the shelf.

But *by far*, the creepiest critter I see, and probably aside from snakes the most frightening, is on my way to chant one night. Almost stepping on the thing outdoors, I am nearly apoplectic. It is an enormous brown worm or centipede or whatever, at least six inches long and a half-inch in diameter. Hanging out near my building, please, please God, keep that thing out of my room is all I can think. But two days later, I do find one in my room, it looking like a baby version of the serpent, one to one and a half inches in length.

Upon awakening this morning, I discover what was biting me—mosquitoes indeed. Apparently, the Indian variety does like this white girl's blood after all for I have dozens of welts on my left cheek, neck, legs, and arms. My middle-of-the-night repellent application was obviously too little, too late. Surprisingly, however, the bites do not itch. Upon seeing Udaar, I ask him about mosquito coils, and he recommends buying the little electronic gizmos that plug into the electrical outlet and release some chemical. He says the mosquitoes come out about 5:00 p.m.

Having a pretty restless and eventful night with the critters, I shut off my alarm when it sounds at 6:15 and roll over for more shut-eye. After lunch about 1:30, I head to town via rickshaw, hoping to be back for Swamaji's 3:30 p.m. satsang, which I have yet to attend. But that is not to be today either. A good rule of thumb seems to be to guesstimate how long something may take, and then double the time.

Business Head Sanjay has done some research, but the results are not reassuring. There are no trains to Goa available on the twenty-sixth. Finally, after various suggestions by me, he finds an opening on the twenty-fifth; there are four seats left. Telling him to book it, he nearly clicks the purchase button when I see the name Margao on his screen. "No," I quickly assert, "I don't want to go to Margao, I want to go to Chaudi."

Searching on the Indian Railway Web site page *after* having phoned twice to their other office in some other town, he says that there is no Chaudi. Clearly, he is not really a travel agent himself. Exasperated, at one point, I inquire, "Who are you talking with?" and he explains whereupon I ask to speak with the person myself, but he won't allow it. Telling me that there are no trains to Chaudi, I argue with him. Unfortunately, today, I leave my guidebook in my room, but I specifically recall a train station on the map and the name starting with a C.

Business Head Sanjay then Googles something. I suggest Googling "train station at Chaudi." Realizing that I read English much better than he, and seeing the name, I point to the spot on the computer screen. The station is at Canacona. We are making progress; I have a ticket from Mangalore to Chaudi, which is near the Canacona stop. He asks if I mind him taking a ten-minute break. Inquiring if it is his lunch time, he informs me that it was earlier and that I can check my e-mails on one of their computers.

Returning from his brief lunch, Business Head Sanjay books my ticket from here to Mangalore, where I then will catch the train for Goa arriving next Monday evening at Canacona/Chaudi, which is near Palolem Beach. That sounds perfect.

And the Oceanic Hotel yesterday confirms a nice off-season rate that I find on the Internet, but it has not answered Business Head's e-mail regarding booking specific nights. He is annoyed, suggesting that the service is not good, and perhaps he should find me another hotel, recommending one with a rate that is one-third higher. Saying I don't want to spend that much and having faith in the *Lonely Planet* research, I shall take my chances. We agree that I will check tomorrow to see if the hotel calls him back. If not, we can look for another.

Getting antsy with how long this whole ticketing process is taking, I ask where to purchase the electronic mosquito gizmo. "Good Knight?" he asks. That sounds right, and I aver. Immediately, he picks up his mobile and calls his associate, who buys one and brings it to me within ten minutes. Now that is service. Obviously, I pay the 100 rupees for it, but he won't allow me to give the employee a gratuity. I am repeatedly overwhelmed by the service and attention here.

At the ashram, the service is the same. Whatever one needs, their goal is simply to serve. Udaar is incredibly helpful. Always reading a book while waiting for the staff to bring dirty linens, he says that he was enrolled in an engineering program, but didn't like it, so he dropped out to work at the ashram instead. He explains that the ashram has many activities and programs, including building low-income housing, various educational projects, and providing medical assistance to the needy.

Not finishing with my travel planning until after 3:00 p.m., clearly, I shall not make it to satsang today either; perhaps tomorrow. I am still not certain if I even know who Swamaji is.

Today, I am thrown out of a second ashram dining room. At least this time, however, we are not screamed at, but merely ushered out. Bhanu and I are gabbing away over dinner when a lady sitting across the aisle hears me mention Arizona. "Are you from Arizona?" she asks. Umisha is lovely; she and her husband Raj, who works for Boeing, live in Mesa. Residents of the United States for more than thirty years, they are devotees of Papa Ramdas, who come to India every couple of years, and have just arrived at the ashram.

Umisha wants my Phoenix contact information. Telling them that I live near the Arizona Biltmore, when she asks for my phone number, I realize there is none to provide her. Too complicated to explain having no home, no car, no phone number, and no life in the United States for all intents and purposes right now, all I have is an e-mail address.

We three women are yakking it up when Dining Hall Lady motions that it is time to leave. Soon, Umisha's husband Raj joins us, and we continue chatting on the way out. They have just come from the north, having visited the sources of three sacred rivers, including the Ganges, and say that it was an amazing trip. Tomorrow, they go to a fourth: Kaveri, the river by the Saccidananda Ashram that I nearly missed seeing. Apparently, there are seven major sacred Indian rivers. I remain impressed that their Hindu faith, like with so many Indians, dictates their vacation or yatra. As I leave them all, Bhanu is still visiting with Raj, speaking in Tamil. It is a fun, fortuitous meeting.

Earlier in the day during chanting at the Bhagvan Hall, a lady pulls me aside and indicates that she knows me from the Shantivanam ashram. Her English isn't good so we can't communicate well, but that I understand. How wild to have these two coincidental meetings in one day.

FRIDAY, JUNE 22, 2012

I spend a lovely day, chanting, meditating, and reading. Udaar tells me to go meet Swamaji, what Swami Muktananda is called, who is in his office. Showing me the way, a gentleman waves me in. Swamaji is sitting at a small table with a laptop in front of him. He asks how I learned about the ashram and if I have been there before. Essentially, I have a private dharsan with him for twenty or thirty minutes. A powerful meeting, I become very emotional listening to him.

He explains the basics of Papa's teachings—that by chanting the name of God (here it is Ram, but it can be God or Jesus or whatever one chooses), eventually one hopes to get a glimpse of peace and harmony. Meditating and doing service are the other cornerstones of the teachings.

Talking about what "spirituality" is, he explains that it is comprised of one's entire life, from awakening in the morning and continuing throughout one's day until going to bed, including dealing with one's family and with honesty and integrity in one's profession. He explains: One's interactions with others define our spirituality. We are all manifestations of God. Simply, he says, "God is love." This is what I believe, and his comments resonate deeply with me. Tears run down my face as he speaks. The message is simple; the goal is trying to live one's life in that way.

I am reading Papa Ramdas' interesting autobiography. Like so many stories about the histories and journeys of India's enlightened holy men, his is also fascinating. Originally named Vittal

Rao, an educated man, he lived the life of a householder with his wife and one daughter, working in the textile industry. Having struggled with many ordeals, including a failed business, many debts, and an unhappy life, he began to chant Ram, a name for God, and not only found comfort, but bliss.

This led to him giving up his family life in the 1920s and taking the ochre robes and the name Ramdas, which means "servant of Ram." He then wandered through India in ecstasy for four years, visiting holy places and shrines. The letter of renunciation that he wrote to his wife is included in the book. During his travels, he too came upon the legendary Ramana Maharshi in Tiruvannamalai.

The Ram chant, which Ramdas chanted, is the mantra Gandhi chanted as well; it was on his lips when he was assassinated. Giving his life to Ram, Ramdas saw everyone as Ram and every directive as coming from Ram.

Papa's very intriguing book details this journey from Mangalore, around the south of India, up throughout the country and back home. Ramdas became enlightened only from chanting this mantra. Hence, this is the only spiritual practice at this ashram. There are no Hindu gods or idols, no statues, just photos and life-sized cutouts of Papa and Mother, who was his primary devotee and who he also helped reach enlightenment from chanting.

SATURDAY, JUNE 23, 2012

After returning from chanting and arati and finishing Papa Ramdas' autobiography, despite there still being some mosquitoes in my room, I fall asleep, but not for long. At 3:27 a.m.—the time I know because I look at my watch, hoping against hope, that *it really is not the middle of the night*—I am awakened by very loud voices of several people and the noise of beds being dragged around.

More new neighbors are moving in next door. Wouldn't you think they might guess folks around them might be asleep and make some attempt at being quiet? No, I have discovered that Indians are utterly oblivious to the concept of being quiet in consideration of others who might be asleep. And obviously, the ashram is a twenty-four-hour joint with people arriving at all hours.

Thinking that this is too incredible, soon, the fan stops running as well. Oh, why not a power outage too? Having no fan translates to there being no muffling of noise whatsoever. One can hear every word, every sneeze, every belch, every cough, and every deep cackle of the throat preparing to spit. Soon, cows start mooing. My room is not far from the goshala (cow barns), and sometimes, I hear them; other times, depending on the winds, I smell them.

Now wide awake, my thoughts wander to pondering why cows moo anyhow. Is it because they are contented (that's what I think)? Or because they are unhappy? Or hungry? Or are they talking to each other at 3:30 in the morning? Having lived around cows on farms as a youngster, I probably should know that, but then again, wondering why cows moo probably was not an earth-shattering query for a kid to research.

Then my thoughts drift to whether these people are planning to sleep or if they are up for the duration. If it is the latter, then obviously, so am I. Should I get up and write? Lying awhile, trying the best earplugs I have with pillows over my head, I chant Ram Nam. I cannot imagine life in India *sans* earplugs, that's a certainty! Actually, being deaf in India wouldn't be such a terrible malady.

Feeling exasperated and achy, I remember Ramdas' stories read just prior to falling asleep. As he wandered India for those four years, he often traveled with other sadhus. Each time there was adversity, from freezing temperatures while sleeping outdoors to mosquitoes eating them alive to wild boars rambling about, he simply considered everything as Ram's wish or gift.

Realizing that I may as well accept this about my new neighbors, I start to laugh. I am receiving my own personal lesson from Papa full-force in my face, right here and now in his own ashram. If part of my quest in India is to become a better, less judgmental and more accepting human being, this is a premier lesson. It is the perfect reminder of how much easier it is to "talk the talk" than "walk the walk" or however that little adage goes.

Heading to the bathroom, in my half-dazed sleep, I fail to lock the door fully and one of the newcomers starts to walk in on me as I sit on the john. Whatever, my pride and dignity are slowly eroding. Deciding that if I desire any more shut-eye for the remainder of the night, I need to take a half ambien tablet and pile pillows on my head, lo and behold, after about an hour, it becomes silent; my neighbors are asleep. I rejoice in the silence. Awakening at eightish, there is no noise next door; obviously, the miracle drug is effective.

In town today, I buy a few items in a supermarket for my train trip. Although Bhanu says the ashram will pack food, it will simply be one more item to carry, so I would rather not bother, despite it certainly being a nice gesture. Continuing to be amazed, over and over, at how absolutely delightful and helpful everyone here is, one of the three tenets of Papa Ramdas' philosophy is providing loving service in your daily lives. It is personified in every aspect of this place. Being of service is something I know must be a part of my remaining years on this planet.

Upon arriving at the travel company, I am happy to discover that Business Head Sanjay has my hotel confirmation. Chatting a bit, I learn that his wife is expecting their first child in one month, that he is Hindu, and that his home is in another place, a short distance away. When I leave, he shakes my hand vigorously for a long time. I like him a lot. Again, the level of service and hospitality is unparalleled.

Barely making it back to the ashram in time for lunch, I take a bus—one of the real ones, the local, brightly-colored vehicles with people packed in like sardines. It's a riot! Jam-packed, I stand holding on to the overhead bar. The total trip, from town until drop off at the ashram road, takes about twenty minutes. This is a good first local bus excursion for me—short and to a destination I know. The money collector/ticket issuer speaks good English and kindly ensures I don't miss my stop. The price is six rupees, about ten cents, compared to forty-five for a rickshaw. I take some photographs inside the bus indicating how crowded it is. Indian buses are always painted in vibrant colors and interesting designs, and this one is no exception.

Attending Swamaji's satsang again today, it is interesting. Yesterday, it is a PowerPoint presentation and series of little homilies and stories. Today's is entirely different and is a talk about chanting—the importance of making it about acknowledging God and not just a parroted routine, how to keep thoughts from cluttering the chanting, and the like. Afterward, I stop by the Bhajan Hall to listen to the children chant, a daily afternoon occurrence. They are so cute and intense.

This ashram is not in the least commercially oriented. There is a book stall, which is open occasionally at irregular times, and manned by Krishna. A tall, very kind, distinguished, bearded older fellow, he is often asleep on the front railing. Loving Krishna the first time I enter the store, he has been at the ashram for more than forty years. Running the book stall is his seva (his service), and he explains that his parents worked at the ashram and that Papa educated him. I have spoken with many, many employees who have been here for decades and received educations provided by the ashram.

Available in various languages are books written by Papa, Mother, and Swami Satchidananda, Ramdas' successor. The prices are dirt cheap—in the range of forty, sixty, and eighty cents, and the place is cluttered from floor to ceiling with old boxes. Stacked outside the door is another six-foot pile of little pink boxes, which, of course, are usually damp and shriveled-looking.

A couple of days ago, I notice a new fellow at chanting. From his mannerisms, jewelry, haircut, and clothing, I guess him to be from Mumbai or Delhi. One evening after chanting, Prasad is distributed at the door on squares of newspaper—interesting serving plates—and the man and his wife are standing nearby.

Striking up a conversation, I learn that they are indeed from Delhi and have been to California where their daughter had gotten her PhD. Her father cannot remember the place, but says that he loved California and was struck by how much room there was compared to India, where he says that unless you go to the jungle, there are no open spaces. Having traveled now through two states by car, I certainly have seen lots of open spaces, but I say nothing.

Indicating that I plan to head to Delhi, they say the weather is abominably hot now and will be miserable for a couple of months. Mentioning that I might be there in September, the woman says that it will be tolerable then. Relying on counsel from these locals, I immediately decide to head further north first and finish my Delhi/Agra/Varanasi stint in September. Varanasi is very, very hot too, probably even more so than Delhi. Spending my birthday at the Taj Mahal in mid-September would be incredibly memorable.

Before coming to India, one of the things that attracted me is that everything in India is sacred whereas nothing is in America, except seemingly money and material things. I am struck both by the multitude of people who come to this ashram annually or more frequently to tend to their spiritual needs, spending their vacations in this manner. The Delhi couple come alternate years and have been devotees of Papa for fifteen years. Travel to spiritual places and pilgrimages are also very important to Hindus and Buddhists.

The Nityananda Meditation
Caves and a Beautiful Beach
Town in Goa

My ARRIVAL IN India was two months ago on April 25. What a trip it has been thus far! "Indescribably" Incredible India would be my added descriptive adverb.

In talking with one of the Reception Gents, I mention having taken my first bus trip. Casually, he mentions that one needs to be certain the bus is heading to Anandashram because there is another ashram in the area also. Unaware of this (more of Kjos' not-so-great research), I need to add to my list of questions: "Are there any ashrams in the area?" Asking Reception Gent which one, he advises it is the Nityananda Ashram. Nityananda? I wonder which one.

Earlier in the trip, I sent an e-mail to the younger Nityananda (and received no reply), the Nityananda who along with his sister was appointed by Muktananda as the co-successor of the Siddha organization. An interesting, but sad, story, he later was thrown out by the sister, and now has his own ashram somewhere in India. I am quite certain that his place is in the north, but I decide to investigate. There are many "Nityanandas," including the flashy, Hollywood-looking one with an "h" in his name, who was recently caught in a sex tape scandal. That one has an ashram in Tiruv, but he certainly might have one here also.

Walking to an Internet café a half-mile away and Googling "Nityananda, Kanhangad," I discover the ashram is of *the real* original Nityananda, the guru of Muktananda. He was a very big deal saint. Realizing that I could have been minutes away and missed it, first I am bummed, but then realize that instead I ought to be grateful to have learned about it before leaving. The universe and my angels continue to direct me.

Deciding then and there that upon arising Sunday, I shall go to the Nityananda ashram. That morning, I see Rickshaw Driver Manoj, who comes daily to take a bath. He picks me up at 9:45 a.m.

What an amazing place it is. All ashrams are lovely and peaceful, this now being the ninth I have visited in India. And although each is different, they share a special serenity. First, I visit the samadhi site of Nityananda's successor, Gitananda. Nityananda died in 1963; Gitananda in 1982.

Then I come to the Mandir, where I am greeted by a kindly old fellow who immediately directs me into the meditation caves. Although there is now illumination in the caves, which were dug out in 1931, the power is out today, so he grabs a torch, and off we go.

This is why I came to India...for these kinds of experiences. Had I known this ashram and caves were nearby, I would have spent more time, possibly even have stayed here. There are forty-four mediation caves, all carved into one hill. Some are very small, but since most Indians are not very tall, they would be of adequate size. A labyrinth of several pathways in many directions with small caves on both sides, there is a breathtaking, powerful feeling inside. Photographs are allowed everywhere on the property, even in Nityananda's samadhi, but not in the caves. I can understand that proscription; the energy would definitely be affected.

There are lots of photographs throughout the property of Nityananda, but the iconic one of him sitting in only his dhoti with big belly and piercing eyes is the one I am familiar with. It is always fun to see photographs of the saints and sages as younger fellows. A constant fire burns in his samadhi site, causing the room to be very smoky. I notice in both his samadhi and later up at Guruvanam a suspended dragonfly. Not then sure of its significance, subsequent research indicates that the dragonfly symbolizes change and going beneath the surface to look for deeper meaning in life.

Stopping by a small office upon departing to buy a couple of books, the kindest fellow, who is the current ashram manager but not a Swami, tells me that Nityananda worked side-by-side with lepers digging out the caves. One reason my bags never lighten is the books added at every ashram.

The manager invites me to stay there anytime, telling me that it is free and that their rooms are very posh. Posh rooms? I wonder how "posh" is defined at an ashram. After leaving, I regret not having looked at a room.

The ashram manager also tells me about Guruvanam, "vanam" meaning forest in Hindi. Rickshaw Driver Manoj mentioned, but rather dismissed it as "being just a forest." After the manager's description of it being absolutely magnificent with water still running from the location where Nityananda caused it to commence decades ago, I must visit. Manoj has a family commitment at 11:30, but returns again for me later in the afternoon.

A little farther out, the scenery on the drive is indescribably gorgeous—green, lush forests, and grass with some water. Upon arriving, Manoj parks the rickshaw, saying that he will remain there, and directs me 400 meters up the road. It is a bit of a trek up a small hill, but speaking of "God's Country," this is it. It is easy to understand why everyone loves Kerala.

Writing about it now makes me weep; it is so amazingly gorgeous. And perhaps, what is more striking even than the exquisite beauty is the silence. When walking, I recall the many spiritual teachers who advise the importance of spending time in nature. In all directions, all I see are trees and trees and trees. This is the personification of God. I stop and say a prayer.

After ten minutes of walking, in a clearing ahead with a beautiful open-air temple is another shrine to Nityananda, tended to by a female sannyasin whose orange robe consists of a sari wrapped around her neck in halter fashion. She blesses me, gives me a flower, and I leave an offering. On the way up to the temple is a large tank with running water. This is the very spot where Nityananda caused the water to commence flowing and where it has continued to pour ever since.

After my blessing, the sannyasin points to the hill behind the temple, saying, "Swamaji's Cave." Little cut-out steps lead up to it. I only walk partway, but get close enough to see it and take photographs. Another very powerful spot, I am awestruck to be in the place where this famous saint meditated and lived. Asking Manoj on the way back more about the place, he tells me that it was the first place that Nityananda came. Spellbound, I am profoundly grateful for having seen both his ashram and this site.

Back for chanting and dinner, tonight is my final visit with Swamaji. Before everyone departs the ashram, he holds darshan with each guest. In our meeting earlier in the week, he asks my departure date, and when I say Monday, he replies, "Why so soon?" I only smile without giving a reply; it seems silly to say that I am leaving because it is so noisy and I cannot sleep. That same day he tells me to come back tonight at 6:30 p.m. Arriving a bit early, sitting outdoors to enjoy the magnificent grounds and take some last photographs, I wander to his office.

Crawling along the step out front is the same awful-looking worm creature that scared the daylights out of me a few nights ago. It must be a nocturnal animal. Watching it incredulously, wondering what the bloody thing is, a couple and a small child come out from Swamaji's office. Asking them, they look at me perplexedly, and the little boy of about age three doesn't even blink. They say, "A small snake, it's not poisonous," and walk off, gazing at me as though I am an idiot.

Seeing other people in his office, I stand and watch the little beast; it is no snake, it has little feet and inches along. Is this what a centipede is? I take a photograph. As I watch it, primarily to ensure it comes nowhere near me, an older Indian lady, walking barefoot, nearly steps on it. I cringe.

Seeing several sadhus near Swamaji's computer table where he sits, I remain outside, thinking that I shall wait my turn. But then a couple of others enter, and remembering Udaar told me just to walk in regardless of who is in the room, I enter and sit on the floor with a few other people in the back. Very animated, Swamaji finishes up with the sadhus, handing them brightly colored bags and books. All are laughing. It is a tender, loving scene.

After the sadhus leave, he motions me up to his desk. He is like the Godfather, seeing everyone, interacting with, and touching us all individually in a special way. Some come to him for advice and counsel, others for darshan. Everyone departs with Prasad and gifts. Upon sitting down, he says something like, "This is it, huh?" and I laugh. He is very charismatic and has an amazing voice when chanting. Asking if he knows who James Earl Jones is; he does not. Explaining that he is a famous American actor, I say that he is "the James Earl Jones of swamis, that his voice is amazing, and that if he ever makes a chanting tape, I want it."

Telling him that my experience at the ashram has been phenomenal, thanking him, and handing him an envelope with my donation, he asks me to write my name on the outside of the envelope. Asking if "Jai" in the chant means "victory," he confirms that it does. He further explains that God is unseen, a presence, inanimate, and everywhere, in everything. We are all of God, a philosophy that I believe and accept, saying that is the reason there are no idols at this ashram. He quickly adds that such an approach is fine, it just wasn't Papa's teaching.

Asking me when I am leaving, I tell him seven the next morning. He says that I should go to the kitchen for breakfast before I leave; he is the third person to mention this. They don't want us leaving hungry. He then hands me a small white cloth bag, saying, "Something for you to eat and something for your soul." Explaining that this saint's work is very good, he gives me two books by Viboda, someone I know nothing about, but learn that he took up Gandhi's mantle after his assassination. Confirming that he already has given me a copy of *Peace Pilgrim*, he asks if I have Papa's books; I tell him that I have bought some. "Hari Om," and I am off.

I am again very moved by my encounter with him, his genuine warmth and kindness, and this special send-off. When I return to my room, in addition to the books, Swamaji has included a couple of Anandashram pamphlets, and in my Prasad bag, are two apples, two packages of biscuits, a bag of banana chips, a small bag of sweets, and a packet of vibhuti, which I shall treasure always.

Wanting a good night's sleep before my 6:00 a.m. alarm, I am in bed by ten. Trying a new strategy of moving my bed away from the wall of my neighbors' room, where currently five men and a woman are staying, cranking up the ceiling fan, and inserting earplugs, my prayer is for good slumber. Gratefully, the coughing, belching, and talking cease a bit after ten so I do fall asleep.

But alas, a full night's sleep is not meant to be. Today at 4:00 a.m., it is the beloved cows who awaken me. Occasionally, I hear them, but they have never awakened me in the middle of the night. Turning up the ceiling fan speed, securing my earplugs more tightly, chanting Ram Nam...nothing works. And the cows are not just mooing; it's a cacophony of loud, continuous bellowing.

Is the universe telling me to get up and meditate? I would rather get eight hours of sleep though. Recalling a sign at the cow shed that says, "Please no visiting during milking times: 5-6 a.m. and 3-4 p.m.," I hope when the milking starts at five, their bawling ceases. Perhaps the cows are lonely or their bags are weighing them down. What am I now? A vet or a cow shrink? Thankfully, finally, the noise subsides about five, and I sleep a bit. Then it commences again. Looking at my clock, it is 5:45 a.m. Giving up, I get out of bed.

Today, upon leaving, my feelings are a mixture of sadness and happiness. Another very, very special place, despite the noise and critters, I would return in a heartbeat. It is good for this spoiled Westerner to have some trying moments.

Very punctual, Rickshaw Driver Manoj arrives at 7:00 a.m. My 8:10 train, the Magdar Express (I love the names of the trains), departs a bit late at 8:30 and arrives in Mangalore, in the state of Karnataka at approximately 10:00 a.m. Still carrying two backpacks, my large wheeled suitcase, and my wonderful daily bag, there is no porter around today. One backpack is water and train snacks and Swamaji's gift.

Having schlepped them all today—up twenty-six steps and down twenty-six more—yes, I counted them—from my arriving platform to a different departure one, I vow to lighten my load. I keep tossing things or sending them back, but my laptop, India guidebook, and *Nirvana* guidebook alone weigh a lot. Those I cannot part with.

With no idea how to locate my car, I check with the information center. One doesn't have much time for a five-minute stop, and with my luggage, I easily could run the entire length of a long platform if waiting at the wrong end. The fellow is very helpful, showing me the area to wait. With two and a half hours to kill and guesstimating the approximate spot, I set up my wheeled bag as a hassock and pull out my laptop.

Hearing announcements for my train, which is to leave at 12:50 p.m. for the Canacona Station in Goa, I see many people boarding a train that has been sitting there for some time. It is now approximately 12:15. Could this be my train, sitting in front of me the whole time? I assumed that it would pull into the station at 12:50, whereupon we would all board. Asking someone, I discover that indeed, this is it.

This is a sleeper car in class 2AC, with each compartment seating four people. We each have a berth; mine is a lower one. Train Man comes through during the trip to check one's ticket. During the day, one sits on the seats, which convert into beds at night. For nearly two hours into the trip, both sides of my compartment are empty, so I move across the aisle where there is a laptop/phone charger. A most enjoyable trip, the time passes quickly.

Not thinking I would be too keen about overnight trains and sleeping with strangers, now having taken this, I would feel comfortable traveling at night. There are curtains that may be pulled across the berths, separating them from the aisle.

The state of Goa is tiny. Known for its party scene, it is a hot traveling spot for foreigners and vacationers. The state of Karnataka, which we pass through, has oodles of rice paddies. Rice production is also Goa's largest source of revenue. Given the amount of rice eaten in this country, most likely, there are rice paddies everywhere. Rice, tea, and spices are staples of the Indian agrarian community. En route, are lots of waterways and still very green and lush. I envision this being similar terrain as Vietnam, Thailand, and Laos.

Train Fellow informs me that the next stop is mine, so I decide to move my luggage to the door and wait for the station. The breeze is cool, beautiful, and refreshing. Standing at the open door and looking out the right-hand side of the car, which is the side where the last stops have been, I watch massive numbers of colorful trucks on train cars. Although the train is stopped, it never crosses my mind that we are sitting in the station. Duh, for some reason, in my semi-blissed out stage, thankfully, I do turn around to indeed discover we are at the station, and the door on the *other side* is open to the platform. Not knowing how many minutes we have been sitting there, I quickly drag out my bags. Calling this "ashram brain," I now add it to both "aging" and "blonde" as excuses for being so spaced out.

The Canacona Rail Station is near Chaudi, the hamlet closest to the beach community of Palolem Beach. Surprisingly, there is only one rickshaw driver at the station, and he quotes me a very high price. Knowing the hotel is closer to the station than the last ashram was, I haggle a bit and get him to drop it twenty rupees. Unfortunately, negotiating is part of the process with drivers trying to take advantage, knowing that especially foreigners have no idea what is a reasonable rate.

Arriving at the Oceanic Hotel, a young, cute employee, Anil, is just arriving and asks if I am staying there. He grabs my heaviest bag, lugging it up two flights of stairs, first to the check-in desk, which also serves as the bar and entry to the dining room, and then up to my room. Manager Sujeesh too is a very nice fellow. I am the only guest at the six-room hotel.

My room is compact with a bed, wardrobe, two small side tables, and a small LG flat screen television. Owned by Germans, it is well-appointed with pretty linens and draperies. It is nice to have a real bed and my own bathroom again with theoretically, at least, hot water. On two occasions, it has been lukewarm; another time, it is scalding hot. When I ask Sujeesh about it, he gives a typically Indian convoluted explanation—something about the solar storage unit, electrical system, and monsoons. Whatever, it is fine; I am very comfortable here.

Having noshed on snacks on the train, I haven't eaten a real meal since 6:30 a.m., when I stop by the ashram dining hall for idlies before leaving. Inquiring about food availability, Anil says there is a restaurant in the hotel. What is available, however, are pool snacks and a few sandwiches. Ordering a tuna sandwich on whole grain bread, it suffices and is tasty. There is a cat in the restaurant, purring away. I inquire if the cat lives here and am told yes. Cats in a restaurant...why not, right, this is India. I only hope that Hotel Pet isn't on the kitchen counters (haha, of course, it is) and that there is no cat hair in my food.

I spend the day doing yoga, writing, checking e-mails, and researching future travel plans. There is free Wi-Fi in my room, something I have not had anywhere other than at the service apartment in Chennai. Even at the luxurious Le Meridien, there was no Wi-Fi in the room, unless paying additionally for it. Since it rains heavily most of the morning, it is nice to accomplish these tasks.

Later, when there is a break in the weather, I ask Anil how to get to the beach. His English is pretty choppy; in classic helpful Indian fashion, first, he tells me to go down the road to the left, or if I want, I can go to the right. Needless to say, I am hopelessly confused so I seek out Manager Sujeesh for better directions. Finally, after asking four more people as I walk toward the ocean, I find it.

Having read that some Goa beaches are filthy and defeca-tion-strewn, this one, Palolem Beach, is not. I later learn that it is considered to be the nicest beach in Goa, another serendipi-tous finding.

Bordering on the Arabian Sea, it is beautiful. There is some-thing magically calming about any large body of water. Looking down the sandy beach and out to sea, I could be in California. I remember my law professor Marcia O'Kelly (a role model and woman I adored, who was our only female professor) once com-menting how rejuvenative the sea is. Off in the distance are some islands, all covered with forests.

Taking lots of photographs, I walk a bit on the beach and into the water. A few people are playing in the water; at a seaside bar, others are having drinks. Since it is off season (as in both Tiruvannamalai and Kerala), it is very quiet. Suspecting that I wouldn't care much for the "drugs, sex, rock and roll" scene of high season, it is bucolic and quiet.

Upon arriving last night, I have similar reactions as when in both Pondicherry and Kerala. Knowing each place to be unique and having gotten glowing recommendations, I expect something more refined and charming, still *forgetting* this is India, a developing country, not a developed one. Therefore, although different from other parts of the country, in many respects, nevertheless, each location is replete with ramshackle shanties everywhere, the same jillion roadside stands selling identical merchandise, mounds of trash on the streets (although to some degree less in Kerala and Pondicherry), cows meandering the streets, and lots of roaming dogs.

Driving into Goa, I remind myself of this again—that this is India, it is *not* Laguna Beach or Coronado Island or even Mission Beach. Yet, arriving today at the beach, the ambience is different.

This being a popular foreign travel destination, it is obvious from how people greet you. All are very pleasant, saying hello, but happily, few ask the "what country?" question. And the dress—even that of the locals—is more diverse. Many young boys sport jeans rolled up below their knees, like clamdigger pants, and some Indian men wear shorts. A few women are in Western-style clothing. There are many more foreigners, several blondes even.

Finding a darling restaurant for an early dinner, Cheeky Chapatti's, it is partially open air, but sufficiently covered to provide shelter from the rains. A bit funky with lots of character, it reminds me of a spot one might find in Venice Beach or other California beach town. My vegetable curry with paneer is *to die for*, running in close competition with Ifran's food in Tiruvannamalai.

In addition to yummy food, I never have seen a restaurant check presented in such a clever manner. Forget the black faux leather folder, little silver tray, or other common variations. The check is inserted in an old copy of a small book titled *Why Men Can Only Do One Thing at a Time and Why Women Never Stop Talking.* I think it is absolutely brilliant—skimming through it to get a laugh. Wondering if they have many copies of the same book or different volumes to present the check, regardless, I love the idea.

My All-Time Favorite Indian Tale Thus Far

A MORNING IN GOA without rain, this is unusual. It is pretty likely that a deluge is forthcoming, however, since it has rained every day. With a break in midday during the last two days, I walk on the beach. The hotel where I am staying is charming. There are two flights of stairs up to my room, and lovely potted plants and Buddhas are sprinkled throughout the property. Outside my room is a little seating area, with plastic sheeting covering the walkway for monsoon protection.

Within an hour, the downpour commences. Sometimes, it is brief; other times, it lasts for hours. Finding the rains refreshing, the temperatures too are delightful. Everyone has major rain gear. Guys on motorcycles or scooters are decked out in complete head-to-toe hooded jackets and pants. One fellow rides a bicycle while carrying an umbrella. Laughingly, I think about using an umbrella, having used the bright pink one purchased in Tiruvannamalai more than I have used one in nearly three decades of living in Phoenix. There, usually the odd time I needed one, perhaps two days a year, I could never even find it.

A couple of days ago, seeing an older chap wandering around and recognizing the Harley Davidson logo in a foreign language on his t-shirt, I comment on it and learn that he, Dan, is from Seattle. The language is Thai so I ask to take a photograph of him to send to my brother, who is both a Harley driver and has lived in Thailand. Quite the chatterbox, I learn that he has traveled extensively all over the world, largely in Asia, for more than thirty years.

With my *Lonely Planet* guidebook and notepad in hand, I take a rickshaw in the rain to Cheeky Chapatti's to eat and do some research. Excited to have an omelet with garlic, feta, and thyme, it is delicious. Today's check is charmingly presented in a different old book. Shortly after sitting down, in wanders Seattle Dan, asking if he may join me. He too is carrying his *Lonely Planet* guidebook with the same plan in mind of working on his itinerary. Within ten minutes, a lovely British woman, Patsy, whom Seattle Dan has already met, arrives with her hostel guidebook in hand, hysterically, with the same objective.

But none of us does any trip planning. Instead we gab, with Seattle Dan mostly holding court. He is quite the smoker, telling us that he smokes hashish three to four times daily and has come to Goa with the objective of completing one item on his bucket list—to smoke hash on the beach in Goa. He must have indulged recently because he literally talks non-stop, barely pausing to breathe. I thought hash made you mellow and relaxed, but apparently not. Spending one's life stoned seems a waste to me, but to each his own, I guess.

To get a reprieve from the chatter, when the rain stops, I simply get up to leave, announcing that I want to enjoy the beach and sea. Or as Dad would have said, "Make hay while the sun shines." Raju, a kindly travel agent across the street with whom I spent a fair amount of time yesterday discussing possible itineraries, is in the office, so I pop in.

After considering various routes, I decide to head northerly to Pune and then on to Dharamsala/McLeod Ganj. Not having any real interest in going to Mumbai since big cities are not my focus on this trip, happily, I learn that there are flights from Pune, which is not far from Mumbai, to Dharamsala via Delhi.

Ergo, the next legs of my journey are set. Tomorrow, I shall take a taxi up north to Old Goa and Panaji to do some exploring. It is very reasonably priced, about $40, to hire a cab and driver for the day. Then the driver will drop me in Margao, located north of here, at the main train depot. From Margao, I shall take my first overnight train to Pune, spend two nights in Pune, fly from Pune to Delhi, and on to Dharamasala, arriving on July 2.

Contemplating my time left in India—still nearly three months—I may stay in Dharamsala for a month. The marvelous energy and Buddhist spiritual sites should be delightful. Melissa from Tiruv has given me names of some guest houses and apartments recommended by her friend Joe, who apparently goes regularly to McLeod Ganj.

Phoning his first recommended property, the kindly Mr. Arjun says that because I am a friend of Joe (I don't mention that I have never actually met the guy), he will make arrangements for me to stay for the whole month. Apparently, someone is leaving about the time I arrive, or possibly I may have to stay somewhere else for a couple of nights. He is most hospitable and pleasant.

I am thrilled. From the Web site, his property looks magnificent with views of the Himalayas and forested areas, and it is only a ten-minute walk from the main center of town. The monthly tariff is a whopping $200 US dollars, less than $7 per night, for a month.

Since Dharamsala/McLeod Ganj is close to both the state of Kashmir and city of Amritsar, the locale of the famous Sikh Golden Temple, I can travel to either or both from there. McLeod Ganj, where the Dalai Lama has his residence and the exiled Tibetan government is located, is a few kilometers from Dharamsala. There is a big celebration for His Holiness' birthday on July 6, and I will be there for that.

British Patsy and I meet yesterday for both dinner and lunch. At lunch, she essentially invites herself along on tomorrow's trip to Panaji and Old Goa, not asking if I mind and adding that she doesn't have much money, which apparently means she doesn't intend to pay half of the taxi fare. Whatever, different people have varying approaches I guess. I am sure we will get along well.

Last night, to fall asleep, I turn on the television, the first I have seen since Chennai. Just like in America, there are more than 100 channels, but little of interest to watch. Having seen no news since arriving in India, I watch BBC and learn about Queen Elizabeth's handshake with the IRA leader, floods in Bangladesh, and fires in Colorado. I also hear about the arrest of a leader of the Mumbai Taj Hotel terrorist attacks and the election of a new Egyptian President of Egypt.

Regarding television, turning it on my first night in Chennai, I discover that there is a Fox Crime channel in Europe and Asia running nonstop crime dramas, including *Law and Order*, *CSI*, and others I am not familiar with. *The Mentalist*, *White Collar*, and some James Bond movies are on other channels. There are at least two cricket sports channels (Indians are crazy about cricket) as well as a plethora of other sports channels, BBC, CNN, and several channels with infomercials selling products similar as in the United States. But there are no Fox News or golf channels.

Having already had many authentic Indian experiences, firsts in India, and a multitude of great stories and memories in two months, last night's, however, receives my *Top Indian Story Yet* designation. Patsy and I dine at Casa Fiesta, about a twenty to twenty-five minute walk from my hotel. Wandering down that way early to return a couple of damaged items purchased from a shop, pick up t-shirts being appliqued, and search for a box for another shipment home, I also have a couple of guidebooks for Patsy to peruse.

Successfully having found a cardboard box, as I walk back to my hotel after dinner, I am carrying it. Having tossed one guidebook in the box instead of my backpack, I decide to stop en route to move it to the backpack in the event of a downpour, which can commence instantaneously and forcefully. My thinking is that if the box gets wet, so be it, but I want my book to remain dry.

Stopping at an outside table of a restaurant, the box is cradled under my left arm. I have pulled off my backpack and am placing the book in it. Suddenly, a man, who with a woman is standing at a house to my left, shouts loudly and begins gesticulating frantically. At the same time, I feel a gentle nudging, thinking perhaps it is a dog at my feet.

But it is not a dog. *Unbelievably,* one of the cows I have just passed on the road has sauntered up behind me, so surreptiously and stealthily that I neither see nor hear her. She is gently tugging the box from under my arm. The fellow yells for her to stop and starts toward the cow to retrieve it.

Not interested in getting into a tug-of-war with a hungry how-many-hundred-pound cow and finding this *the most* comical experience of my life, I laugh hysterically, telling the guy, "Oh, no, no, please let her have it." With no resistance and her mission accomplished, the cow happily goes on her merry way, dragging along and chomping away on her box! Oh, for a photograph of that little incident. I chuckle all of the rest of my walk home. Welcome to India! I wouldn't exchange these crazy, yet precious, moments with anyone for anything. Going back to America is likely to seem pretty mundane by comparison, I fear.

Picturesque Old Goa
and My First Overnight Train

Tomorrow is Nick's wedding; actually in the United States, due to the twelve-hour time difference, it is the day after tomorrow. My little brother is getting married. Single for fifty-five years, this is a big deal. Athough sorry that I am missing it, at least his other two sisters will be there to celebrate with them.

Today is spent up a bit farther north in Old Goa and in nearby Panaji, or Panjim. Taxi Driver Damin is great, not in the least talkative, but knowing exactly where to take us and the major attractions to visit, obviously having done the trip many times.

Nick e-mails, having gotten quite a kick out of my experience with the "attack cow" as he calls her. Having lived in Pakistan eons ago, he more than anyone reading my journals can relate to life here. Successfully obtaining a replacement box after my cow-snatching incident, yesterday I race into Chaudi around 3:45 p.m. for the linen box wrapping routine. However, I learn that the India Post Office parcel posting counter is open from only ten until two. Great; new post office rules. Therefore, today on our way to Old Goa, we stop at the Margao post office.

Happily, I now have pared down, carrying *only* my purple wheeled bag (the bloody thing weighs a lot even when empty though), and one, instead of two, backpacks. So that is major progress. Actually, Patsy, who is at least 5'10" tall, carries a few smaller bags and an enormous backpack the size reminding me of Mt. Everest-bound mountaineers. The thing is probably as heavy as my wheeled bag. Ergo, after seeing her bags, I don't feel so embarrassed by mine.

Never in my life have I managed to travel truly "lite" with only one bag, but I would love, someday, to conquer that weakness. Always marveling at people able to do that, certainly, one of the tricks is a willingness to wear the same clothes *ad nauseum* and live *sans* some daily comforts. Recalling when all Nick carried from one end of the globe to the other was a giant canvas knapsack-like bag, it still amazes me. He actually packed lots into it, including thrilling gifts for family from exotic faraway lands.

But then, guys don't need the girl stuff and products that we do, and living in the same jeans and shirts for weeks on end seems easier for the male gender. Of course, still not even owning a pair of blue jeans, I may never master the 'one-bag travel' drill.

Proudly, though, I exist without curling irons, blow dryers, or hot rollers and with limited jewelry and makeup. So that simplifies life and lightens one's luggage. Believing a leopard's spots don't change, however, I cannot envision ever becoming a hippie-like granola girl. After this many decades, I likely am doomed to requiring some girlie goods and styles.

But I badly digress. Apparently, back in the day, the prior capital city of Old Goa competed with Lisbon for being *the* hot spot, and its population in the 1500s exceeded that of both London and Lisbon. Now, a sleepy little place, charming and lovely, the main sightseeing destinations are several churches. Since Goa was colonized by the Portuguese, the churches are Catholic. Most of India is overwhelmingly Hindu, except Goa and Kerala where Christianity is more prevalent.

We are able to enter several churches and cathedrals in Old Goa. Those we visit include: the Chapel of St. Catherine, which is more rustic and smaller; the Church of St. Francis of Assisi, with exquisite massive gilded, carved, and woodwork with murals of St. Francis' life; Se' de Santa Catarina Cathedral, the largest church in Old Goa in Portuguese style with a Gothic exterior, Corinthian interior, and an altar and paintings representing St. Catherine of Alexandria; and the Basilica of Bom Jesus, famous throughout the Catholic world for containing the tomb and remains of St. Francis Xavier, who spread Christianity among the Portuguese colonies in the East.

Although I enjoy the history and architecture of churches, after a couple of hours, it becomes repetitious, and my brain is on overload. One should probably institute a "three-churches per day" rule to truly appreciate them.

Heading the fifteen kilometers or so to Panaji, the current capital of Goa, we find a little local dive for an inexpensive lunch. It proves to be the first Indian food that I don't much like. I order something called upatta, which the restaurant chap describes as like pizza; unfortunately, it is essentially onions in a bread-like crust.

After lunch, we wander to the beautiful Church of Our Lady of the Immaculate Conception, a gigantic white and blue-trimmed structure located in the center of town. Still a functioning church, it is not open today, however. Then following a portion of a walking tour recommended in the *Lonely Planet* guidebook, we stumble upon cute shops, restaurants, great architecture of the street buildings, and an impressive, gigantic orange-colored Hanuman temple atop a large hill with many flights of steps to climb.

Running out of time, we are unable to linger in the temple, but take many wonderful photos. Finding Driver Damin at our taxi, Patsy throws a wee snit at a pay toilet for paying five rupees to pee, asking the attendant if he charges the locals the same price or gouges the tourists. I laugh. Five rupees is a pretty high urination tariff; usually, it's one or two. On our way to the train depot, we are both tired; it is a relaxing ride back.

Learning the rail system a bit better, there is a massive electronic board at this station, indicating the track location of each car once the train stops. Not seeing mine, thinking I am in 2 AC, I ask the nice information fellow and discover that I am in a different section. Incredibly helpful and probably feeling sorry for this doting American (one nice benefit of aging is that people do seem to take pity on you, and, of course, my Indian standards, I am an old lady), he leaves his office to show me the marker and precise location where my car will stop.

Patsy goes off to find an Internet café (she is blogging, doing Facebook, uploading photos, and the like), but I am happy to look for some vittles and rest a bit. Shortly before the train arrives, Patsy comes to say good-bye.

So I experience another Indian first—an overnight train trip—arriving in Pune at approximately 10:30 a.m. today, June 30. Raju, my Palolem travel agent, gets me a lower berth seat. On a future trip, however, I might experiment with an upper berth, where there would be a bit more privacy and less activity. The train leaves forty-five to sixty minutes late. Until everyone retires around tenish, we read, chat, and nap.

My Seatmate is a very nice fellow, an engineer—of course, every second male I meet is an engineer. Commenting on that, he explains the reason is that engineering is a very good career path, with people knowing they will find jobs even if not actually working as an engineer.

From Pune, Seatmate provides helpful suggestions about places to visit and answers some of my questions about the history and culture of India. I make note of some books that he recommends. For example, I have forgotten that Gandhi was assassinated by a Hindu who was unhappy about the partition of India. Gandhi always believed partition was a colossal mistake, and ultimately, his life was snuffed out in 1948, only one year after the British left India. Interestingly, Indira Gandhi was assassinated in 1984, remembering because of my mnemonic device of transposing numbers of the years.

A sweet shy woman, Pamal, who never speaks unless answering my question, is in the seat across from me. Another nice, younger guy, with whom I never speak, is in the berth above her. Happy for a lower berth and that my next sleeping mate is another woman, little do I know that at lights-out time, a game of musical berths is to ensue.

As people begin to prepare for bed, with no explanation, Pamal simply leaves her berth and is replaced by an Older Gent in his sixties or seventies. Great, I am to be in the same bedroom with a strange, older Indian man! Having noticed a similarly aged woman in the berth behind us, I assume her to be his wife.

In conservative India, it seems odd to have him sleep there, or is it because there are also two men in this compartment where the young girl would be? Who knows the reason. Actually, Older Gent is well-dressed, genteel, and kind, instructing me how to pull down the seat backrest for the bed. Happily, he also is quiet. I hear him snore a bit only once while awake during the night.

Another reason a single woman traveler might consider reserving an upper berth is if some chap opts to get friendly during the night, it is far likely to happen if she is in an upper bed. And guidebooks recommend against single women traveling in 1AC. It is a closed compartment shared with only one other person. And in this country, statistically, since Indian women rarely travel alone, one almost certainly would have a male companion, and be less safe from inappropriate advances.

In the morning, Pamal and Older Gent return to their original seats. Another possible explanation for the switcheroo may be that because Pamal is younger, it is easier for her to crawl up the ladder to the upper berth. I simply should have asked her.

In the morning, Older Gent and I are the last to crawl out from under the covers. On overnight trips, the Indian Railway provides a set of sheets (the only place other than a five-star hotel that I have seen *two* sheets actually), a blanket, and a pillow. Gratefully the shouting Food Chaps don't commence their rounds until about seven.

One of the two Keralan young boys in the berths at the end compartment moves over to talk with me. Indians love speaking with Westerners and Americans in particular, it seems. After the usual questions of "name," "what country," and "what do you do there?" he tells me that his brother works in Austin, Texas. He and his travel companion are off to Pune to start new jobs on Monday with an auto manufacturer. Of course, they are engineers—mechanical—who have just finished their bachelor's degrees.

Very pleasant and well-mannered, he explains, in answer to my questions, that most engineering students get their BS degrees, work a year or two, and then go on to get their master's degrees. The most common places to take their master's studies are Australia, Great Britain, and the United States.

Laughing to myself, truly *every* young man from Kerala is either an engineer or engineering student. Kerala does boast the highest literacy rate and education level in India. After selling my house in Phoenix and briefly sub-leasing an apartment from a young Indian fellow before leaving, a couple of his ASU buddies were helping him move, and I stopped by to collect the key. Telling them that I was going to India, they told me that I should go to Kerala, and specifically to Cochin. As it happens, I have done both. Inquiring what they were studying, one laughingly replied, "We're Indians from Kerala, we all study engineering!"

The Indian populace seems to be where America was in the '60s and '70s *vis-a'-vis* an emphasis on education. American college-aged kids, by comparison, have a much different philosophy about the importance, considering education more an entitlement than we did. Perhaps the reason is because today's US kids are so many generations removed from their immigrant ancestors, who strongly valued it.

To my surprise, I actually do get some sleep; however, taking overnight trains will not be particularly high on my must-do list again. A primary benefit, of course, is that one doesn't pay for a hotel room if traveling at night. It would be more enjoyable, I think, if traveling with a companion. Awakening a couple of times, thinking it pretty hot, I conclude the air conditioning is less effective than others I have traveled on.

The next day, when mentioning this, my Seatmate says the air conditioning was not working; I guess an engineer would know that. Sleeper class traveling with open windows would be more comfortable.

Day trains are more pleasant. First, one can actually enjoy the scenery, and second, sleeping on a train poses some challenges, such as sleeping in one's clothes, not having great toilet facilities, no shower, and feeling grungy upon awakening. Actually, my trips for remainder of my time in India will be relatively short, by comparison to this leg, and should easily be managed as daytime travel.

A Most Powerful Moment
of My Life and My Most
Poignant Yet in India

ARRIVING AT THE train depot in Pune is major sensory overload. This is the largest city I have traveled through by train. Crowded, noisy, confusing, and pretty overwhelming, standing amidst throngs of people with my large wheeled bag, another backpack, a cloth bag with food, and my day bag, I have no sense of which direction to go, where the actual train station is, the location of the street, anything.

Seeing no signs, I venture a guess as to which direction to begin walking. A couple of porters descend on me. The first looks drunk or stoned, so I say, "No, thank you" to him. Knowing that I can manage the bags myself, having one less and the other lighter than when I last schlepped them up and down flights of stairs, a porter may not be required.

About the time I notice more flights of stairs, similar as at the other station, another young red-shirted porter approaches me. Feeling more comfortable with him, he quickly wraps a red turban-like scarf atop his head and tosses my quite heavy wheeled bag up, balancing it on his head, and insists on grabbing my other two bags. Smashing, I am not carrying *that* bag on *my* head that's for sure. Quite the sight, I grab my camera, hoping to get a good shot of him ahead of me. Maneuvering through a morass of humanity, literally jammed with a body-to-body crowd, it is quickly obvious having assistance is an exceptionally good idea.

Again, there are two sets of stairs, one up and one down, so crowded I barely can see the porter ahead of me, having gotten stuck behind a lady struggling up the stairs with *her* bags. Only his bright red shirt and my large purple bag keep him within distant eyesight.

Train depots in India, at least in larger cities, are not for the faint-hearted. Grateful for the young porter's aid and well worth the 100 rupees, he delivers me to a rickshaw outside the depot in which he deposits my bags.

In answer to my query about hiring rickshaw drivers here, my Pune train Seatmate says that they all should use meters. What a refreshing change from haggling over every trip. But of course, this *is* India after all, so *should* doesn't necessarily translate to *will*, and why would one expect that protocol to be followed? Later, when checking into my hotel, Hotel Desk Clerk informs me that not only is it *the law* that drivers use meters, but there is a number to call to report someone who fails to use it. Of course, I know not whether any consequences attach to such violation.

Rickshaw Driver, where the porter delivers my bags, refuses to use the meter, so when he quotes me 200 rupees, I remove them. Knowing my hotel is a five- to ten-minute ride, his quote is an outrageous overcharge. After go-rounds with a couple more rickshaw drivers along the street, all who refuse to use meters, I begin walking down the street. Finally, I jump into one who quotes me 100 rupees.

Arriving at the Grand Hotel, which is far from "grand," Hotel Desk Clerk says the charge should only be fifty rupees. Then after checking the room, accepting and paying for it, I notice Rickshaw Driver still hanging around and ask why. Hotel Desk Clerk says he is waiting for his commission. *What?* In addition to double-charging me for the trip, he gets paid a commission to boot? Even though I booked the room myself, he receives an eighty-rupee commission from the hotel simply for dropping me there. What a system; apparently, the hotels all pay this to the rickshaw drivers. Gotta love India!

Although the room he shows me at the "Not So Grand Hotel" is pretty shabby and is nearly twice the rate listed on the Internet and in my *Lonely Planet* guidebook, Hotel Desk Clerk explains the rate I found for a single room has a community bathroom in the hotel lobby, and because drunks can use that bathroom, they don't give those to single ladies. Whatever.

But I feel rather stuck since I am only here for two nights, and I certainly have no interest in running around Pune with a rickshaw driver looking for another hotel. Really wanting to remain "unplugged" to the extent possible, wandering around in my own little zone, I remain determined not to have a cell phone. This, however, would be an instance where it would be helpful to call around to other properties.

Assuring me that there is hot water 24/7, the first thing I most want, after my all-night train ride, is a hot shower. Guess what, there is no hot water! Having quite vast experience—soon qualifying for some certificate of knowledge about Indian plumbing, I would think—on the intricacies, oddities, and perils, I try every knob, spigot, and faucet. There most definitely is no hot water, so I take a cool shower instead.

When later I go to the front desk, Hotel Desk Clerk assures me that there is hot water and says he will send Hotel Boy to show me how it works. Explaining that I have just taken a shower, and there is no hot water, "Oh, no, no," he says, "no hot water in shower, only faucet." Of course, silly me, why would anyone in her right mind assume that "24/7 hot water" might actually mean it would be dispensed through the shower head?

Tired, and experiencing another crabby moment, I tell him my assumption about what "24/7 hot water" means, explaining that where I come from, hot water pours from a showerhead. He launches into some typical, nonsensical prattle, a drill I am becoming accustomed to, about how this is a very good rate for a hotel in this area, yada, yada, yada. What that has to do with the price of tea in China, I have no idea.

Hotel Boy accompanies me to my room for a hot water demonstration. Ah, why did I not think to check the wall outside my room to see if a particular switch is engaged? Yes, *outdoors* and around the corner from my room. How foolish of me. Hotel Boy flips on that switch, and a light comes on which activates the hot water heater, a.k.a. geyser, hanging on my bathroom wall. Lights on the geyser come on as well. Next, he turns on the hot water faucet. Noticing a couple of drops coming out, I say. "Fine," and dismiss him, assuming that I have hot water.

Upon returning to my room in the evening, I decide to shower in Indian bucket fashion. However, not only is there *no* hot water, actually no water whatsoever flows from the purported hot water faucet. Traipsing outdoors again, I flip the same switch. It must take some time to fill up the geyser because a few hours later, plenty of hot water is available.

Since visiting the famous B.K.S. Iyengar Institute is my sole reason for coming to Pune and noting in my guidebook that it is closed tomorrow on Sunday, I decide to head there immediately. If I stay and rest in my room awhile, I fear falling asleep.

Why I am here at all is most interesting. Never had I ever contemplated coming to Pune (pronounced "poo na"). But over the past few weeks, I receive on several occasions, both while in meditation and on the mat, internal messages that I ought to go to Pune to pay tribute to Iyengar and that I will meet him. Knowing that my intuition, which I now understand is simply God speaking, is incredibly powerful in India, I never dismiss, or take lightly, any of those messages. The fact that it repeatedly comes up, especially causes me to pay heed.

Thinking it highly unlikely that I shall be fortunate enough to meet the illustrious yogi, paying homage to B.K.S. Iyengar, in and of itself, seems an important thing to do. A true genius and certainly *the most* famous yogi in the world, he is responsible for introducing hatha yoga to the western world.

And, in an indirect way, his work is the reason I am in India at all, my spiritual journey strongly intertwined with yoga. His books and those by his students were my bibles, especially the manual I call the red book—the one with photographs of yoginis in red leotards. All of my early yoga teachers were Iyengar-trained, and many were his direct students, including Sandra Summerfield Kozak, Rama Vernon, Judith Lasater, Elise Miller.

Very excited about my mission as I leave my hotel, I ponder how truly amazing it would be *if* I am blessed enough to get a glimpse of his eminence. Having no idea of his precise age, if he remains in good health, or if he even is still involved in the Institute's work, it matters not. I become misty-eyed merely contemplating that possibility, and feeling especially grateful to be in his town in India.

Luckily, just down the street, I find an older rickshaw driver. This is my new tack. Having noted several elderly drivers and assuming them more experienced, I seek them out. Indeed, he knows exactly where the Institute is.

Arriving in ten or fifteen minutes, I am moved to see the hallowed premises of this great man. A bronze bust of Mrs. Iyengar stands in front of the multistory, pleasingly pale pinkish-colored structure. The Institute, named for B.K.S.'s long-deceased wife, is called the Ramamani Iyengar Memorial Yoga Institute. Adorning the building's exterior are gorgeous, huge white plaster castings of Iyengar himself in various yoga poses, including Triangle and the Dancer.

In requesting entry, both the security guard and Other Employee inform me that the office is closed for lunch, with Other Employee pointing rather obviously to the sign, as if to say, "Lady, can't you read?" It indicates hours are from eight to twelve and four to six-thirty. He tells me to return at four o'clock.

Asking Other Employee about restaurants in the neighborhood, he glowingly recommends Charros. Wandering the direction he tells me to go, I stop at the large Toyota dealership on the corner, figuring car salesmen always know eateries in the area. There, I am advised that Charros is closed. With three hours to spend, I meander off, assuming I shall run into something in India, the land of a jillion food establishments.

Coming upon the Ambience Hotel, which looks moderately nice and a good place for a long, leisurely lunch, there are even several tables of women-only diners too, a real rarity. Managing to lollygag for a couple of hours, I eat and peruse my guidebook.

On my way back to the Institute, seeing several Western women in tights and leotards, I assume they are going to class. At the gate, they walk right through. Hoping to do the same, but Other Employee, now seated in the guard's chair, advises me that it is not yet 4:00 p.m. and that the office manager is still not there. Therefore, I must wait. That's fine; this is my only planned outing today.

Patiently and somewhat anxiously I sit for another thirty minutes on a small elevated ledge along the sidewalk, keeping a vigilant eye toward the gate with the thought that perhaps I shall be lucky enough to spot Mr. Iyengar enter the property. Later, having been inside the gate and Institute, I realize that his residence is located behind the Institute.

At precisely 4:00 p.m., Security Guard returns to relieve Other Employee, and both walk through the gate. Sensing that I am not being invited in, I follow them and inquire if the office manager is there yet. Told that this important person has arrived, Other Employee instructs me to sign in at a register book.

Other names signed above me are Liz with an address of Russia, Sue from Italy, and the like, so I similarly provide nominal information. Interestingly, all of them—many others enter as I wait—are Westerners with addresses of Italy, Russia, and France. Security Guard and Other Employee walk me to the door where I leave my shoes, and then escort me inside and upstairs to the office.

In the inner sanctum of perhaps the world's most gifted, and certainly the most influential, hatha yogi, I am mesmerized simply to be in *his* space. Essentially ignored by the few people about, I gaze at numerous glass-enclosed cabinets brimming with awards, honors, plaques, and photographs. Hanging on walls are a magnificent painting of him with a very large image of Hanuman and another beautiful, serene portrait.

Looking through a flip portfolio with photographs of a very young Iyengar performing poses, I recognize them from *Light on Yoga*, one of his early classics. A note on the portfolio indicates that orders may be placed for 8" x 10" copies as long as they are not used for marketing purpose. The photographs may be displayed in one's studio or practice space, and a disclaimer to that effect is to be signed.

After ten or fifteen minutes, with various students and teachers wandering in, one is familiar as having studied with in Tucson many years ago. This is exceedingly bizarre because earlier in the day when trying to recall the Iyengar-trained teachers I have studied with, there is only one name I cannot recall. It is likely selective memory because I didn't care much for his teaching style.

All I remember is that his first name is Dick and that he is from Texas. Recognizing a guy standing across a table from me wearing a Texas State cap, I ask his name, and it is him. I am *beyond* amazed. What is the likelihood that *the one guy*, whose name I have been trying to remember for some time, suddenly materializes in front of me. Chopra's "synchronicity" occurs over and over again here.

Assuming that a fellow sitting at a desk might be the infamous office manager, I introduce myself, telling him that I am from the United States, that all of my early yoga instructors were Iyengar-trained, and that I have come to pay my respects to Mr. Iyengar. He says to give him a few minutes, and he will show me around. Fabulous, I think; I am going to get a little tour. It is thrilling to think that I might see an asana room.

While wandering around, I notice the schedule of classes posted on a board. Iyengar's children, Geeta and Prashant, teach only a few of the regular classes, but there are several each day. Fees are based on several categories of students, one of which is for beginners. It's 900 rupees per month for one class per week (just a bit more than $4 per class; that's quite a contrast from US classes, which can run up to $20 apiece if paid for individually); 1,800 for two classes per week; 2,700 for three; and 3,600 for four. Rates for advanced are higher than beginning classes, and still another higher rate is charged for remedial classes.

Teachers are arriving for a teachers' training session. The waiting list to study at the Institute is several years, and only teachers who have studied with Iyengar teachers for many years are permitted the privilege of coming here. It is refreshing that he has maintained an integrity and high standards, unlike the Western mode now where one can become a yoga teacher in a brief time, simply by paying the course fees. It matters not in the United States, for example, in some programs if a yoga teacher even knows what Patanjali's yoga sutras or pranayama are. I have even met new yoga teachers who never had a personal asana practice before signing up for a teacher training program.

Soon, a sweet, older woman, Mrs. Jarin, who is setting books and CDs out on a table for purchase, calls my name and says, "Come with me." Beginning to follow her down a flight of stairs, she asks, "Would you like to meet Guruji?" *What! Is the Pope Catholic?* I am *really* about to meet Iyengar! I am in utter shock. "Of course, very much," I reply. On the short way down, she asks who my teachers were; the only name I get out is Sandra's, to which she says, "Fine, fine." Not knowing if she recognizes her or merely wants me to provide some name, I am overwhelmed with anticipation, which is brief because in less than a minute, we enter a room at the foot of the stairs.

To the left, in the flesh, is the "Lion of Pune," B.K.S. Iyengar, or Guruji, as Mrs. Jarin respectfully calls him, dressed in flowing, pristine white clothing. Sitting quietly at a small desk or table, there is a commanding, yet peaceful, elegance about him. In the room, seated at long tables, are several young Indians, I assume students or perhaps participants in a yoga teacher training program, whom I notice are reading one of his asana books. Thinking to myself, *I wonder if these young kids appreciate the man who sits in front of them—his energy, his genius, his passion, his gift?*

Mrs. Jarin drops to her knees, bowing to his feet, and hands him a book with an attached note. She then introduces me, and I do the same. This is one Guruji to whom I unhesitatingly and conscientiously can bow in abject homage. In Indian culture, the greatest tribute to someone is bowing to or touching a person's feet.

Telling him how honored I am to meet him, that my early teachers were all trained by him, and that I am here to pay my respects, I am so overcome to be in his presence, while speaking, I am moved to tears. He smiles endearingly, and says simply, "God bless you." It is simultaneously a very tender and powerful moment, one that shall remain forever ingrained in my heart and memory as one of the most poignant experiences of my life.

Mrs. Jarin ascends the stairs ahead of me, leaving me alone in the stairwell. I stand for a couple of minutes in tears, before regaining my composure and returning upstairs. Thanking her profusely, I tell her what a great privilege it is to meet him.

On her table are some wonderful color photographs of Iyengar, four or five different poses taken on his ninetieth birthday. She tells me that he is "ninety-four years young." Wondering if he still has an asana practice, I would imagine that he does. Having just seen him, I would never guess him to be that old. He is certainly a living testament to the benefits of yoga.

Deciding to buy a few for myself and as gifts for yogi friends, Mrs. Jarin tells me that if any I choose are not signed, Guruji will be happy to sign them. One I select is unsigned, so she asks me to wait a few minutes. Inquiring if I want to join her when she takes the photo to him, I, of course, do. So I have the rare privilege of seeing him again and thanking him. How very blessed I feel not only to meet him at all, but to experience his powerful energy twice. Each time since that I reflect on those moments, I weep.

Upon purchasing my photographs and a CD on the *Yoga Sutras*, I meet another Institute fellow, Datta, who is in charge of the book sales room. Another stop, a few more books to add to my luggage weight, and an amazing calendar later, I stop in the rest room, which is spotlessly clean, As I depart, I again thank Mrs. Jarin profusely.

While purchasing books, I notice a gorgeous calendar hanging on the wall and ask Datta if it is for sale. It is, and honestly, I've never seen anything quite like it. The photographs, taken by Datta's son, are breathtaking, showing small features of Iyengar in various poses. One, for example, is only of his feet; another shows just his hands; and one is only his back in shoulder stand.

After leaving the Institute, I am enthralled and in a complete daze. Ready for something to drink, I stumble upon a modern shopping mall just down the corner, the Pune Centre. Up escalators, the market and food court are on the fifth floor. Now, in this larger and more modern city (Pune is renowned as an educational center), the attire is much more casual and less conservative.

All of the kids could be living in the United States—wearing black t-shirts, blue jeans, tennis shoes, or sandals. Women's attire too is more diverse and far less conservative. They are, of course, still wearing saris or salwar kameez ("suits"), but many are in Western clothing, especially jeans.

Returning to my hotel, I have another classic Indian rickshaw experience. Despite giving the driver *both* the hotel's business card *and* map showing the precise location of the hotel with street names identified (and he can read English), he still is unable to find the hotel. This just reaffirms that rickshaw drivers in India don't know where *anything* is, except perhaps in their own limited area; the Institute is about seven kilometers from my hotel.

Ergo, three stops later to ask directions, we finally arrive at the hotel, and the trip costs thirty rupees more than the same ride to the Iyengar Institute. The rickshaw driver actually is very nice, however, apologizing profusely for the extra distance. Both rickshaw drivers today use their meters; however, I did pass up two at the shopping mall, who quote a fare and refuse to use meters.

Upon returning to my room, I keep crying aloud as I dance about, "I met Iyengar," "Oh, thank you, God, I met Iyengar," "I can't believe it, I met Iyengar," "I met Iyengar today," "I met Iyengar!" I feel like a little child who has seen Santa Claus for the first time or an adolescent meeting her rock star idol.

Assuming that the Taj Mahal will be amazing and impressive, meeting Mr. Iyengar certainly is the most incredible experience thus far for me in !ncredible India. And never shall I consider disregarding a strong intuitive message from God. Perhaps the other piece of this message is that I am supposed to teach yoga again. Aside from some private lessons, I haven't taught classes for awhile.

This always will be a most memorable day, one of the *most* ever in my life—the day that I met B.K.S. Iyengar! *And* the day of my baby brother's marriage. Okay, so he is far from being a baby, but he remains my little brother always. Realizing that June 30 actually is a day later where Nick is, nevertheless, the day shall be an important one in both of our lives, rather an international connection between two siblings.

Never did I really believe that I would meet the great yogi, who has had the greatest single influence on hatha yoga in the West. He is responsible for teaching thousands of teachers, who themselves have taught countless students around the world.

Analogizing the importance of Iyengar's contribution to the study, understanding, and teaching of yoga would be asking a lawyer which Supreme Court justice he or she most admires as having impacted jurisprudence in a powerful or important way, a William Douglas or a William Brennan perhaps. Or a physicist about the brilliant Steven Hawking. Or a Tibetan Buddhist about being in the presence of the Dalai Lama. Or a psychologist having been fortunate enough to meet Milton Erickson, Sigmund Freud, or Carl Yung. Or a golfer meeting Arnold Palmer (aren't I dating myself?) or Tiger Woods. A guru's guru, a master's master, a teacher's teacher.

SUNDAY, JULY 1, 2012

It is July 1 in India, but June 30 in the United States. This is Brother Nick's and Vicki's wedding day there. They must be so excited. I hope that they have a beautiful day and great celebration, and I send them good energy from afar. Nick sounds very happy in his e-mails. How very nice it is for him to find love later in life.

Inquiring about a city tour at my own hotel, Hotel Desk Clerk hands me a tourist-type pamphlet with a variety of information, but it is not what I am seeking. There are definitely disadvantages of staying at budget hotels.

So while lunching yesterday at the Ambience Hotel, I stop by the front desk and a fellow kindly shows me a brochure, saying they can arrange a car and driver for me. It is agreed that the driver will pick me up at the Grand Hotel today at 10:00 a.m., and I reconfirm that information with him at least twice. Seemingly an easy arrangement, after waiting fifteen minutes today and calling the Ambience Hotel, I learn that the driver is mistakenly waiting there for me.

While waiting for the driver and chatting with Day Hotel Clerk, he informs me that the airport, from where I depart tomorrow, is only seven kilometers away, that I indeed can take a rickshaw, and that it will cost 100 rupees. This is substantially different from what Hotel Desk Clerk Pedey tells me yesterday, claiming the airport is more than an hour away and I need to take a taxi. When I mention this to Day Hotel Clerk, he just shrugs his shoulders and says that perhaps he thought I meant the Mumbai airport. This is a perfect example of why one can never rely on only *one* source of information.

Now I am thoroughly confused. Do I listen to Hotel Desk Clerk Pedey or Day Hotel Clerk? While with my driver during the day, I ask him, and although his English is not great, I think he says that it is fifteen kilometers and that his charge would be 600 rupees. When responding that the amount seems high, he says he has to drive from his house.

Doing additional research on the issue, I walk to the rickshaw area not far from the hotel and inquire of three different drivers. The consensus of all three is that it will take a half hour, and the tariff is 200 rupees. Going to a nearby more upscale hotel, there the concierge says it is eleven kilometers and that 200 rupees is reasonable.

Feeling more comfortable about this information, on my way back to the hotel from dinner, I engage a rickshaw driver who assures me he will be at the hotel at 8:00 a.m. That prevents my having to walk down the street in the morning, find a driver, and haggle for the fare. But having a back-up plan in India is always a good idea; if he fails to materialize, I still have more than three hours until my flight leaves.

This hotel room, although disgustingly dirty (the blankets are absolutely filthy and I do not use them), otherwise, it's not that bad. My spoiled American friends probably would cringe at the place, but I've become pretty comfortable with lesser levels of comfort. At least, there is no noise whatsoever back by my room, and I sleep well. The pathetic paint, also filthy, I suppose could be described as having character. Most importantly, the ceiling fan works exceedingly well; no air conditioning is needed here either.

Both the entry and bathroom doors are old and dilapidated, and all windows and doors bear the requisite three sliding bolt locks apiece. But hands down, my favorite unusual aspect of the place is *once again* the bathroom. Next to the commode is a full-sized door which opens to the outdoors. There is a screen on the door, which I examine carefully to ensure there are no holes for animals or people to climb through. But how bizarre, a door outdoors from the toilet seat.

This morning, when exiting my front door (as far as I can tell, I am the only guest in the entire place), there is a young, good-looking guy fast asleep on the large lawn outside. Lawn Guest is lying on a mat, with a pillow and blanket, his sandals tossed off to the side. Needless to say, I am rather taken aback.

Another "India first," or first anywhere in the world for that matter. Did the guy have too much to drink and just pass out here? Is he staying here and decides to sleep on the lawn rather than in his room? Did his girlfriend or wife throw him out? Although amused, as a single woman, I am cautious, especially since he is right outside *my* room. He appears to be asleep as I depart.

Deciding to eat breakfast before leaving on my sightseeing outing, I sit on the patio out front and inform Day Hotel Clerk that I wish to order something. He yells for another employee to take my order. Ordering scrambled eggs and toast with butter (no jam here), it takes forty minutes before *only* the eggs are finally delivered. Knowing how long it takes to scramble eggs and seeing not another soul around, I have no idea what the delay is, other than this is India. I suspect that someone had to run out to purchase them.

Tasting them, they are awful. A huge plate of eggs—probably four to six eggs, doused with massive amounts of onions, other finely cut vegetables, and very, very spicy, they are pretty dreadful. I ask my server to remove them, and to skip the still undelivered toast and tea since my taxi is to arrive in five minutes anyhow.

Noticing a spot on the white t-shirt I am wearing and with still no food or cab at that point, I dash back to my room to change. Lawn Guest is still sleeping out front; however, when I pop back once more to use the bathroom before the delayed driver arrives, I notice him sitting on the steps behind the kitchen looking at a menu. Thinking perhaps that he is a guest, or is at least planning to eat breakfast here, in the evening when I leave the hotel for dinner, I see Lawn Guest dressed in a server's uniform. He is an *employee* working in the beer garden attached to the hotel. What a riot! I guess one way to ensure not being late for work is to sleep on the property lawn.

Taxi Driver eventually arrives. Throughout the day, we visit some of the recommended local sightseeing stops, including Parvati Hill, the highest point in Pune. At least a thirty-minute climb to the top, I opt to view it from the ground. We drive past the beautiful Dagduseth Ganpati Temple. No parking is permitted out front, and there is a long line of devotees awaiting entry.

Our next stop is the magnificent Shaniwar Wada. Formerly a seven-story fortress-like palace, there remains part of one multistoried structure. I climb the stairs and look out over the rest of the grounds, comprised of ruins of former buildings. A palace of Peshwa rulers, it was built in the 1700s. Nearby, within walking distance is the Lal Mahal, remains of a red-colored palace where a Maratha king named Shivaji spent his childhood. Its exterior architecture is interesting, but there is not much to see inside.

Our final stop is the Aga Khan Palace and Gandhi Memorial Center. This magnificent white palace sits in impressive gardens and is where Gandhi, his wife, and a couple of his aides were imprisoned from 1942 to 1944. The British held him there after his famous Quit India Resolution in 1942. Both his dear friend and loyal secretary of thirty-five years, Mahadoebhai Desai, and his wife, Kasturba, died there, and their ashes are maintained in memorial samadhis on the property. Some of Gandhi's ashes also were brought to a memorial samadhi site adjacent to theirs; the remainder of his ashes were spread at sea at the tip of India where three seas merge.

An interesting and moving exhibit, we are not allowed to enter the rooms in which Gandhi lived, but can view them through glass doors. It is an emotional experience to see where this phenomenal human being spent time. After exiting the hall, and near the samadhi sites, is a small gift shop comprised of a few tables. I buy some wonderful t-shirts with his image and khadi cloth (made famous by his protests) towels. Several little statuettes are appealing, but they are too heavy to carry. Some are of the infamous "see/hear/speak no evil" monkeys; apparently, that famous statement is attributable to the Mahatma Gandhi, which I am amused to learn in India.

After six hours of sightseeing, ready to call it a day and return to my hotel, it has been a good day and well worth the reasonable fee of 1,000 rupees. Deciding to wander out for dinner, I find a Subway and eat a tuna sandwich, which tastes the same as in the United States. Sometimes, it's refreshing to experience the familiar.

Back in my room, I reflect upon the first part of this quest. It has been truly amazing! I adopt my Kerala boat mates' favorite adjective. Already, in this brief time, I feel shifts in my consciousness, a deepening of my spiritual connection, an appreciation for the little things in life, and tremendous gratitude to the wonderful Indian people.

Meeting Iyengar certainly is the crowning moment of these first two and a half months. I now am eager and excited to experience the north, visit the home of His Holiness the Dalai Lama, and have more contact with the Buddhist aspects of India. I have another two and a half months here.

Epilogue

TWO AND A half months in south India provided me experiences, joy and clarity—much more even than my optimistic, adventurous spirit imagined or dreamed possible. A plethora of wonderful books have been written by travelers, and seekers, in India. Having read many, the similar thread running through them is that all came away with momentous experiences from their time there…some good, others painful.

Spending time—at least if for a substantial period—in a culture so vastly diverse than the modernity of America naturally means one will be challenged. But despite moments of frustration or discomfort, and sometimes sheer exasperation, the positive, exciting aspects so vastly overshadowed the difficult, I quickly forgot about them. And, I didn't go to India to be comfortable; that lifestyle was available at home.

Upon returning, one friend asked me if I had found God, my defined reason for going. My answer was an astounding, "Oh yes in spades!" When answering a question, before departing, of why I was going to India, posed by another girlfriend who has been there at least six times, she replied, "If that's what you seek, you'll find God in India." I suppose one can find his or her version of the god experience anywhere, even in the United States. But to find what I yearned for, I had to leave the self-absorbed, materialistic West.

Although sharing my daily meanderings with family and friends, I also kept a private journal of my spiritual experiences and evolution, believing that should remain personal. If it becomes public fodder, I reasoned, how does one keep his or her connection with the Divine intimate. After my journey, I reread those entries. I wept, smiled, and felt profound thanks for my relationship with God that deepened enormously during my time in India.

Those journals included a wide range of thoughts and perceptions. I wrote about my parents, about values derived from my Midwestern roots, about forgiveness, about trying to be nonjudgmental, and about finding a passion. I pondered the power of thoughts, the need to be of service, living and dying, finding enlightenment, living in the present, and most importantly, finding God everywhere, and trying to live in the light.

Chanting in ashrams, visiting temples, meditating, doing yoga, praying, and living with large blocks of daily silence—all became important to the journey. But the simple joys of living amidst India's sacred landscapes, along with her remarkably kind and loving people, afforded me the richest, most powerful breakthroughs. Self-realization, in the manner I ultimately seek, may be eons away, but the process itself is marvelous.

After departing south India, I was going north for the last half of my journey. It too was an unplanned itinerary, other than to head to McLeod Ganj, home of His Holiness the Dalai Lama, and, of course, to visit the Taj Mahal. Thrilled with anticipation about what lay ahead, I would leave from Pune via Delhi to arrive in Dharmasala shortly before the Dalai Lama's birthday celebration. The odyssey continued.